Introduction to
FAMILY CAMPING

Boy Scouts of America

CONTENTS

Author: Fritz Hines
Color illustrations by: Ruth Pisano
Black and white illustrations by: Joe Snyder

FOREWORD

About The Author

"Fritz" Hines' interest in camping led to a career in professional Scouting spanning 38 years. During that time he served in five local councils, the national office (twice), and the World Scout Bureau in Geneva, Swizerland. Mr. Hines, who holds a degree in Physical Education and Journalism from the University of Minnesota, has written many Scouting publications including the eighth edition of The Official Boy Scout Handbook. *We asked him for a recounting of his family camping experience to establish his credentials for writing this book. Following is an account of his lifelong lodging in the out-of-doors.*

I can't remember my first family camp because every summer from the year I was born, my family lived for 3 months in a cabin on Beaver Dam Lake near Cumberland, Wis. We also made many family trips fishing, hunting, and enjoying the great northern Wisconsin forests, lakes, and streams. In 1932, in the heart of the great depression, Daddy, Mother, Sis, and I packed up our Studebaker and headed out for a summer vacation in Yellowstone National Park. My father had read how to cut the front seat of a car so it would fold back to join the rear seat, making a bed. This made a nice double bed which, coupled with an umbrella tent carried in the trunk and a great wooden box fastened to the running board to carry the cooking gear, gave us everything we needed for camp living. My sister and I, after more than 50 years, still fondly remember that great family camp.

By the middle 1940s I had a family of my own, wife Eddie, daughter Sandra and son Gary. Our first camps were enjoyed fairly near our home in Superor, Wis. In 1949 we moved to Phoenix, Ariz., where I worked for the progressive Theodore Roosevelt Boy Scout Council. For 8 years I served as camp director of Camp Geronimo. This camp had family facilities for members of the camp staff, so summers under the Tonto Rim were eight summers of family camping—each lasting more than 2 months. After the Phoenix experience, I joined the national staff of the Boy Scouts of America, then headquartered in New Brunswick, N.J. During those years we participated twice in the family camp at Philmont Scout Ranch's Volunteer Training Center. We also vacationed as a family on my mother's lake property near Cumberland, Wis., and camped in, of all places, Washington, D.C. and a few assorted sites like Maine, Pennsylvania, and Ohio.

My first wife died in 1966. Family camping stopped until I married Loretta 4 years later and inherited her three sons to join youngest daughter, Cathy. Philmont was

our first camping experience together, followed by trips from New Jersey to California, camping along the way in a tent trailer. This was followed by another tent trailer trek to the world jamboree at Farragut, Idaho. On this trip we visited Banff, Lake Louise, the Calgary Stampede, Glacier and Yellowstone National Parks, and the Black Hills.

In 1974 I joined the staff of the World Scout Bureau in Geneva, Switzerland. Soon after our arrival we brought a travel trailer, or caravan as it was called in Europe. We realized that a family of our size couldn't afford to see Europe any other way.

Our trailer made it possible to spend Easter vacation in Verona and Venice, Christmas and New Year's in Florence, Rome, and Naples, and a summer vacation on the Costa Brava in Spain. These were the long trips. We also took many weekend trips in Switzerland, and nearby France.

We returned to the United States in 1977 and bought another travel trailer. In 1982 Loretta and I were joined by Rich, still in high school, Ron, a junior at the Massachusetts Institute of Technology, and Bob, a senior at the University of California in Berkeley for a Christmas ski week at Lake Tahoe. The nighttime temperatures reached 10 degrees, and the snow was so deep in the campground that the top of the trailer could just be seen above the drifts on the sides of the trailer space. But the skiing was great and the trailer was warm.

As I look back to that first trip in 1932, and all the things we've done and seen because of family camping, I'm grateful beyond words. Very little of it would have been possible had not my three families been campers.

—Fritz Hines

3

WHY GO FAMILY CAMPING? CHAPTER I

Thousands of tired, nerve-shaken, over-civilized people are beginning to find out that going to the mountains is going home; that wildness is a necessity; and that mountain parks and reservations are useful not only as fountains of timber and irrigating rivers, but as fountains of life.

"Climb the mountains and get their good tidings. Nature's peace will flow into you as the sunshine into the trees. The winds will blow their freshness into you, and the storms their energy, while cares will drop off like autumn leaves."

John Muir

You might ask, what's in it for me—or better yet, what's in it for my family? What can be done in a camp setting that we couldn't do at home? What's out there that I couldn't more comfortably enjoy in my easy chair in front of a TV set? Why risk failure by tackling something new and possibly beyond my capability? Why invest in camping gear when I'd really rather stay in a motel?

These are good questions—particularly if you don't have a camping background. Perhaps it will help if you know that millions of camping families have asked these same questions and have decided that the pluses far outweigh the negatives.

Parental Quality Time

Be honest with yourself. Between your job, social and community activities, phone calls, and similar things that fill your waking moments, how much quality time do you have left for your family—particularly your children? Quality time is time when you have direct and meaningful interchange with them. It's not time generously given as a spectator at their activities, but rather time directly shared with them.

The family camp offers you a great chance to give a lot of quality time to your children. It starts with the first planning, and doesn't end until the final trip wrap-up.

There's the first talk about where to go and what to see, and studying maps and campground guides—not telling, but sharing. Then comes menu planning, food buying, assembly of gear, and packing to leave—all shared.

A good family camp must be a safe camp, so lessons about sanitation, first aid, and safety must be learned. A discussion of campground courtesy can ingrain a deep feeling for the rights of others.

Then it's time to leave on the trip. You'll have hours and hours to spend with your family during days and days that are uninterrupted by all those distractions that seem so important the rest of the year—things that take you away from your children.

The Economics of Camping

In these days of $75 motel rooms and $15-plus-tip dinners, camping has become the only way that many families can afford a vacation. A $10 campsite and meals for about the same cost as eating at home brings "nature's peace" as described by John Muir to millions of families.

But, the affordable vacation isn't the only reason for family camping. If it were, then why are so many families that are able to afford luxury hotel vacations opting instead for the outdoors?

The Outdoor Atmosphere

There are sounds, sights, smells, and experiences in the outdoors that can only be imagined in the city — and not even that if you've never camped.

The air is clean and crisp, "polluted" only by the fragrant smell of pine and the pungent odor of campfire wood smoke.

Skies are bluer than you can remember. At night the velvet darkness is splashed with stars so brilliant they seem unreal. When was the last time you looked skyward and saw the Milky Way? You can in camp.

In the quiet of the night, you hear the rippling water of a stream as it rushes over rocks, and the crazy cry of a lonely loon. The hoot of an owl adds the bass to the symphony of croaking frogs and chirping crickets.

Camping will give back to you many of the things that civilization has taken away from you and your family.

Honking horns and the drone of traffic, the scream of fire and police sirens, and the rumble of freight trains are alien to the peace of camp.

In the out-of-doors, evidence of your Creator surrounds all with eyes to see. You may seem closer to Him than you ever were in the city. In this environment there can be a sermon in silence and lessons learned by listening to it.

Sharing Family Responsibilities

Making camp, building fires, cooking meals, cleanup, and all the related camping tasks become a sharing experience. Since earliest childhood, children want to do "grown-up" things. In a sharing camp relationship with their parents, they often find that things they thought were childish chores are really part of the essentials of "grown-up" living. Children need adults as role models. Don't let it be someone else for your kids.

Your children will learn that by sharing responsibilities, no job was as big as it seemed. This shared living in camp can't help but strengthen your family. Someone once described family camping as "Making Moms out of Mothers and Dads out of Fathers." More than that, it provides a setting where children can see you as friends and not just disciplinarians.

Fun

In camp you can have fun without losing your dignity —or if you do, who cares? Camp is a place to let down your hair and become one of the gang. If it's good for the kids, it's good for you, and if it's fun for them, it will be fun for you, too.

It's in the fun of camping that the kids find out you're an OK guy or gal. They'll see that you can share the fun with them, and maybe they'll learn they can share other things—things like their problems, their dreams, and those thoughts they were afraid you'd laugh at.

New Skills

The skills of outdoor living have been part of Boy Scouting since 1910. This was partly because they were so useful in the camping program, but mostly because they instilled a sense of self-reliance in those who mastered them. An early Scout official was asked, "Why learn to start a fire by friction when it's so much easier these days to just use a match or a lighter?"

He answered, "First of all, what makes you think we didn't have matches way back when it was decided firebuilding was an important skill? And, have you ever seen a boy down on one knee, his other foot on the board of a fire-by-friction set, cranking away with his bow as sweat streams down his face? Clouds of acrid smoke drift up until he thinks he has a coal on his tinder. Quickly, he lifts the tinder to the heavens in his two hands, and gently blows through it until it bursts into flame. The expression of success on his face is something that using a match can never bring."

The skills of camping are the skills of self-reliance, and they are fun. A person may never need to find North without a compass, but there's a feeling of confidence and pride in knowing how to do it. You may never need to use first aid to save a life, but isn't it great to know you can?

These skills can be invaluable in an emergency when the vagaries of nature and humankind might take away the normal structure of civilization. Tornadoes, floods, hurricanes, earthquakes, and, heaven forbid, war could

all draw deeply on your family's ability to survive. The skills of camping could be the plus that carries you through.

Memories

Memories are pretty intangible, yet they will strengthen family ties now and in the future. Over the years, the memories of close-knit family living, and playing together in camp will form a bond that is harder to forge in the home situation.

Why? Who can say? Perhaps it's because so many unusual things happen in camp. Certainly situations are faced that you would never expect at home. And,

strangely, it's the most disagreeable camping experiences that bring out the best, and so are the remembered highlights years after they happen. The blown-down tent in the middle of a storm, a burned dinner caused by the cook forgetting it in his rapture over a gorgeous sunset, and even the family sitting disconsolately with a steaming radiator waiting for help on the turnpike become memories to recall at family reunions years later.

That's why the Camping Log mentioned in "Planning" (Chap. 5) is so important as a means to stimulate the recall of those memories in later years.

Lifetime Activities

There are a few activities that can be enjoyed by all—children, teenagers, young adults, middle-agers, and senior citizens. Among them are sports like camping, fishing, bowling, bicycling, golf, and swimming. Camping is high on the list because it can easily involve the whole family regardless of age.

Just look at the mix at the next campground you use. The people enjoying camping are of all ages, all walks of life, all family lifestyles, all religions, and all races. Camping is a universally shared experience.

Start your children on the outdoor path, and they'll say thanks in their hearts when they join the millions of retired persons who are filling their lives with travel, exciting activities, and the pleasure of meeting new friends through their enjoyment of camping.

Need More Convincing?

The rest of this book is designed to help you get started and to succeed in outdoor living. Some of it may seem complicated and fraught with danger, but remember, it is aimed at all types of campers and all the situations they might, but probably won't, face.

A. C. Nielsen studied participation in sports by Americans in 1982. The study revealed that some 64 million of us took a camping trip during the preceding 12 months. Once upon a time, all 64 million were beginners. A veteran camper is a person who has camped more often than the person to whom he is talking. After your first trip, you, too, can be a veteran. All you have to do is get started.

FAMILY CAMPING GEAR CHAPTER II

*"Camping is the art of living as comfortably
as possible in the out-of-doors."*

Daniel Carter Beard

It's your camping gear that makes comfortable outdoor living as envisioned by Dan Beard a reality. It's housing, cooking, clothing, comfort, and tools. In each of these categories, the limit is how much you can afford, and want to spend.

The early scouts, trappers, and guides in America lived in the wilderness for months with one set of clothing, a bedroll, rifle, ammunition, flint, and steel. You can't get by that way today, even if you want to. Laws won't let you hunt for your food with a rifle, or build a fire to cook wherever you happen to be. And, that one set of clothing will make you very unpopular after a few days.

This doesn't mean you can't camp cheaply, if you want to. You can sleep under the stars, or build a simple shelter from a sheet of plastic. Your bedroll can be blankets from home with a piece of plastic for a groundcloth. Eating utensils and dishes from home will double in camp. You can cook on an open fire with a few rocks to hold pots off the coals.

Few families would even consider camping under these conditions, much less enjoy it. Unfortunately, some families have tried to camp that way. A few liked it, but many more resolved to never camp again.

The other extreme puts you in a self-contained motor

home or luxury travel trailer—self-contained meaning it has electricity, and LP (liquid petroleum) gas to fuel the kitchen stove and oven and to heat hot water in the storage tank. It has a toilet and shower with holding tank to collect sewage until it can be dumped later. The modern RV (recreational vehicle) has comfortable beds, closets for clothing, and ample drawer and cabinet space in bedroom and kitchen areas.

Between these two—primitive camping and the luxury of an RV—there is the kind of camping gear you need and can afford.

If you are starting out in family camping, take many small steps before you begin to run. Read everything you can find on the subject. When you think you know the kinds of gear that will fit your pocketbook and family needs, consider rental. Check the Yellow Pages under Tent Rentals, Camper Rentals, Trailer Rentals, Camping Equipment Rentals, etc.

A few trips using rental gear will tell whether it's what you want. You won't tie up a lot of money finding out. Then you can buy your gear without making a costly mistake.

When you're camping with your rental gear, you'll see lots of people with other kinds of equipment. Get friendly. Stop by and ask them about their gear, and what they would recommend. Just remember that people often have

prejudices in favor of things they own. After all, they won't want you to think they made a mistake.

Before starting out on that first big trip to a distant campsite, it's smart to have a test camp in your own backyard or some nearby campsite where failure won't be a disaster—where you can go back in the house or drive a couple of miles to get the can-opener or other important item you forgot. This shake-down camp will pay off in confidence and enjoyment when you are out on that first big trip.

Housing

Play a little game with yourself when you drive on the Interstate. See if you can spot the kinds of family campers coming towards you on the other side of the divider.

The station wagon with a covered cartop carrier or towing a small cargo trailer? Probably a tent camping family.

The trailer with the low, flat profile towed behind a family car is most likely a pop-up tent trailer.

The pickup truck, a lot higher than normal and with a window across the top front, is a camper. The pickup

rig that looks like a semi truck is a 5th wheel travel trailer.

And then there are the vans, motor homes, and travel trailers looking like narrow houses traveling along.

Here's a quick look at the kinds of camp housing available.

Tents

The smallest investment you can make for adequate camp housing will be for a tent. When you start shopping for tents, beware. The cheapest product often isn't the best buy. Look for quality in workmanship, material, and design.

Design is important. Review your needs and choose the design that fits your family. Common tent designs include:

Free standing. No lines to trip over, easy assembly, and good for areas where space is restricted.

Backpacking. Lightweight and easily packed into a compact unit.

Cabin tent. More conducive to family camping because of ceiling height and square footage.

Dome tent. Superior stability and ventilation.

Fly tent. Very versatile; can be used to protect food, supplies, kitchen and dining areas, and for sleeping in the open.

Wall tents. Heavy-duty fabric adds years of life to tent, and is the traditional group tent.

Station wagon tent. Fits over open rear gate to allow wagon campers more room. Can also adapt to pickup shell and van rear or side doors.

Once you have decided on a design that will fit your family's needs, shop with an eye to value as well as price, and then take care of your investment.

The great enemies of canvas are fire, rain-shrunk ropes, poor pitching, clumsy feet, and mildew. Good construction and materials can withstand much of this kind of abuse, but there's a limit. A tent-repair kit for immediate patching is worth carrying. Small rips become catastrophes if not caught at once.

To prevent mildew, pack wet canvas (if you must) loosely and then thoroughly dry it as soon as you can. This happens when breaking camp in the rain.

The fabric used in the manufacture of your tent determines its weight, durability, and ability to keep out rain. Two common tent fabrics are 50/50 polyester-cotton blend, and rip-stop nylon. You can still buy canvas duck tents, but most have been replaced with the two fabrics mentioned.

Good workmanship is important. Look for uniform and careful cutting, hemming, and stitching. Check the grommets—they should be firmly set. Grommets with rolled rims are better than flat ones because they aren't as rigid.

Look for reinforcement at stress points like the peak, eaves, and corners. Every place exposed to extra wear should be reinforced. Where tabs or ties are attached, they should be supported with one or more layers of extra fabric stitched in place to spread the strain.

Several kinds of tent poles are available—some sectional, some one-piece. If poles are not included with the tent, you can choose the kind you like best. Make sure your poles are sturdy. A strong wind puts great pressure on

the pole. If not strong, it might collapse at a poor time—in the middle of a storm.

Tents come with floors, sod cloths, or neither. Sod cloths are strips of canvas about 3 or 4 inches wide, stitched all around the bottom edge of the tent. The tent has no floor until you put your groundcloth on top of the sod cloth. In effect, this gives you a tent with a floor that can be removed for easy cleaning.

It is recommended that your tent or tents allow a minimum of 30 square feet of floor space per camper, with headroom to permit dressing and undressing while

standing. A 7 x 9-foot tent has 63 square feet—adequate for two people. For a family of four, the 30-square-foot formula translates into a 120-square-foot tent. So, you need a tent about 10 x 12 feet.

Think about it. Two 7 x 9's would probably be more practical—easier to pack, easier to move and set up, and give the privacy available in a two-bedroom home.

Pop-Up Tent Trailers (Also called Camping Trailers)

When you move into the tent-on-wheels category, your vehicle now classifies as an RV (recreational vehicle) along with vans, motor homes, travel trailers, 5th wheelers, and pickup campers, all of which are discussed in this chapter.

> **HINT** *Some bridges, tunnels, and ferries are off-limits if you are carrying LP gas. A few aren't open to use by trailers at all. Check your latest campground guide for specific information.*

The tent trailer is just that—a tent on wheels—so everything that's been said about tents is true for the tent part of the tent trailer, except design. While layouts of the trailers vary, most tent designs are quite similar.

Weight is a factor in choosing any tent, but overall weight is even more important in a tent trailer. Today's high gas mileage cars aren't powered to pull as much trailer weight as the old gas guzzlers. Before buying a

trailer, ask your car dealer for the towing capacity of your car. Buy a trailer at or under that capacity or plan to buy a more powerful car.

With a trailer, you are entering an area of motor vehicle regulations beyond that of a single vehicle. There will be connections between your car and the trailer, the first being the trailer hitch itself. You'll need a permanent hitch installed on your car. It doesn't pay to try to use a portable hitch. It is illegal in some states and you'll probably want to travel in more than just your home state.

Other connections between car and trailer include wires to activate brake, turn signal, and backup lights; and brakes themselves, depending on the weight of the trailer. There will be a safety chain connection between car and trailer and you'll need special rear-view mirrors. The

Solid state pop-up trailer

trailer is wider than the car, so unless the mirrors extend out on each side it's hard to see cars behind you. Some states require a mirror only on the driver's side, but others call for one on each side. These mirrors can be a clamp-on type so they can removed when not trailering. If your trailer is low enough to see over with your conventional mirror, you won't have to add extra towing mirrors.

A big advantage of the tent trailer over travel trailers is its low profile, offering less wind resistance, hence easier towing and better gas mileage.

Another advantage of most tent trailers is in the amount of sleeping capacity crammed into a relatively small and light vehicle. Most have beds that slide out at each end of the trailer. These have space for two people to sleep at each end. More can sleep in the main trailer by converting seats and tables to beds at night. Sure, it's snug, but for a large family it's a great way to go.

Modern tent trailers have gas stoves, sinks with a water supply, electrical and water hookups, an icebox or refrigerator, and plenty of storage. They don't have built-in toilets, but a portable chemical toilet can meet this need.

Time spent in setting up on arrival at the campground and taking down before leaving are disadvantages of the tent trailer. Check out the tent-raising mechanisms to see which are the easiest to use.

HINT *When backing a trailer, the rear of the car must go in the opposite direction from the way you want the trailer to go.*

Another disadvantage inherent in any trailer can be overcome with patience. Until you learn how, and practice, backing a trailer can be difficult. Frequently you will have to back your trailer into a campsite space—frustrating if you haven't practiced. Some tent trailers are light enough that you can unhitch and push them into a camping space, but it's still wise to learn how to back a trailer with your car.

Cars with trailers don't have the pickup they have without them, and together they are longer. It takes longer to pass slower cars, and because of your added length, it takes longer for faster cars to pass you.

You will have to register your trailer with your State Motor Vehicle Department, and pay a license fee. You probably won't need special liability insurance (trailer liability will be included in the car's coverage). You will

HINT *Always check your tires for wear before a long trip and be sure they are inflated properly for the load being carried. Carry a tire pressure gauge to check pressure periodically during the trip.*

have to pay an extra premium for comprehensive and collision insurance, if you want that protection.

Station Wagons

You can use a station wagon as supplemental sleeping quarters when tent camping, or even as regular camp housing. A couple of air mattresses in the back can accommodate two people.

HINT *Air shocks on the rear of a station wagon will prevent that "camping sag" that makes it feel like you're driving uphill all day.*

There are tents available that attach to the rear of an open station wagon. These provide extra space for dressing, and even an extra sleeping area.

If using a wagon for sleeping, you'll want interior curtains on the windows to give privacy and keep the early morning summer sun from waking you too soon.

HINT *Attach Velcro® tape to your station wagon privacy curtains, and the mate around the windows. This makes it easy to put up curtains at night and take down in the morning. Sew one side of Velcro® tape to curtains and fasten the other side to wagon with contact cement.*

Pickup Campers

These vary from low shells that cover the cargo space of a pickup truck to a full living unit that mounts on and around the truck.

The shell merely gives a protected area in which you can sleep. Just put a couple of air mattresses on the deck, and crawl in. Protection from the weather is better than in a tent, but living space is much less, and lacking in headroom. You can add a connecting tent as described for the station wagon. The shell can be stored when not in use.

Pickup campers with full living space have many more conveniences than tent trailers—electric or gas refrigerators, water tanks with sink and pump, toilets, and comfortable double and single beds. You can hook up to electricity and water in a trailer park or run appliances on LP (Liquid Petroleum) gas where hookups aren't available.

HINT *Carry a fire extinguisher and first-aid kit in your RV and car.*

Advantages of the pickup camper are many. You don't have the inconvenience of towing a trailer. It's easy to back into a campsite. The truck will handle rough roads. It's legal to ride in the back of the camper, but not in a trailer, so your family can relax while on the road.

Disadvantages include the problem of driving from the campsite for sightseeing, trips to town, and similar excursions. You have to move your home with you each time. It's possible to jack the camper up off the pickup and leave it at the campsite, but this takes time and effort. Unless owners plan to be in a campsite for several days, they usually don't feel it's worth the effort to separate the two. Some carry mopeds or bicycles, or tow a small car or dune buggy to use for excursions from the campsite.

5th Wheel Trailers

Those land yachts you see cruising along the highway behind a pickup truck are among the latest innovations in travel trailers. Their interiors are roomy and luxurious, sporting modern home conveniences.

They usually have dual tires on the trailer section. This adds up to four wheels. The pickup truck which acts like the semi of a semi-trailer rig, is considered to be the 5th wheel. Hence the name.

There are several advantages to the 5th wheeler over a motor home or camper. When you arrive at your campsite,

you can disconnect the trailer from the truck as easily as a semi driver drops his trailer. Then you have a pickup truck to use for excursions. If there are more than three in your family, you'll need a stretch pickup that has front and back seats in the cab. Carrying passengers in the cargo space of a pickup is very dangerous.

Another advantage is the ease of parking the trailer section. You've seen those huge semi-trailers being maneuvered into tight spaces at loading docks. That will give you an idea of the backing ability of a 5th wheeler.

HINT *Rust is the cancer of steel. Check your vehicles regularly. At first sign of rust, remove it by wire brushing, scraping or cutting out. Coat with rust resistant primer and paint. Replace cut-out areas with fiberglass or body putty.*

An extra room is gained over a regular trailer of the same overall length — trailer plus towing vehicle. The 5th wheeler's design puts a bedroom at the front over the cargo space of the pickup, adding a room without adding length.

A disadvantage is the need to use the pickup as a family car when not camping. Or you will need a second family car.

Vans

Vans can be commercially or owner converted for camping. With a good conversion, a van can serve camping needs as well as providing comfortable transportation for non-camping use. The extent of luxury and facilities in a van depends on the wishes of the owner and customizer.

Advantages of the van lie in the ease of driving and parking, the legality of passengers relaxing in the back while on the road, and its year-round use for other than camping.

Disadvantages include the need to "break camp" even if you just want to leave for a short time, and its rather cramped conditions for more than two or three people. However, the station wagon type connecting tent can be used at the rear or side doors to give more space. Another disadvantage is the need to find a level area in which to

Van and truck trailer

FAMILY CAMPING GEAR

set up camp. Vans usually don't have leveling jacks to use on uneven terrain. Living on a slant isn't fun.

Travel Trailers

For years travel trailers have been the last word in camping comfort. They still are, although they have been joined by motor homes and 5th wheelers.

Trailers have packed into their interiors all the comforts of home, albeit in compact form. Most late models are self-contained. This means they can be used with full facilities for days without any connection to outside utilities such as water, electricity or sewage. They have climate control with air conditioners and furnaces. Hot water heaters provide water for dishwashing and personal bathing.

There are other advantages. You can set up your trailer at the campsite and use the towing vehicle for excursions.

HINT *Road flares must be carried in RV's and tent trailers in most states.*

A well-built travel trailer will depreciate slowly, and last for many years if you care for it. There's no engine to be

cared for, and overhauled when things go wrong. And, you can camp in luxury.

They aren't inexpensive, although it's possible to start small with a compact trailer that can provide tight quarters for a family of four. Another option is to carefully choose a used trailer.

Disadvantages include the need for a more powerful car to tow the larger models, and overall length, which makes for problems in passing slower cars and for faster

HINT *Breakaway brakes are required in most states if your trailer weighs 3,000 pounds or more. It is as low as 2,000 pounds in some states. The breakaway activates trailer brakes if the trailer accidentally separates from the towing vehicle.*

cars getting by you. If you've ever been in one of those long lines waiting to pass a slow travel trailer, you know about this. Towing larger trailers will cut your gas mileage, although the amount will vary with the size of the trailer, and the amount of wind resistance in its design.

Mention was made earlier about the difficulty of backing trailers into confined spaces. Another disadvantage that can be overcome by trailer selection concerns the rules of some campgrounds, both public and private, limiting the length of trailers permitted. Some restrict trailer length to as little as 20 feet, but most common is a 30-foot restriction.

You'll have to register your trailer with your State Motor Vehicle Department and pay a license fee. You must follow all state regulations related to your equipment, such as connections to the car, and rear-view mirrors.

Motor Homes

Like travel trailers, motor homes are self-contained. They have all the facilities of home, but can cruise down the highway at legal speed limits.

They have the advantages of a camper and van. While traveling, members of the family can relax "at home" in the back. They are almost as easy to park as a car, and shorter models aren't so long that faster traveling vehicles find it hard to pass.

You can buy motor homes with diesel engines giving better mileage and longer engine life than a gasoline engine.

The main disadvantage is that a motor home is designed for one purpose: travel camping. It isn't a vehicle to use around town or on short trips from home, except to go camping. At the campsite, where it is your home, you must break camp to take a side trip unless you carry supplemental transportation as mentioned for pickup campers.

Another disadvantage comes when passing slower cars on the road. The motor home is heavy. Engine power, while adequate, can't provide the quick pickup needed for passing on narrow, winding, hilly roads. Be a courteous driver, When you see traffic lining up behind you, pull off the road to let it pass. In some states you can be fined for not pulling over when five or more cars are lined up behind you.

HINT *Carry wheel chocks in your trailer. A 4 x 4-inch piece of wood about 6 inches long cut diagonally makes two fine chocks.*

Cabins

It probably seems strange to think of a cabin as a form of housing for family camping. Too soft, you say? Living in rental cabins in National Parks and some State Parks isn't as luxurious as a travel trailer or motor home.

These facilities offer bare necessities such as beds, kitchens, central toilets and showers, and trash and garbage disposal.

The cabin is an inexpensive alternative to hotels and motels in the park or outside the park boundaries. For information about park cabins, including reservations, write to the park you will visit and ask for a brochure on cabins. There's no charge for this.

Another kind of cabin camping is in a permanent cabin you own, rent, or borrow from a friend. This is usually on private or leased government land. It restricts your camping pretty much to one location, but if that location is right, it can be great.

Houseboats

In many parts of our country you can own or rent a houseboat for family camping use. These offer a relaxed vacation of fishing, sightseeing, swimming and sunning. You'll find ads for rental houseboats in travel magazines.

16

Many RV stores and repair facilities have dump stations for disposal of holding tank sewage. These are listed in campground guidebooks.

There are now pontoons with frames that can be bought or rented. You can back your trailer onto the pontoon frame, fasten it down, and by adding an outboard motor have a great houseboat.

For a fantastic, but not inexpensive family vacation, consider traveling on the canals of Europe in a houseboat. Biggest extra cost is getting there.

Care and Maintenance

Care and maintenance of tents has already been discussed. It applies to tentage on tent trailers as well as to separate tents.

When you move from tents to RV's (recreational vehicles), care and maintenance is a whole new proposition. RV's are a combination of vehicles and homes. Anything that can go wrong at home can in your RV. There can be electrical, plumbing, sewage disposal, appliance, and gas problems, along with a myriad of little things like locks that stick, hinges that squeak, and cupboards that won't stay closed.

These usually aren't things to fix during a trip. Sure, some demand immediate attention, and may even call for a stop at a garage or RV service shop. But, attention

HINT *Campgrounds are like communities, and communities have thieves. Protect your property under lock and key whenever you'll be away from your site.*

to the maintenance schedule that came with your RV owner's manual will help you avoid those unhappy breakdowns that will spoil a vacation.

Manuals are written for each kind and make of RV. It isn't possible to list details here as comprehensive and specific as you'll find in your own manual, so read it, keep it, and use it.

Don't forget the care and upkeep of your motive power either. Motor homes and vans have maintenance for the power train in their manuals. If you are using a pickup to carry your camper, or as a 5th wheel, or the family car as a towing vehicle, be sure to maintain it properly.

Cooking Gear

The kind of camping you will be doing is a major consideration in your choice of cooking gear. Utensils,

pots, pans, skillets, cleaning supplies, coolers, and storage facilities are all part of your cooking gear.

You can't cook without groceries, but their selection will depend on your cooking source — your fire and stove.

Grills

Your simplest fire is on the ground in a stone fireplace to hold your kettle or skillet. The next step up is a grill, either on those same stones or with its own legs.

The grill will support your pots and pans and can also be used for broiling over the coals. Some campgrounds have fireplaces with built-in grills at each campsite. But if you plan to do most of your cooking on a simple grill, don't count on having a built-in one at every campsite you visit.

HINT *It's easy to waterproof packages of matches by surrounding one wooden match with six others in a rosette. Wrap together by winding cotton cord for about 1½ inches starting near the heads. Finish with a clove hitch, leaving about 4 inches of cord before cutting. Hold this end and dip bundle in melted paraffin. When cool, wrap each firestarter in foil for safety. To activate, remove foil, and strike matches on rough surface.*

Charcoal Stoves

Charcoal camp stoves are a little more sophisticated than camp grills. They hold charcoal within metal containers, usually with legs to bring the working surface to table-top height. They often have adjustable grills so you can raise or lower their height above your coals. Vents that can be opened or closed permit control of heat by cutting the air supply. Most have removable fireboxes or ash pans, making cleaning easy.

These stoves come in round, square, or rectangular styles. Many have lids for giving an oven effect. These are the type stoves most commonly used for backyard barbecues.

Heat localizer rings of heavy gauge steel concentrate the heat of charcoal directly under kettles or pots. They also are

HINT *A rack from a junked oven makes a good grill. Put a piece of heavy duty aluminum foil on top to make a smooth cooking surface.*

fuel savers since you don't need coals over the entire area, just in the localizer.

Even if you plan to use wood for cooking, these stoves can be used in areas where open flames aren't permitted.

Gas Barbecue Grills

The addition of gas to backyard barbecue stoves has made it possible to cook this way without charcoal. The gas fire heats permanent coals that act like charcoal, but don't burn. There aren't any ashes to dispose of with a gas barbecue grill.

Fuel supply can be either natural gas piped to the unit, or a tank of LP fuel that can be refilled when low. You'll use LP gas for camp cooking.

HINT *Melt paraffin or wax in a double boiler. Make your own double boiler by putting paraffin in a 1-pound can sitting in boiling water on small stones in a 3-pound can.*

Heatabs or Canned Heat Stoves

These tiny stoves consist of a framework to support the heat source and a kettle above it. You can buy the heatabs or canned heat at sporting goods outlets.

These are single burner stoves that work fine for heating a one-serving dish or water for hot beverages.

Canned heat may be lighted, used, and extinguished by putting the lid back on the can. You can keep using the fuel in the original can until used up.

Gasoline Stoves

These were the original camp stoves that took campers away from dependence on wood for fuel. They use white gasoline, usually available at stores selling the stoves and at some campgrounds.

Gasoline stoves are a practical camp stove providing a good, clean, hot flame. Heat can be controlled by a

HINT *Adult supervision is recommended when using LP or gasoline appliances.*

burner valve much the same as your gas stove at home.

The gasoline must be converted into a vapor to be efficient, so these stoves take a few minutes to generate the heat needed to vaporize the liquid gasoline. They have wind deflectors that should be used when cooking in a breeze.

Gasoline camp stoves are found in one-, two-, and three-burner models in most sporting goods stores.

LP (Liquid Petroleum) Stoves

These stoves were a natural outgrowth of gasoline stoves. Their fuel in disposable containers takes the danger inherent in gasoline stoves out of storage, transportation, and refueling.

LP stoves don't need generation. They light as soon as turned on and a spark or flame is touched to the burner.

If you plan to use an LP stove for most of your cooking, you'll want to invest in a bulk cylinder and adapter to

provide a cheaper source of fuel than using small disposable cylinders. Bulk cylinders can be refilled at most campgrounds and at RV supply stores. Most common LP stoves are either single- or double-burner types.

Stoves in RV's are the LP type operating off a refillable cylinder. They usually have four burners and an oven.

Kerosene Stoves

There are kerosene stoves available for camp use, but they are much less common than the kinds mentioned earlier. If interested, check with a camping supply store.

Electrical Appliances

If your campground has a 110-volt outlet at your site, electrical appliances can save cooking time and mess. You'll probably need a grounded (3-wire) extension cord of 16-gauge wire or larger to run from the outlet to your work area. It's hard to say how long the cord should be,

but to be safe get one at least 25 feet long.

Some appliances to consider are grills, fry pans with dome lids, toasters, and hand mixers. With an RV you can use these on your 110-volt system once you connect with the camp's power supply.

Incidentally, you will have to pay a little more for your space if you want to use the electricity.

Cookware and Utensils

These are the "tools of the trade" for cooks. You'll have to decide whether to develop a complete set of cookware and utensils just for family camping or bring these from home each time you camp. A compromise is probably best—some from home and others in your camping kit.

Outdoor cooking can be hard on good kitchen gear. Pots and kettles become dented, knives are nicked and dulled, and eating utensils are lost. Consider carefully those that should come from home.

Kits

If space and weight are factors in your consideration, an aluminum cook kit probably is for you. Many choices

HINT

The Dutch oven and the 4-N-Tote System should be considered. They convert a bed of coals into an oven.

are available in different gauge aluminum, with an assortment of contents. Most have nesting pots with lids, one or two skillets or frying pans, a hot beverage pot, and cups. If the cups are important to you, choose a cook kit that has plastic rather than metal cups. Metal cups are lip burners when used with hot beverages.

Also check the method of attachment for detachable handles. The system should give a secure hold on the pot or pan, yet be easy to attach and detach.

Another kind of cooking kit has basic tools such as knives, spatula, long-handled fork, ladle, bottle/can-opener, and peeler. An advantage of the tool kit is its packaging—usually in partitioned canvas that can be hung in a handy place near your work area.

Camp Griddle

This supplements your skillet. It is a flat piece of cast iron or aluminum that's easier to use with a spatula than the skillet with high sides. A non-stick surface is an advantage when cleaning, but you'll have to use a plastic spatula to keep from scratching through the surface.

Tongs

You'll find these helpful for lifting hot lids, lightweight pans, Dutch oven lids, and fry pans in use without their

detachable handles. Long-handled tongs are useful for picking up coals to put on a Dutch oven lid, and to turn items on a hot fire without singeing your hair.

Water Buckets

If you aren't using paper or plastic disposable dishes and utensils, you'll want a couple of large metal pails to heat dish and rinse water for dishwashing. These can also be used to carry water to your site.

Consider plastic collapsible water carriers with spouts. The spouts make it easy to pour small quantities of water.

Canvas water bags, also called desert water coolers, are useful in keeping drinking water cool, and for serving drinks. Soak them before filling and they'll work better.

Ice Chests

There are light foam ice chests of many sizes and prices. These make an inexpensive cooler, but won't last very long in use. More durable chests are made of insulated metal or plastic. A drain is handy, because ice does

HINT *Some foods can spoil just sitting in a warm car while driving to your campsite. That's a good reason for having an ice chest.*

melt. It's hard to dip the water out, and if you do you'll lose some of the box's cold, just as in leaving a refrigerator door open. In use, open the door or lid as little as possible. Temperatures will rise quickly if the box is open for long in warm weather.

HINT *Find a source of ice for your ice chest before you run out.*

These chests are more efficient when they cool down, so put a block of ice in several hours before the food, and don't let the ice supply get low during use.

Check the temperature of your ice chest while it's in use. Consider this: at 36 degrees F, large cuts of meat will keep for 3 or 4 days, but hamburger is safe for only 24 hours; poultry may keep 2 days. If held at 45 degrees F, eggs, butter, cheese, vegetables, fruit, and fluid milk will only keep a few days (more or less), depending on the item.

HINT *Avoid leftovers. Eat it or throw it away. This doesn't apply to things like bread, butter, jelly, peanut butter, and syrup, which will keep for awhile if packed away properly. Sealable plastic bags and plastic containers are good for this kind of storage. Also the original food container may be adequate.*

Holding these temperatures in an ice chest in summer heat is difficult. Finding spoiled food is bad—not finding it can be fatal!

Hand Protection

Cooking gloves are a necessity in outdoor cooking. Insulated flexible gloves have replaced asbestos since the cancer/asbestos connection was made. With these gloves you can pick up and move hot coals, lift a hot Dutch

oven lid, take aluminum foil off coals, and open the packages without burning your hands.

You can get by with leather gloves or hot pads, but don't try handling hot coals with them.

It has been said that if you use a pair of cooking gloves long enough, you'll never fear going hungry. Just put the gloves in boiling water for a nourishing stew!

Measuring Cups and Spoons

You can't follow recipe directions without accurate measuring. Get a set of plastic or metal measuring cups from ¼ to 1 cup size, and spoons from ⅛ teaspoon to 1 tablespoon. You might even find a 2- or 4-cup measure handy, too.

Dishwashing Tools

In addition to two hot-water buckets, you'll want a dish mop, rubber plate scraper, or dish brush, and pliers or tongs to hold dishes while washing with hot water. If using paper or plastic disposable dishes, you can dispense with these.

Scouring pads, either disposable or long-lasting, will help in cleaning pots and pans.

Mixing Tool

A hand operated rotary egg beater or chef's whisk are helpful for many mixing jobs in camp. You can get by with a fork or stirring spoon, but results will probably not be as good.

Dining Area

If you are sure your campsite will have a picnic table and benches, fine. Just bring along a piece of oilcloth or sheet of plastic to make a tablecloth.

In the long haul, though, it might be helpful to buy a

portable table and chairs. Then you can be sure you won't have to eat crosslegged on the ground—kind of uncomfortable after you reach a certain age.

You'll probably want a dining fly over your kitchen and dining area. It gives protection from sun and rain.

Storage of Cooking Gear

The cowboys of the Old West developed a simple item called a chuck box. It kept cooking gear and some non-perishable foods in one place, and provided work space for preparing food. If you'll be doing a lot of camping, a chuck box may serve a real purpose.

Here are rough plans for a chuck box that you can adapt to your needs by building to your own dimensions. It's not hard to make. Just be sure to use lightweight materials and don't make it so big it's hard to move around.

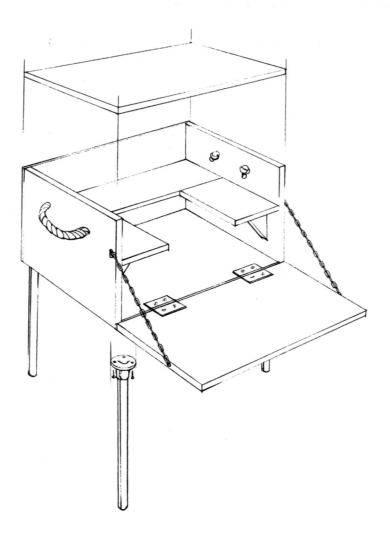

Chuck Box

Use ½-inch exterior grade plywood for sides, bottom, and top. Screw and glue together.

The back can be ¼-inch plywood screwed and glued all around to the ½ bottom, top, and sides. Since the front will be a work area, it should be of ½-inch thickness.

Hinge front at bottom so it opens for a work area. Keep it from dropping below 90 degrees by a light chain on each side. Put a hasp at the top to hold or lock shut. Install shelves mounted on cleats on sides and back.

Legs are made of threaded ¾-inch metal or 1-inch PVC pipe screwed into pipe mounts at the bottom corners. You can make the worktable more stable by fastening wedges under the front pipe mounts to slant the front legs forward.

Make handles of rope knotted inside holes drilled near the top on each side.

Finish by painting or varnishing. You may want to cover the work surface with countertop covering.

Other Cooking Items

There are many other things shown in the following checklist, but their functions are obvious, so descriptions aren't needed.

This checklist looks formidable and it is if you think you have to buy all of these things. This is an all-inclusive list. You decide which items are necessary for your kind

---

HINT — *A pressure cooker with regulator can save cooking time, especially with stews.*

---

of cooking. When you have decided, you might develop your own checklist to use each time you are getting ready to go camping. This will be important if you are using some items from your home kitchen.

Cooking Gear Checklist

_____ Camp stove and fuel (could be grill over wood fire)

_____ Heat localizer rings

_____ Ice chest

_____ Dining fly

_____ Kettles (preferably nesting)

_____ Dutch oven

_____ Reflector oven

_____ Skillets (large and medium—consider one of heavy cast iron)

_____ Griddle

_____ 2 pails

_____ Water storage container with pouring spout

_____ Desert water bag

_____ Serving dishes

_____ Mixing bowls

_____ Cutting board

_____ Strainer or colander

_____ Spatulas (metal and plastic to use with non-stick surface)

_____ Butcher knives

_____ Paring knife

_____ Peeler

_____ Can/bottle-openers

_____ Long-handled fork

_____ Serving spoons

_____ Ladles

_____ Wooden stirring spoons

_____ Rotary beater or chef's whisk

_____ Tongs (both short- and long-handled)

_____ Grater/shredder

_____ Insulated gloves

_____ Leather gloves or hot pads

_____ Extension forks for marshmallows, hot dogs, and toast

_____ Skewers for kabobs

_____ Wooden matches or match firestarters

_____ Plates, cups, bowls, knives, forks, spoons

_____ Plastic wrap

_____ Heavy duty aluminum foil

_____ Paper towels

_____ Napkins

_____ Self-sealing plastic bags

_____ Plastic food containers with lids

_____ Foil cooking pans

_____ Oilcloth or plastic tablecloth

_____ Sharpening stone

_____ Sponges

_____ Dish mop

_____ Dish scraper

_____ Scouring pads

_____ Liquid detergent

_____ Portable table and chairs

_____ Chuck box

_____ Electric fry pan

_____ Electric griddle

_____ Electric hot plate

_____ Electric mixer

_____ Electric toaster

_____ Extension cord

Camp Comfort

Housing and cooking gear aren't the only items important to camp comfort. Among the others are clothing, bedrolls, air mattresses, foam pads, cots, lanterns, insect protection, toilets, and personal grooming articles.

Clothing

This is a personal thing that you take care of every day at home by going to your closet and dresser drawers. It's a little different in camp. You have to bring everything you'll need from home. Most camp clothing will consist of the things you wear around home. Differences depend on the climate of the camping area, activities available, and the kind of campground.

You'll need bathing suits and towels if going to a lake, ocean setting, or a campground with a swimming pool. If there will be horseback riding, you'll want a broad-brimmed hat, boots, and jeans. A camp in the mountains will probably require warmer clothing, particularly at night. A camp in a hot humid area will call for shorts and T-shirts. If there are mosquitoes or biting flies, you'll want long sleeves and trousers. So, follow the Boy Scout motto. "Be Prepared."

The kind of camp will influence your clothing plans. Your needs for a two-day weekend camp will be quite different from those of a week-long trip.

Many private campgrounds have complete coin-operated laundries. If the campground where you'll be staying on a lengthy trip has laundry facilities, you won't have to bring a change of clothing for each family member for every day. These camp laundries usually have dryers as well as washing machines, but a clothesline and clothespins will come in handy after a rain.

Whether you will be doing laundry in camp or wait until you get home, you'll want to bring a mesh or duffel bag to hold soiled clothing until wash time.

Packing

Experienced family campers have found it an advantage to pack each person's clothing in a separate suitcase, packsack, duffel bag, cardboard carton, or other container. They label each container with the name of the person to whom it belongs.

An exception to this is with raingear. You never know when it might be needed, and it's foolish to have to dig into separate containers for rainsclothes every time they are needed. You'd better make one more container just for the raingear.

Special Clothing for Special Conditions

Clothing to protect you from rain is the most obvious. You'll want a rainhat, raincoat, and rubbers as a minimum for each person. A rain suit will probably keep you drier if you'll be doing things in the rain. These two-piece outfits have a drawstring hood, waist and ankle cuffs, and elasticized wrists. Get rain pants with legs large enough to put over your footwear.

Unless you and your family are inveterate hikers, anxious to tackle rough backcountry trails, you won't need

special hiking boots. Sneakers or moccasins are fine for most activities around camp, and for short hikes of 5 to 10 miles.

Cold weather is another special condition to think about. It is recommended that you use the layer method of keeping warm. Many layers of clothing are warmer than one thick layer, and you can take off or put on layers to match the weather. The first of the layers to wear in very cold weather is thermal underwear, followed by a wool shirt and trousers. You'll want to consider a windbreaker to stave off the chill caused by wind. A hood or parka-type garment is good because it keeps the heat from your body from escaping around your neck.

Head covering is extremely important in keeping you warm. Antarctic explorer Paul Siple did a study on body comfort in cold climates, and found that the head is the body's thermostat. If you keep your head warm and dry, you'll be avoiding chilling the rest of your body.

Mittens are warmer than gloves because there isn't a heat loss all the way around each finger, just around the thumb. If you find that hard to believe, just put that single cold thumb in with the fingers and see how fast it warms up. Carry gloves with you to wear when a job calls for use of fingers.

Sleeping Comfort

Sleeping Bags

You'll probably sleep warmer in a sleeping bag than in blankets of equivalent weight. The bag is designed to eliminate drafts. Unless well fastened with blanket pins, blankets have a tendency to develop drafts during the night.

The problem with a sleeping bag is the inability of a single bag to meet all temperature conditions. A summer bag won't do in the winter, nor will a winter bag be comfortable in the heat of summer.

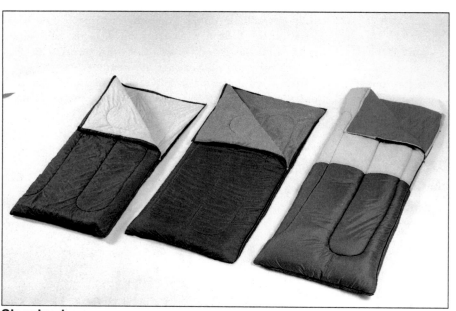

Sleeping bags.

Air mattress, pillow and pad.

Some manufacturers classify their bags according to seasonal suitability—spring, summer, fall, and winter, or combinations of two or three. They will go so far as to list a bag as OK for spring, fall, and winter, but few will claim a four season capability. Best for most use is the three season kind. You can always sleep on top in the summer.

Check out sleeping bag shapes when buying. A mummy bag is warmer than a rectangular bag of the same weight because there is less heat loss from your feet and around your shoulders.

There are also mummy bags with hoods. Remember what was said about the importance of keeping your head warm? There are some who find the mummy bag too confining for comfort. It's hard to roll over in one, for example. You have to learn to roll the whole bag.

An advantage of a rectangular bag is that if you buy two matching bags with full zipper, you can open each bag and zip the two together to make a double bag in which two people can sleep comfortably, and warm since two bodies in a single bag have less heat loss than just one. The stocking cap worn to bed by our ancestors in their cold homes is useful in camp if you don't have a sleeping bag hood.

Today's sleeping bags are machine washable. Many campers find that the convenience of a light sleeping bag outweighs any advantages of sheets and blankets, even in a trailer or motor home. They are easy to put

away in the morning, and to get out at night. They don't come apart in use the way sheets and blankets do when used with foam mattresses common in RV's that have beds that double as couches during the day.

Air Mattresses, Foam Pads, and Cots

You'll want some kind of padding under you when sleeping. Air mattresses are fine for this. They pack into a small space when not inflated, and are comfortable when inflated properly. Air mattress users generally recommend that you first overinflate your bag. Then sit on it and slowly deflate it until your rump just touches the ground. When you lie down on it your weight will be distributed over a wider area than when sitting, and it will be about right. If you try to sleep on a fully inflated air mattress, you'll tend to roll off during the night. Experiment a little to find the best inflation pressure for your comfort.

You can save weight and cost by buying a short air mattress like the ones used for riding the surf at ocean beaches. They'll support your head, shoulders, and hips. Many feel that leg support isn't needed for comfort.

Air mattresses come in rubberized fabric and plastic. The fabric mattresses are heavier and more expensive, but will last longer and be less subject to puncturing.

Foam sleep pads have gained popularity in recent years. These are similar to the pads found as mattresses in many RV's. They come in different lengths, the most popular being only 24 inches long. This is ample to

support your head, shoulders, and hips. A short foam pad compresses to the approximate size of an uninflated sleeping bag and doesn't have to be inflated and deflated each time you set up or leave a campsite.

If you are using either of these on the ground, you'll want a groundcloth. A plastic sheet is adequate to keep moisture from the ground from dampening the underside of your mattress. A groundcloth that fits the inside sod cloth of a floorless tent seals it against crawling insects.

You might want to consider a folding cot for sleeping in a tent. The flexibility of the canvas in a camp cot provides enough give to spread your body weight evenly. Canvas cots can make for cold sleeping unless there is a good layer of insulation between you and the canvas.

You'll find a wide range of cots today. There are the original wood frame cots with canvas still for sale, and to these have been added light aluminum framed cots with vinyl-impregnated poly-duck covers.

Pillows

Pillows are important to sleeping comfort. In a tent trailer or RV you can either bring your down or polyester filled pillows from home, or buy a second set to store in the vehicle.

Where space and weight are important, you can get an air pillow that inflates quickly and stores compactly.

Insect Protection

If you are going where there's even a remote chance of mosquitoes, you'll want a mosquito net or screen. These are easy to set up over sleeping bags or cots, and will assure you of a good night's sleep undisturbed by a single mosquito buzzing around your head.

There are also good insect repellents on the market. Some are liquid or cream that can be rubbed over exposed areas of skin. Others are sprays that kill bugs in a confined space like a tent, trailer, camper, or motor home.

Still more elaborate are the electric "zap" systems that attract flying insects to a light and then kill them when they touch an electrically charged grid. These are also effective used around your kitchen and dining area.

Camp Lighting
Battery Powered

Battery powered lights are the safest to use in camp. There's no flame in these so there's no danger of fire when using them in tents or even while reading in your sleeping bag.

There are tiny hand lights, larger flashlights, camp lanterns, and table lamps. Some camp lanterns have fluorescent tubes and operate off batteries, 110-volt power with an adapter, or a 12-volt adapter that can plug into your car's cigarette lighter.

Gasoline Lanterns

These were the common camp and cabin lanterns in places without electricity years ago, and are still an excellent camp lantern. They give a steady, bright light

LP (Liquid Petroleum)

The most common LP fuels are propane and butane. Most camp lanterns operate on bottled propane. The light a propane lantern produces is comparable to that of a gasoline lantern.

Propane cylinders are safe to use and easy to attach to the lantern unit. Some lanterns use the cylinder as part of the lantern base.

If you are using propane for your cooking stove, and have the adapter mentioned in the cooking gear section, you can hook up your lantern to the cylinder and use it

Gasoline lanterns

that's easy on the eyes, and capable of lighting a sizable area of your campsite.

They use white gasoline and must be pressurized with a self-contained pump. If you are using a gasoline cooking stove, a gasoline lantern is a fine mate since it uses the same fuel.

If you've ever used one of these lanterns you know that the gasoline lights up a fragile mantle. This mantle glows brightly to give a light comparable to an electric bulb. But, the mantles are delicate. You'll need a supply of mantles unless you are extremely careful in handling the lantern, particularly in moving from campground to campground.

Kerosene Lanterns

There are two main types of kerosene lanterns—the wick, and the mantle. A wick lantern burns with a steady, but rather dim flame that is adequate for lighting small areas of your campsite. The mantle lantern burns with a light similar to that of a gasoline lantern or electric light bulb.

Kerosene isn't as volatile a fuel as gasoline, so it is safer to transport and to fill lanterns with than gasoline. It is a little harder to find than propane or white gasoline.

at the same time you're running a couple of stoves.

Mantles in propane lanterns are as fragile as those in gasoline lanterns, so bring along extra mantles.

Camp Toilets

Most campgrounds today have some type of toilets. The more primitive have the old pit type, but most, particularly the private campgrounds, have regular flush toilets.

If there aren't toilets at your campground, you should have a portable chemical toilet that can be dumped after use in a flush toilet or RV dumping station. These are easy to clean, completely sanitary, and use a chemical deodorant. You'll want to have a piece of canvas and poles to make a screen around your toilet for privacy.

Self-contained RV's have their own holding tanks that operate the same way as portable chemical toilets. In campgrounds with full hookups, a sewer outlet makes it possible to run sewage through a flexible hose directly from the RV to the sewer.

Except for wilderness backpacking trips, the day is past when you can dig a latrine and build a rustic toilet atop the hole. Any digging leads to later erosion problems, so it's best to use modern toilet facilities.

Even if you will be using campground toilets, it's wise to bring your own supply of toilet paper. Campgrounds are noted for running out of both toilet paper and paper towels.

Grooming

RV's have their own sinks with running water to use for personal grooming. Most have a hot water tank that provides hot water for showers and washing hands and face. Campgrounds with central sanitary facilities usually also have hot water at sinks, and in showers.

Wash water is called "gray water" in campground terminology. In some campgrounds you can either run this out on the ground, or into a bucket that you can then use to throw the water out over grass or at the base of trees that can use the water. In other campgrounds, "gray water" must drain into the sewer outlet. Campgrounds distribute a set of rules to arriving campers. Rules on "gray water" are usually specified.

If you're camped at a site without washing facilities, you'll want to provide your own. There are portable sinks available that have their own water tanks with a hand pump to bring water to a faucet. They have built-in drains.

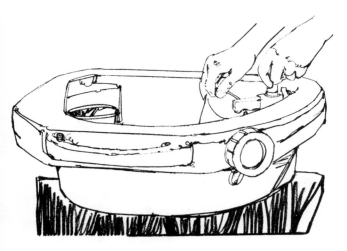

A plastic washbasin on a tripod stand is an alternative to a portable sink. You can get by with an old-fashioned washbasin sitting on a table.

Portable showers are also available. They have a privacy enclosure around them that can double as a screen for your chemical toilet.

HINT *If men are accustomed to using electric razors and the site doesn't have electricity, consider getting a battery operated rechargeable razor, or face up to razor blades.*

A few things to make your outdoor grooming more convenient may be found in grooming kits containing soap dish, mirror, comb, toothbrush, and washcloth. These items will be needed singly anyway, and in a kit you have a container that holds them all together.

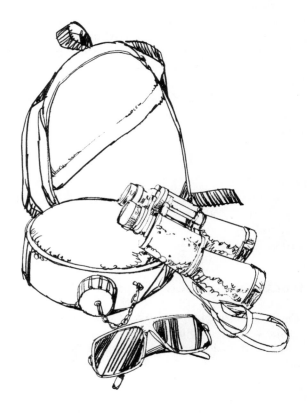

Miscellaneous Comfort Items

Consider bringing sewing materials to handle torn clothing. A few buttons of different sizes will come in handy.

A tent repair kit is invaluable if you accidentally tear your tent. Rips that aren't fixed while they are small get big fast.

A collapsible drinking cup is useful. Campgrounds often don't have drinking fountains. When hiking with a friend or two, you can use the personal collapsible cups to all drink from the same canteen.

If you'll be taking day hikes from your camp, you'll probably want a small hike bag to carry your lunch and items like camera, binoculars, canteen, and insect repellent.

It's smart to bring extra eyeglasses if you wear glasses.

If you break or lose your regular pair, you can survive until you get home.

A travel alarm clock will come in handy even though you don't plan to get up early. It's handy to use for timing cooking, and you might need the alarm to waken from an afternoon siesta.

A portable radio will keep you in touch with the world and bring weather reports that might influence activity plans. Just keep the volume down so you don't disturb fellow campers. Chances are that one reason they came camping was to get away from the blare of a radio or TV.

Lightweight canvas folding chairs are great for just sitting around camp reading or chatting with friendly neighbors.

Camp Tools

The first items on the following list are primarily for tent campers, although they will be useful for RV campers, especially if they are going to do any wood cutting for campfires or barbecues.

Tent Camping Tools

Saws. The original camp saw was called a bucksaw because it was used to buck wood (cut into usable lengths). It was used with wood held in place for sawing on a sawbuck.

The camp saw you use today is an offspring of the bucksaw. Camp saws use narrow blades that are replaceable. Blades are held tight for use in a variety of frames. Use a 5-inch ignition file to touch up the edges of the blade when it gets dull while in camp. After the trip, replace the blade rather than trying to sharpen it unless you happen to be an expert. The frustration of a dull blade or one that cuts in a curve isn't worth the cost of a new blade.

These saws' blades are very sharp and need to be masked (covered) so they don't cut when and where they aren't supposed to. A length of garden hose with a slit cut along one side makes a good mask.

There is also available a small folding pack saw with a blade similar to that described. The blade folds into the handle of this saw, thus being self-masking.

Another handy little saw is the pocket cable saw. This is a flexible steel cable with sharp cutting spurs on all sides. It has thumb rings on each end for easy use in pulling back and forth through light wood. It's handy for sawing off lower dead tree branches for kindling wood.

Don't downgrade the value of a saw in collecting wood. If you've ever seen someone hacking away at a piece of wood with a hatchet, and then watched someone slice through a similar piece in a tenth the time with a bow saw, you'll be sold.

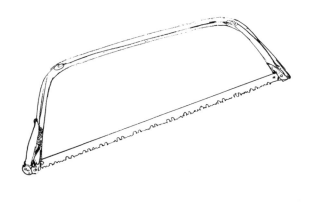

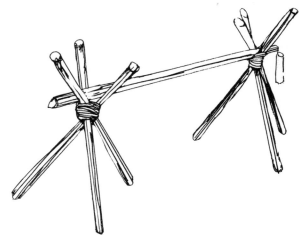

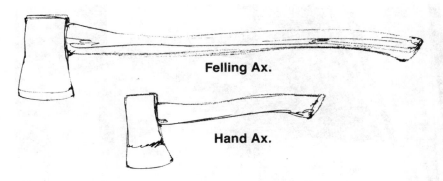

Felling Ax.

Hand Ax.

Hatchets and Axes. A hand ax is fine for light camp chores. It is quite capable of cutting and splitting wood up to 2 inches thick when used with a chopping block to give support. Remember, split wood burns better than in the round. A hatchet is meant to be used in one hand and is awkward if you try to make it a two-handed ax.

HINT   *Keep your cutting tools sharp. A sharp tool is safer than a dull one.*

A felling ax is for cutting larger branches. As its name implies, it's also for felling trees. It has a heavier head

and longer handle than a hatchet. It is a two-handed ax and is awkward and dangerous to use with one hand.

As in the case of a saw, axes should be masked when not in use. They can be masked in their sheaths or by sinking the blade solidly into a dead log, stump, or chopping block. Keep your ax or hatchet off the ground. Your ax is designed to cut or split wood, but if you do use the butt or poll to drive tent pegs, be sure to remove the sheath first. Even if your sheath doesn't cover the butt, you'll ruin it as the force of the blows drives the sharp blade through the end of the sheath.

Keep your ax sharp by filing with an 8-inch mill file. You can touch it up with a sharpening stone if it's not real dull.

Other Camp Tools. A camp shovel will come in handy, although you won't be allowed to dig in most campgrounds today. It's good for moving hot coals, and may help you get your vehicle out if you get stuck.

Your shovel need not be a long-handled type. For your use, a small trench shovel or large trowel will be adequate.

You'll find use for lengths of cord, along with some elastic shock cord. Some soft wire is useful, as are side cutting pliers. Safety pins and wire clothes-hangers will also come in handy.

RV Camping Tools

Many of the tools described for tent camping are useful for RV campers. But there are other tools that are specifically for RV's. You'll want a substantial mechanic's

---

HINT   *An awning attached to the side of an RV adds usable outdoor space protected from sun and rain.*

---

toolbox, large enough to pack all these tools, and any others you think you might need.

Pliers are perhaps the handiest of tools. Include a pair of standard pliers, needle-nose, clamp type, wire cutters, and adjustable channel lock pliers.

You'll also want an assortment of screwdrivers. Include different sizes of each kind—slot, Phillips, and clutch heads.

You'll want a couple of crescent wrenches, one 6-inch, the other 12-inch. Other wrenches should include a $\frac{3}{8}$-inch drive socket set with sockets from $\frac{1}{4}$ to 1 inch. These are great for getting into hard-to-reach places. You may even want to add a universal joint adapter. Another set of wrenches that will reach places and do

things the sockets can't handle are box and open end combinations from ¼ to 1 inch.

For electrical work you'll want a 12-volt circuit tester, a combination crimper and wire stripper, a soldering iron with rosin core solder, and a roll of electricians' tape.

A small pipe wrench will handle stuck nuts, and miscellaneous plumbing repairs. A hacksaw will be useful for these jobs, too.

A pop rivet setter with steel and aluminum rivets will let you replace rivets that have come out during travel. You'll want an electric drill with an assortment of bits up to ¼-inch diameter. You'll need these for making holes for rivets to strengthen areas where old rivets have come out.

Many fasteners in RV's need nut drivers to tighten, so carry a set of these from 9/32 to 1/2 inch.

A few other valuable items for your toolbox are a hammer, spare electrical fuses (check your car and RV

for correct sizes and amperage), a 10-foot tape measure, a can of light oil, some penetrating oil, white glue, and contact cement.

HINT *You'll need extra batteries, bulbs, lantern mantles, and fuel unless you're sure they will be available in your campground's store.*

These will all go in your mechanic's toolbox. You'll also want a tire gauge, but will want that in the glove compartment or a handy drawer in the trailer.

!!Caution!!

The following checklist, combined with the Cooking Gear Checklist, may seem so overwhelming it could scare you from even considering family camping. Please use the list with a big dose of caution. Items are optional, based on the kind of camping you'll be doing. As mentioned earlier, gear from regular home use may double as camping gear.

Camping Gear Checklist

Tent Camping Gear

_____Personal clothing including rain and special activity items

_____Personal grooming articles— soap and dish, comb, mirror, washcloth, toothbrush and toothpaste, curling iron, razor, etc.

_____Laundry bag

_____Sleeping bags or blankets

_____Pillows

_____Groundcloths

_____Air mattresses, foam pads, or cots

_____Mosquito nets or screens

_____Insect repellent

_____Flashlights

_____Camp lanterns

_____Table lamps

_____Extra batteries, extra bulbs, propane, gasoline, kerosene, extra lamp mantles

_____Portable chemical toilet and chemical deodorant

_____Toilet paper

_____Toilet privacy screen

_____Portable sink

_____Portable shower

_____Sewing kit

_____Tent repair kit

_____Collapsible drinking cups

_____Hike bag

_____Extra eyeglasses

_____Travel alarm clock

_____Portable radio

_____Folding easy chairs

_____Camp saw

_____Hatchet or ax

_____Sharpening instruments— ignition file, mill file, whetstone

_____Camp shovel

_____Cord, wire, clothesline and clothespins

_____Side cutting pliers

_____First-aid kit

RV Camp Gear (in addition to some tent camping items)

_____Mechanic's toolbox with the following contents:

Pliers

_____Regular

_____Needle-nose

_____Clamp

_____Channel lock

_____Wire cutters

Screwdrivers

_____Slot

_____Phillips

_____Clutch head

Wrenches

_____6-inch crescent

_____12-inch crescent

_____Socket set

_____Combination set

_____Nut driver set

_____Pipe

Electrical

_____12-volt circuit tester

_____Combo wire cutter/crimper

_____Soldering iron and rosin core solder

_____Electricians' tape

Miscellaneous

_____Hacksaw

_____Pop rivet setter and rivets

_____Hammer

_____Electrical fuses

_____Tape measure

_____Can light oil

_____Can penetrating oil

_____White glue

_____Contact cement

_____Tire gauge

HINT
You don't need everything on the above list. Be selective. Use a transparent felt-tip marking pen to highlight the items you'll need for your kind of camping. Ignore the rest for now. You can add to the list as your experience dictates the items you may want later.

HEALTH, SAFETY, AND FIRST AID

"First aid is immediate help right after an injury. First aid isn't playing doctor. It's doing the things that must be done before expert help arrives."

Scout Handbook

Bits and pieces of health and safety are scattered throughout this book. You'll find references to them in every chapter. That's how important these are to family camping.

It may seem repetitious to read about fire safety here, and then again in later chapters, but if one life can be saved or a child spared from lifelong scars, the repetition is worthwhile.

Family camping should be a learning and growing experience for those taking part. Lessons learned in camp about health and safety can last a lifetime.

It has been said many times that an example is better than a lecture. In family camping, you have a chance to teach by example, but be sure your children understand what you are doing and why you're doing it.

For example, in this day of the self-service gas pump, there's a tendency to overlook those safety precautions we used to count on from the attendant, things like checking oil, water, tires, hoses, fanbelts, and wiper blades. The pre-camp check of your car, shared with your children, can teach them its importance.

Precautions taken before building fires, when swimming, on the highway, and in the use of camp tools should be pointed out, explaining what you are doing and why.

Do your children really know why they shouldn't drink from just any water source? Or why garbage should be disposed of properly? Or what could happen if gasoline is transferred from a can to a gasoline stove tank near an open flame?

You have a great chance to teach basic first aid in a meaningful way in a camp setting—not just to teach your children something new, but to prepare them to help themselves and others.

The way to really learn something well is to teach it to others. In the process of teaching first aid to your children, you'll imprint these concepts in your own mind. They'll be there whenever they're needed.

Vehicle Safety

Before Leaving

Passenger Cars

You've checked your car, and it passes inspection. Now make sure it isn't overloaded with cargo and passengers. Chances are it's normally able to carry family members in comfort, but how about those same passengers and all the gear needed for a camping trip?

One way to tell with a passenger car is to eyeball it from the side. It shouldn't look like it's going uphill—low

in the rear, and high in front. Another way is to check the center of your car headlights high beam on your garage door when the car is unloaded. Check it again with the car loaded. If the center of the beam strikes well above the normal mark, you're overloaded.

HINT *Keep all doors locked when your vehicle is in motion.*

Follow the advice in "Getting There" (Chap. 6), and buy or rent a cargo trailer. A car can pull a lot more than it can safely carry.

Another car problem might be lack of space. Passengers and excess gear are so crammed into the vehicle there's little room for comfort. Don't expect children to ride for hours in a space so small they are uncomfortable.

The answer to this problem, if you aren't also weighted down, is a cartop carrier, also discussed in "Getting There."

RV's

If your RV is overloaded based on the gross weight capacity on the RV's specification plate, the answer depends on your RV type. If it's a motor home or pickup camper, you can follow the advice given for a car: get a cargo trailer.

HINT *Seat belts should be installed and used by all passengers, not just those in the front seats.*

But, if your RV is a tent or travel trailer or a 5th wheeler, you can't expect to tow another trailer behind, so there's only one solution. Cut weight.

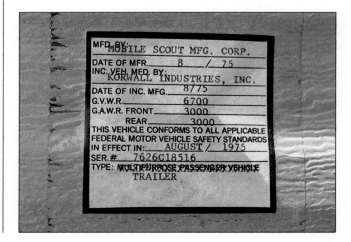

Test Run

If the camping trip you're about to take is your first—first ever, or first with your present car or RV—a test run can be invaluable. This test run should be with the loaded car or RV including the passengers that will be making the trip.

You'll find out several things. Are you overloaded either in weight or bulk? Does the engine overheat? If you will be climbing hills on your trip, find a hill and go up and down several times to check overheating and towing ability. Remember that if it's a struggle, it will be worse if you're traveling to higher elevations in mountains. Gasoline engines with sea-level carburetion lose a great deal of power at higher altitudes.

So, what do you do about what you find? Take your vehicle to the service department of a dealer for that vehicle. The service manager can tell you whether overheating can be corrected by installing a supplemental electric water cooling fan, transmission oil cooler, or crankcase oil cooler. It may take one or all of these to overcome a heating problem. Before spending the money for these cooling devices, you should receive assurances from the dealer that they will do the job.

Lack of power is another story. It can be overcome by installing a rear end with a different axle gear ratio, but that's expensive and will cut gas mileage. That's one reason for making sure your vehicle has enough towing power to handle the load before buying a trailer.

Your test run will also give you a feel for the road in your RV. It's longer than your car. You can't take corners

HINT *Use your turn signals when leaving or returning to the highway, and when changing lanes. Remember, they are on your trailer, too.*

as sharply as you're used to. Acceleration isn't the same with a heavy RV or trailer behind a car. You can also practice using your new rear-view side mirrors, and with a motor home or van, the bullet lens on the rear window. Practice stopping. It will feel strange when towing a trailer with brakes, so get used to it.

You'll notice when towing a travel trailer on a highway where speeding trucks are traveling in both directions that your trailer may sway badly from the turbulence caused by these passing behemoths. It's possible to install an anti-sway bar between your car and trailer to control sway. It will also be helpful when driving with a strong wind blowing from the side. You probably won't have this sway when towing a low profile tent trailer.

HINT *Double your normal following distance behind the car ahead of you when towing or driving a heavy vehicle. It will take more time to slow down or stop because of the extra weight.*

On the Road

The unexpected can always happen despite all pre-checks and obedience to traffic conditions and laws.

Accidents

If you have an accident:

1. Don't leave the scene.
2. Help the injured but don't move them unless they are endangered by fire or other life-threatening condition.
3. Call police. Use C.B. if available; call Channel 9. Ask for an ambulance if needed.
4. Write down names, addresses, license numbers, and insurance company of persons involved.
5. Get names and addresses of *at least* two witnesses.
6. Write down a description and registration number of vehicles involved.
7. Diagram the accident showing how each car was moving and approximate distances involved.
8. Notify your insurance company.

Breakdowns

Get out of traffic as soon as possible if your vehicle breaks down. Pull off the road if you can. Turn on your emergency lights, and raise the hood of your vehicle. If you don't have flashers, tie a white cloth to the antenna or roadside door handle. Stay near, but not in your car. Set out flares or emergency reflectors, especially at night.

Overheating

The first sign of overheating will show on your temperature gauge. Stop in the right stopping lane. Some expressways have stopping lanes at the dividers on the left, too, but these are dangerous because they are near the fast lane, and there's no place for your family to wait, out of the vehicle. Put on your emergency lights and brake. Shift into neutral. Keep the engine running a little faster than idle to keep your water pump circulating water through the radiator and block. Turn your heater on full. Though it seems strange, that helps dissipate heat from the engine. Have passengers get out on the right side, and move away from the vehicle. Open the hood, but not the radiator cap. Keep the engine running. Wait a few minutes.

Your radiator has a pressure cap. It takes two separate turns to open completely. Put on a glove, or protect your hand with some rags. Turn the cap the first turn. This will release steam, so be careful. It will scald you if it

HEALTH, SAFETY, AND FIRST AID

hits bare skin. After the steam has stopped, make the second turn to open the cap.

Shut off the engine, and wait for the block to cool down. Meanwhile try to find the source of the problem. Is your fan belt in place? Check the oil level in the crankcase. OK? Any hoses leaking? Maybe your trouble was trying to pull the weight while using your air conditioner.

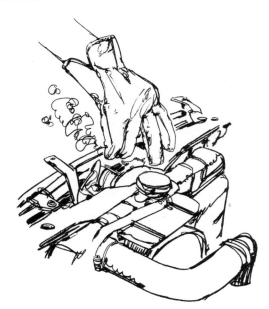

If you are carrying extra water, start your engine, and add water slowly, checking for leaks. Let the engine run awhile and check the temperature gauge. If it looks all

right, load the family and head out, taking it easy, and without using the air conditioner.

If you don't have extra water or the car continues to overheat, you'll have to get help.

Tire Problem

When a tire goes flat, don't slam on the brakes. Just let up on the gas, turn on your emergency flashers, and coast into the right stopping lane. Set the emergency brake. Put out warning triangles or flares if at night.

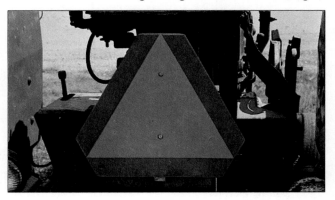

Unload passengers from the right side of the vehicle and have them move away. Put blocks in front of and behind the tire that is diagonally opposite the flat. Loosen each wheel nut about a half turn before raising the vehicle on a jack.

If the flat is on a car, follow normal tire-changing procedure. Put on the spare, load up, and drive to a service staion for tire repair.

If you have a flat on one of the dual rear wheels of a motor home or pickup truck, you have a choice. You can drive a few miles slowly with the flat tire in place, or you can stop and take it off, and drive to the nearest service station on the remaining dual. This will protect the flat tire from possible further damage. If the flat tire is one of the front tires and you don't have a spare, you can take off one of the dual tires and put it in place of the flat tire.

You also have a choice if towing a tandem-wheeled travel trailer. You can drive slowly with the flat tire in place, or you can take it off. Your trailer torsion bar will keep the hub from lowering to the road. With a tandem trailer, you don't need a jack. Just back your trailer up on one of your leveling blocks so the good tire is on the block. This will raise the flat tire off the road, making removal easy.

If you have a blowout, don't overreact. Keep a firm hold on the wheel but don't make a sharp turn toward the stopping lane. If you have to brake, do it gently.

Emergency Equipment

Carry the following emergency items in your vehicle at all times:

_____Spare tire, tool kit

_____ABC type fire extinguisher

_____Road flares, flashlight, triangular portable reflector kit

_____Jumper cable

_____Gloves

_____Spare can of oil and opener

_____Empty 1-gallon red gasoline container

_____Gasoline siphon hose

_____Spare parts—fan belt and fuses

_____Special for winter—chains, ice scraper, spray deicer, shovel, gallon milk carton filled with dry sand

_____First-aid kit, blanket

_____Roll of 1″ repair tape

Health and Safety at the Site

Site Selection

If you have a choice of sites, safety should be a main consideration. There are things to look for.

Avoid sites under large trees, especially if they have any large dead branches. In a storm, the branches could fall on your tent with fatal consequences. Even an RV can be severely damaged by falling limbs.

Lightning tends to strike the highest points in an area, so avoid camping near the tallest trees.

Never camp in a gully or under an overhanging cliff. The gully could become a raging river and the cliff a landslide.

The site should have reasonable security against fire.

Battery operated smoke alarms work as well in RV's and tents as they do in your home, and are as valuable in warning you of fire. They are a cheap investment in your safety.

Hookups

Make sure any extension cord running from an outlet to your RV or tent site has wire big enough to safely handle the load. This should be at least 16-gauge wire. Larger, meaning a smaller gauge number, would be even better.

Check the location of hookup facilities in your site, and then position your vehicle to take advantage of the location. You'll need to have the holding tank outlet near enough to the sewer to reach your hose. Your water hose and extension cord will need to reach the outlets.

After moving to the best site location, chock your wheels before hooking up.

Personal Cleanliness

Family members should be clean when it counts. Soap-and-water scrubbing is important before cooking, handling eating utensils, and eating, and after using a toilet.

A lightweight plastic, canvas, or metal washbasin is a must, even in a permanent campsite that has washing facilities. The cooks should have a way to wash their hands as needed during meal preparation.

If you camp near a lake or stream, don't soap bathe in the water. A quick dip to rinse off dirt or a supervised swim is fine, but a lake or stream isn't the place for soap bathing.

Bathe regularly—if possible every day. Showers are usually provided at established campgrounds. If not, arrange for your own portable shower.

Drinking Water and Milk

A constant supply of pure drinking water is essential. Thermos jugs, plastic water containers, and sterilized milk cans with covers work fine. Water should be dispensed into each person's own drinking cup, or preferably into paper cups.

Don't take a chance on using water you're not sure of. Salmonella, polio, cholera, dysentery, hepatitis, and typhoid can be contracted by drinking unpurified water.

If there is any doubt about the purity of the water, one of four purification methods may be used:

1. Boil water for 10 minutes, cool, and aerate by pouring back and forth from one container to another rapidly several times.

HEALTH, SAFETY, AND FIRST AID

2. Add water purification tablets and let the water stand for 30 minutes before drinking. Follow instructions on container.

3. Add 5 drops of 2% tincture of iodine to 1 quart of water and let stand for 30 minutes. *Never* use iodine drops or tablets in aluminum containers. Iodine reacts with aluminum to poison the water.

4. Add 2 drops of household bleach to 1 quart of water. Let stand for 30 minutes.

Plan for 1 quart of milk per day per person, including that used in cooking. Use pasteurized, canned, powdered, or the new packaged long shelf-life milk. This last item has been used in Europe for several years with great success. It will keep unopened for up to 6 months without refrigeration (an expiration date is stamped on each carton). It requires refrigeration after opening, but since it comes in 1 quart size, there should be little left after a normal family meal. *Under no conditions should raw milk be used.* Don't buy more fresh milk than will be used before it turns sour. How long milk may be safely stored will depend on the temperature of your refrigerator.

Sanitation

Garbage can be disposed of by burning, putting in campsite garbage cans subject to daily pickup, or carrying to such facilities in other locations. Don't throw aluminum foil in the fire with your garbage. It won't burn.

The importance of proper garbage disposal was emphasized by the first Director of Camping of the Boy Scouts of America, L. L. McDonald, who said, "When inspecting a camp for health and safety I make it a point to check the garbage dump at mealtime because that's when the flies are up at the dining hall." The connection between garbage, flies, and your food is indisputable, and flies carry germs.

Additional suggestions about disposal of garbage, waste water, and wilderness area latrines can be found near the end of "Setting Up Camp" (Chap. 6).

Woods Tools

An ax and hatchet top the list of dangerous camp tools. There are a few precautions that can make them safe.

Always use a sharp tool. It will cut and not glance when it strikes. If you do cut yourself with a sharp edge, the cut will be clean, and not torn and jagged as with a dull blade.

Be sure the head of your ax or hatchet is on tight. Most modern ones have the head bonded to the handle, so this isn't a problem with a new tool. But, older axes and hatchets have wedges driven into a wooden handle through the eye of the tool. When the wood dries out, it

shrinks. The head loosens and could fly off in use. You can re-wedge the head or soak it in linseed oil. This will make the wood swell and tighten.

HINT *Don't cut wood held in your hand or underfoot with a swing of your ax or hatchet.*

When getting ready to chop, be sure there aren't overhanging branches or other obstructions to interfere with a free swing.

The safest way to cut and split wood is with the contact method. This is described in "Setting Up Camp" (Chap. 6).

HINT *Knives, axes, and saws should be properly sheathed when not in use.*

Human Hazards

Whenever you set up camp, you create hazards to health and safety that weren't there when you came.

It's easy to trip over tent ropes and pegs anytime, but especially in the dark. Tie pieces of white cloth to the ropes and the tops of pegs to mark their location.

A clothesline is a hazard that's easier to overcome than a tent rope. Just tie it so it's higher than your head. Then no one except an NBA center will get caught on it.

Keep your campsite free of clutter. Don't have gear sitting here, there, and everywhere. Your family will be very "trippable" in such a site.

If your RV windows swing sideways or up to open, hang a strip of cloth from the corner of each window to warn people of the danger. They are often at head height and the sharp edge can give a bad gash.

HEALTH, SAFETY, AND FIRST AID

Air out your sleeping bags if you have them dry-cleaned. Some dry cleaning liquids leave a residue that is dangerous to breathe. If you have a clothes dryer, run the bags through a cycle. If not, hang them out on a line all day, turning them inside out at least once midway through airing.

boat turned upright than to hang on the sides for a long time. The secret to getting in is to keep your weight low and slide in over the gunwale while another person steadies the craft from the opposite site.

If the boat has an outboard motor, be sure it has oars and oarlocks or paddles in case the motor fails.

Canoeing and Boating

If you own your boat or canoe, you already should know the related safety precautions, but if you are borrowing or renting the craft, you may not.

There should be a U.S. Coast Guard-approved life preserver (P.F.D.) aboard for each person in the craft, and they should be worn all the time by non-swimmers or poor swimmers.

Never allow more persons in the craft than it is designed to carry. Insist that everyone remain seated all the time.

Instruct passengers that if the craft overturns, they should stay with the boat. Wooden boats will float by themselves, even if capsized, and plastic, fiberglass, and metal boats are required to have built-in flotation tanks, so they, too, will float when capsized.

It takes less energy to sit on the bottom of a capsized

Swimming

The Boy Scouts of America has a Safe Swim Defense Plan to protect group swimmers. All aspects of the plan

Skin specialists advise the use of lotions for sunburn protection that contain a chemical called PABA for short. It will be shown on the container. Sunscreen lotions are rated by number according to their effectiveness in blocking out harmful rays. The higher the number, the more protection.

won't fit a family, but the sense behind the steps should be considered. The plan includes:

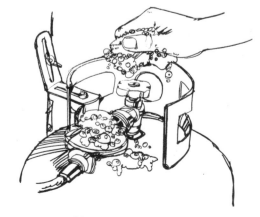

1. Qualified supervision.

2. Good physical condition of each swimmer.

3. A safe swimming area that has been checked for underwater hazards, and limits set according to the ability of swimmers.

4. Lifeguard on duty. For the family swim, there should be one person on shore watching.

5. Lookout. For the family swim, this could be the same person designated as Lifeguard.

6. Ability groups. Each person tested as to swimming ability, and restricted to the depth in which he or she can swim according to that ability.

7. Buddy system. The heart of the BSA plan calls for each two swimmers to team up and be responsible for one another.

8. Discipline. A responsible adult in charge with authority to uphold all swimming rules and regulations.

Gasoline, Propane, and Other Chemical Stoves and Lanterns

Keep fuel containers away from hot stoves and fires. Store them below 100 degrees.

Never fuel a stove inside a tent. Always do so outside. Never operate a stove in a tent. The fire danger is too great.

Check fittings on compressed-gas stoves and on pressurized propane stoves for leakage if you smell gas. Put a soap and water solution around each fitting. If it bubbles, you've found the leak.

HINT *PFD's (life preservers) are now required in most states for all who use boats and canoes. It's much more convenient and cheaper to take them with you than to be forced to buy or rent them at your destination.*

HEALTH, SAFETY, AND FIRST AID

Follow all manufacturer's directions when using stoves. They are usually posted inside the stove lid. They cover operation, safety, and maintenance.

Keep fuel bottles, cans, and other containers away from the stove. When lighting, keep your head to one side in case of flare-up. Open the valve slowly. Light carefully with no part of your body over the burner.

Put the stove on a level, solid surface before using.

Store flammable liquids where they will be safe from discovery by curious children.

One danger in using gasoline comes when refilling the main tank from the storage supply. Move well away from any open flame when you do this. Recap both the stove or lantern tank and the fuel container when finished. Make sure there is no unevaporated gasoline on the stove or lantern before lighting.

Don't carry fuel in a plastic or glass container that could be easily broken or punctured by a sharp object.

Butane lighters are cheap and do a better job than matches in starting a fire. They work when wet, and don't blow out as easily in a wind.

It's easy to put too much weight in big pots and kettles on a camp stove. If anything over a couple of quarts is needed, set up a grill with legs to hold the pots, and put the stove under the grill.

Don't cook with the stove valve wide open. It isn't necessary, and it wastes fuel and overheats the stove.

Teach children how to use these stoves and lanterns, and let them light and use them, but always under your supervision.

HEALTH, SAFETY, AND FIRST AID

Wild Animals

Major danger from animal life in the wild is the possibility of a bite from a rabid animal. Carelessness around "tame" animals in the wild can make them bite. That cute little chipmunk or adorable baby skunk could be rabid. An animal bite leaves a puncture wound and the danger of rabies is always present. Preventive shots for rabies are very painful, but not necessary if the animal that did the biting can be captured and found to be free of rabies. This is almost impossible to do with a wild animal. Even if you could catch an animal, it would be hard to identify it as the one that did the biting.

HINT — *If you meet a wild animal, stay still or out of sight until it moves on. Don't run from it.*

Another danger, depending on the location of your camp, is with bears. Generally bears are dangerous only in National Parks and Forests where they have been "civilized" by tourists. They have lost their fear of humans, and have learned to look for and take handouts. The common black bear isn't as dangerous as the grizzly, but both can inflict serious injury and even death if startled into an attack. They are particularly dangerous when they have cubs, and are protective of them if they feel they are endangered.

So, what can you do? First of all, leave them alone. Next, don't leave any food out at night, and above all, don't keep food inside your tent or tent trailer. One swipe of a paw can rip open a tent.

You can protect your food at night by putting it in a sack and tying the sack on the end of a rope. Throw the rope over a high branch, and pull the sack up until it is at least 8 feet above the ground. Tie the free end of the rope to the tree trunk to hold the sack at that height.

Above all, don't think that bears are like Yogi or Bubba in the cartoons. Don't let your children approach them, pet them, or, as some do, ask your children to pose with a bear for a picture.

Lightning

Danger from lightning is minimal. In the woods you are quite safe in a storm if you are under trees of roughly the same height.

The worst lightning storms take place in the mountains. If caught on a mountain or high hill, stay low and keep off exposed slopes. Stay near the lowest cover possible, even if it means just lying on the ground and getting soaked. The safest place to be is in your car or R.V.

The greatest real danger zone in a lightning storm is water. Never swim when a storm is approaching. Stay out of small boats.

You can estimate the distance of a storm from you by counting the seconds from the lightning flash to the sound of its thunder. Count "one thousand one," "one thousand two", "one thousand three," and so on. Each count takes about a second to say. Every fifth count stands for one mile. Suppose you count to 25. That would mean the storm front is about 5 miles away.

You can determine how fast the storm is approaching by waiting one minute and counting another flash-to-thunder time. A count of 20 means the storm has moved one mile in the one minute you waited. This is about 60 miles per hour. It also gives you something like 4 minutes to find shelter.

Lost Training

This is a must for any family going camping in almost any type of area. It's tragic when a child is lost—tragic for the parents, and tragic for the child. Don't let this happen to your family. Take steps before you ever leave home to eliminate the possibility.

Each of your children should carry a whistle on a cord around the neck. Each should be taught that the whistle is a life-saving device to be used only to attract attention when lost. The whistle

44

they should pick a nearby tree and hug it—even talk to it, if they feel like it. This may comfort the lost child, and will tend to keep a child in the location of the tree instead of wandering around.

Children who have been lost have been asked why they didn't call out when they saw someone nearby, and some said they were afraid their parents would be mad at them for getting lost. Let your children know that the last thing in the world you would do is to be angry at them for getting lost. All you want is for them to be found.

Fear of animals, particularly at night, might cause a lost child to panic and run from the "safe" tree. Explain to your children that if animals do approach them, they should blow their whistles or yell to frighten them away.

Often searchers belong to organizations whose members wear uniforms—forest rangers, members of sheriff's departments, Boy Scouts, and members of the military. Some children might be afraid of people in uniform, and hide from them. Tell your children that anyone in uniform is their friend, not just in the woods, but at all times.

Once you have discussed these things at home, review them with a fun quiz in the car on the way to your campsite. It's important enough to review again the first evening around a campfire.

You should recognize that you, too, could become lost in the outdoors, and that much of what you have told your children will then apply to you. A survival expert facetiously said one time that he would recommend that everyone who went in the woods should carry a deck of cards as a basic survival tool. When you get lost, find a flat stump, take out your cards, and start playing solitaire. Sooner or later, he said, someone would tap you on the shoulder and say, "Put the red nine on the black ten." The point being, of course, that the best thing you can do is to stay put.

uses less energy and its sound carries farther than the human voice.

Teach children that there's great danger in wandering around trying to get back after they become lost. They need to know that you will report their loss and hundreds of people will be mobilized to find them. If they stay in the place where they first realized they were lost, they'll be found much sooner than if they leave the spot.

An organization called "Hug A Tree and Survive" recommends that children be told that if they become lost

HINT *To get a topographic map, first send a post-card to the Map Information Office, U.S. Geological Survey, General Services Building, 18th and F Streets N.W., Washington, D. C. 20405, requesting a free Topographical Map Index Circular of the state in which you intend to use it, and a free folder describing topographic maps. This will tell you how to order a map for the area in which you are interested.*

HEALTH, SAFETY, AND FIRST AID

There are things you need to do immediately if one of your children doesn't come back to camp when expected. Call the local law enforcement office quickly. The sooner you do this, the better the chances of finding the child before he or she wanders.

Give authorities every possible clue that might help them in their search. Hold nothing back. It could be the difference between success and failure.

Basic First Aid

Hurry Cases

Some accidents call for quick action to save life. This is a must for severe bleeding, stopped breathing, or internal poisoning. Bleeding must be stopped—right now! Breathing must be started—right now! Poison must be made harmless—right now! That second—right now—may save a life.

Severe Bleeding

Spurting blood comes from a cut artery. The bleeding must be stopped quickly or the patient will bleed to death.

Apply pressure directly on the cut. If you don't have cloth to press on the wound, grab it with your bare hand and press down hard. Help control bleeding by raising the cut arm or leg above body level while applying pressure.

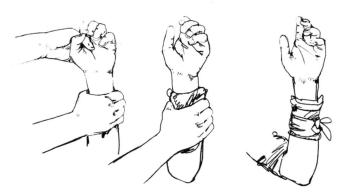

Quickly use your free hand to get a pad of cloth of some kind. Use anything. Don't worry about whether it's sterile. Your problem at the moment isn't the possibility of infection, it's stopping the bleeding. Let go of the wound just long enough to put on the pad, and then reapply pressure.

Finally, wrap something around the pad to keep it in place. Use a triangular bandage made into a cravat, a tie, or a belt. Tie it snugly. If the pad gets blood soaked, don't take it off. Just put another pad on top of the first. Tie it on tightly, and send someone for medical help.

How to Make a Cravat

A cravat for holding a bandage can be made by folding a triangular bandage. It can be used on head, hand, arm, knee, leg, or foot.

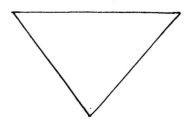

Start with the point of the triangle toward you.

Fold up the point to about 2 inches from the long edge.

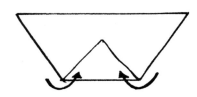

Fold the long edge down over the point.

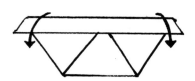

Fold once more from the top.

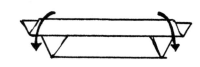

Make a final fold to make the cravat.

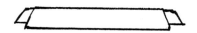

46

HEALTH, SAFETY, AND FIRST AID

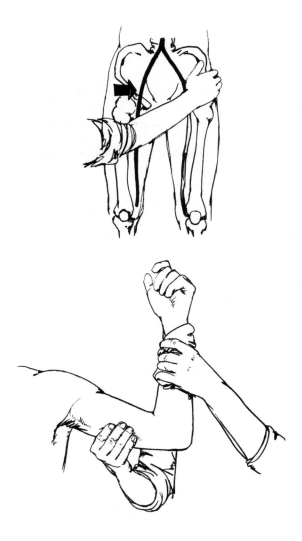

A. Put cravat, belt, neckties, or other strong piece of material around the limb just above the cut. Tie with an overhand knot.

B. Put a strong stick, screwdriver, wrench, or other stiff object over the first overhand knot.

C. Tie it in place with a square knot in the ends of the cravat.

D. Twist the secured stick or tool until bleeding is stopped. Tie another bandage around the end of the stick and limb to keep it from untwisting.

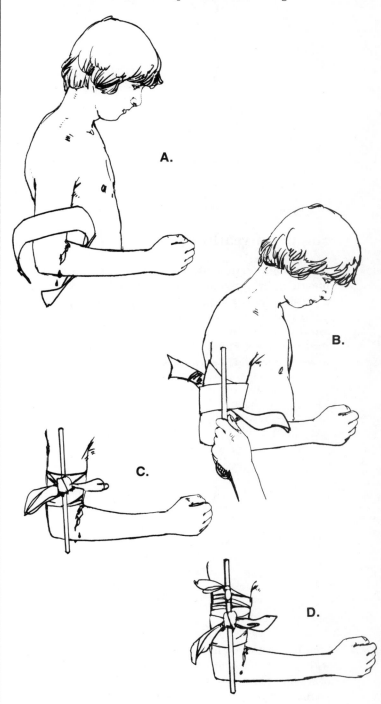

Pressure Points

If direct pressure and elevation don't stop the bleeding of an arm or leg, you can use a pressure point. Press the artery against the bone at the pressure point. It acts just like stepping on a water hose.

Control bleeding from a leg by pressing the pressure point with the heel of your hand.

Control bleeding from an arm by squeezing with the flat of the fingers on the pressure point.

Tourniquet Use

For many years, the Red Cross and Boy Scouts of America taught the use of the tourniquet as standard procedure to control severe bleeding. Recently, doctors have recommended that the tourniquet not be used except in cases where bleeding is so beyond control that life will be lost. When an arm, hand, foot, or leg is severed, or nearly so, then and only then is use of a tourniquet justified. You may never face this situation, but if you should, it's good to know what to do. Study the diagram.

HEALTH, SAFETY, AND FIRST AID

Poisoning by Mouth

The first thing to do is to dilute the poison. Get the victim to drink a glass of water. You'll need to find out what poison was taken. Look for the bottle or can. Get expert help right away. In large cities, phone the poison control center.

The container label may tell the antidote. Follow the directions.

It can be very dangerous to make the victim vomit. Some poisons do serious harm to the lungs, throat, and mouth when they come back up.

If you are sure the poison is too much medicine (like aspirin), it will help to make the victim vomit. Press down on the back of the tongue with your finger or a spoon.

Never make an unconscious person vomit.

Stopped Breathing

You could save a life if you know how to do rescue breathing by breathing into the victim's lungs. Use it on a person who has stopped breathing. Speed in starting is important. Don't waste time moving the victim to a comfortable place. In a water rescue, for example, you can start rescue breathing while carrying the victim from the water to dry land. Learn the steps shown.

Step. 2. Put your ear close to the victim's mouth, listen and feel for breathing. Watch for the chest to rise and fall for at least 5 seconds.

Step 1. Tilt the victim's head back as far as you can. Lift with your hand beneath the neck. Push down with your other hand on the forehead. This step may be enough to enable the person to start breathing.

Step. 3. Keep the victim's head tilted back. Pinch nostrils shut.

HEALTH, SAFETY, AND FIRST AID

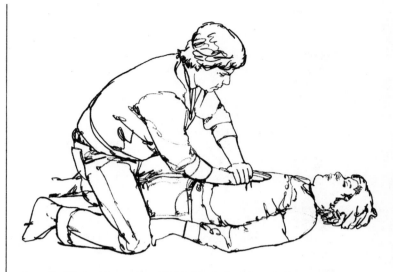

Step. 4. Take a deep breath. Put your mouth over the victim's mouth. Blow in hard with four quick, full breaths. Continue blowing in with one breath about every 5 seconds for an adult or every 3 seconds for a child.

Step 7. If the airway is still blocked, lay the victim on his back. Face him, kneeling beside or astride his hips. Put the heel of one hand on the abdomen just above the victim's navel and below the rib cage. Press into the abdomen with four quick upward thrusts.

Step 5. Let the victim breathe out between each of the times you blow in. When you are blowing in, the victim's chest should rise. It should fall during this Step 5.

Step 6. If air isn't getting into the lungs (the victim's chest isn't rising when you blow in), check the tilt of the head (Step 1). If still blocked, turn the victim on one side, facing you. Give four sharp blows with the heel of your hand between the shoulder blades, over the spine.

Step 8. If air still won't enter, open the mouth with your thumb on the lower teeth and check for obstruction. Sweep the index finger inside the victim's mouth to remove the foreign object. Be careful not to force something farther down the airway.

Persist! When the victim is deprived of oxygen, the muscles often relax. Continuing the back blows and manual abdominal thrusts may dislodge the object. Once the airway is open, check again for breathing. If necessary, continue mouth-to-mouth breathing until the person revives, someone else relieves you, a physician pronounces the victim dead, or you are too totally exhausted to continue. If the victim begins to breathe on his own, you can stop, but keep checking. If he stops, immediately start rescue breathing again.

Shock

Every serious accident brings shock. It's a quick loss of strength caused by pain, fear, and sometimes loss of blood.

A shock victim is very weak. The face is pale. Skin is cold and clammy. The person shivers from chills, seems dazed, and may vomit. In extreme cases, the victim may pass out. Shock may come with the accident or soon after. It may even strike a few hours later.

SHOCK IS DEADLY SERIOUS. DON'T WAIT FOR THE SYMPTOMS TO SHOW. Assume that shock will always be present in an injury. Treat for it, and you may prevent it.

Keep the patient lying down. In cool weather, cover the victim, and put blankets or clothing underneath, too. It's essential to keep the person warm. If the weather is hot, covering isn't necessary. Elevate the feet from 8 to 12 inches unless there is a head injury or the person has trouble breathing. Make the patient comfortable.

Let the victim, if conscious, sip a little water, but only if the shock was not brought on by head, chest, or abdominal injuries. Don't try to force water between the lips of an unconscious person. It may cause choking.

Fainting

This is a "blacking out" caused by not enough blood going to the brain. If a person faints, loosen the collar. Raise the feet. Keep the victim lying down even after consciousness returns.

If the person doesn't come to right away, treat for shock. Get expert help.

If you ever feel faint, sit on a chair. Bend forward with your head between your knees. This will force blood to your head, and keep you from blacking out.

Heat Exhaustion

Heat exhaustion hits suddenly. It causes the same symptoms as shock, and treatment is the same as for shock. Even though the condition is called heat exhaustion, keep the victim warm. Give sips of salted water.

Heatstroke

This is usually caused by long exposure to direct sunlight. The victim's face is red, hot, and dry. Breathing is slow and noisy, and sounds like snoring.

The victim should lie down. Take off outer clothing. Sponge the head and body, especially the head, with a wet towel or other cloth. Use cool or lukewarm water, or alcohol if available. If conscious, the victim should drink all the water desired.

Heatstroke is life-threatening. Call an emergency rescue ambulance immediately.

Poisonous Plants

First, make sure everyone can recognize the poisonous plants common to the area in which you will be traveling and camping.

Poison Ivy

This could be a low-growing plant, shrub, or vine. It has three shiny, green leaflets, usually with coarse teeth. At certain times of the year it has white berries. In the fall the leaves turn bright red, then yellow.

Poison Sumac

This grows as a shrub or small tree in damp places. It is related to poison ivy. It has compound leaflets and white drooping berries. Unlike non-poisonous sumac, its leaflets are smooth and grow in a V-shape from the midrib.

Poison Oak

This is closely related to poison ivy. Poison oak has three to seven lobed leaflets that look like small oak leaves but are hairy underneath. Poison oak is common in the southern and western United States.

It is dangerous to burn any of these poisonous plants. The smoke they make contains molecules of poisonous oil The oil in the smoke is even more dangerous to your skin than the touch of the plant itself.

Here's a saying to help remember poisonous plant identification:

> "LEAFLETS THREE,
>
> LET IT BE.
>
> BERRIES WHITE,
>
> POISONOUS SIGHT."

Treatment of Skin Poisoning from Plants

If you think you have come in contact with a poisonous plant, wash the part that was touched with soap and water. Unscented soap is best. Then clean the area even more thoroughly with rubbing alcohol. If a rash develops, apply calamine lotion. If it gets worse, see a physician, who can give shots to control the spread of the poison to other parts of the body.

Insects

Mosquitoes, gnats, chiggers, black flies, horseflies, bees, and wasps can inflict bites and stings that hurt long after they are inflicted. In some parts of the world, mosquitoes can transmit malaria to humans when they bite.

Irritation and itching from these bites can be eased by applying household ammonia, a baking soda paste, or calamine lotion to the affected area.

Bee stings are serious only if the person stung is allergic to them. Most people who are allergic know they are, and carry a prescription medicine to counteract the

HINT *Be careful when spraying insecticide inside your tent. Direct spray on some fabrics can damage them.*

allergy. If a bee-sting victim doesn't have this and feels sick, has trouble breathing, or has excessive swelling, rush the person to a hospital emergency room.

If the victim is not allergic, remove the stinger by pulling it out with tweezers or scrape it off gently with your fingernail. Apply any of the remedies for itching mentioned earlier.

HINT *Don't disturb beehives or hornet nests.*

Ticks carry a serious disease in some parts of the country. Learn to identify a tick. If you are in tick country and feel one crawling on you, brush it off. If a tick has fastened on you, don't pull it off. The head may break off and stay under your skin. This could cause infection. Cover the tick with grease or oil. It will let go in time because the oily substance stops its air supply.

Learn what scorpions *and* brown recluse and black widow spiders look like. Avoid them. Check shoes and clothing before putting them on if you are sleeping in scorpion or spider country. A scorpions sting or spider bite can be dangerous.

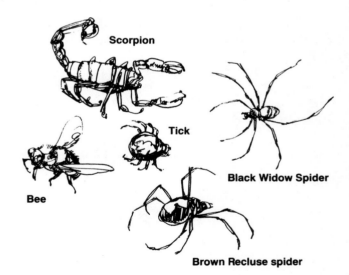

Treatment of Scorpion Stings, Spider Bites, and Allergic Reactions

Treatment for all of these is the same.

1. If the bite is on an arm or leg, tie a constricting band above the bite. It should be just tight enough to stop the blood in the skin, not the blood under the skin.

2. Put ice water or ice in a cloth on the bite.

3. Take the band off after 30 minutes.

4. Keep the arm or leg lower than the body to slow the spread of poison to the rest of the body.

5. Take the person to get medical care. Be sure the victim keeps breathing. Give rescue breathing if breathing stops.

6. Treat for shock.

Snakes

There are four types of poisonous snakes in the United States. Learn to identify them and to tell the difference between poisonous and non-poisonous snakes.

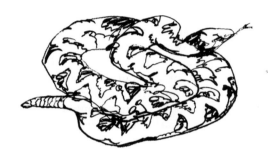

Rattlesnakes

They occur in every state except Alaska and Hawaii. Their color depends to a certain extent on where they live.

Pale-colored rattlesnakes live in deserts, darker ones in forests. They are all characterized by their rattle, a horny jointed structure at the tip of their tails. The snake can shake this rattle so fast you can hardly see it, but you can hear the warning buzz.

Copperhead

The copperhead can be found in the eastern half of the country. You can recognize it by its copperish-brown color with hourglass shaped crossbands of a darker shade. It prefers rocky, wooded areas.

Cottonmouth Moccasin (also called Water Moccasin)

This snake lives in streams and swamps of the South, up to southern Illinois and Virginia. It is muddy brown or olive in color. When angry, it raises its head and opens its mouth wide, showing the cotton-white inside.

Rattlesnakes, copperheads, and cotttonmouth moccasins are called pit vipers. They all have broad, triangular heads and seem to have four nostrils. The triangular head is characteristic of these three poisonous snakes, and few non-poisonous ones. It is a key to identification.

Coral Snake

This is the fourth of the poisonous snakes in the United States. It ranges from Florida to North Carolina, through the lower Mississippi Valley, and through states bordering on Mexico. It is a small, slender, brilliantly colored snake, with broad black and red bands separated by narrower bands of bright yellow. Its head is small and *not* triangular in shape. It is seldom seen because it spends most of the day underground, only coming out at night or after a rain to find food.

This snake is often confused with the harmless scarlet kingsnake. They both have the brilliantly colored bands, but the arrangement of the colors in the king and the

HEALTH, SAFETY, AND FIRST AID

coral is different. Red and yellow bands touch each other in the coral snake. Red and black bands touch each other in the kingsnake.

There's a little poem that will help you remember the difference. It goes like this:

"Red on Yellow—Kill a fellow!

Red on Black—Friend of Jack."

A few words about harmless snakes. They are great friends of humans, helping to control insects, rodents, and other pests. In nature, the snake population of an area is in balance with the number of rodents and other animals available for food. If the food supply decreases, so does the number of snakes. If the food supply increases, other snakes move in to balance the supply.

That's why harmless snakes shouldn't be killed or captured, particularly in or around a camp. As the number of harmless snakes is reduced, the rodent population increases. Snakes from the surrounding areas move in—and these could be poisonous!

HINT *Wear high-topped shoes or boots and loose-fitting pants in snake country.*

Snakebite Treatment

Any snake—poisonous or non-poisonous—will bite if cornered or startled. For non-poisonous snakes, treat the bite like a puncture wound. Let it bleed. Wash it it with soap and water. Cover with a sterile pad held in place with bandage or adhesive tape. Treat for shock.

If the bite is from a poisonous snake, take the following steps:

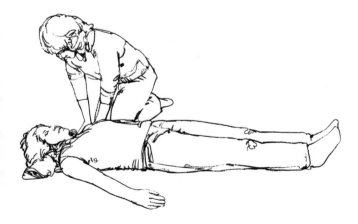

1. Have the victim lie down and stay very quiet. Put the part that was bitten lower than the rest of the body. Make the victim comfortable. Stay calm, and keep the victim calm.

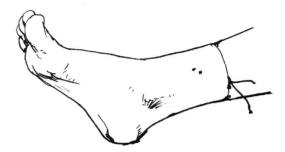

2. Put a constricting band 2 to 4 inches above the bite. Make it tight enough that it's not easy to push your fingers between the band and the skin.

3. Call for medical help and report the kind of snake, if known. Medical personnel may need time to locate the antivenin.

Desperate Snakebite Cases

If you know that medical help will be long delayed, more than 4 to 5 hours, treat as follows:

1. Carry out steps 1 and 2 in the treatment listed above.

2. Sterilize a sharp knife or razor blade.

3. Wash the bite area with soap and water.

4. Make shallow cuts into the fang marks. Cuts should be about ¼ inch long running up and down the limb, not across. These cuts should only break the skin.

5. Apply suction by mouth or suction cup for about an hour.

To be effective, this treatment should start immediately—in no case more than 15 minutes after the victim is bitten.

Razor blades and suction cups are part of standard snakebite kits that should be in your first-aid kit when you're camping far from medical help in poisonous snake country.

HEALTH, SAFETY, AND FIRST AID

ESTIMATION OF WIND VELOCITY IN MILES PER HOUR

INDICATIONS	Velocity	INDICATIONS	Velocity
Calm; smoke rises vertically.	0-1	Large branches in motion; whitecaps on most waves; tents billow and strain.	25-31
Smoke shows wind direction.	1-3		
Wind felt on face; grass or leaves rustle; snow eddies.	4-7	Whole trees in motion; walking against wind difficult; loose snow rises in air.	32-38
Leaves and small twigs in constant motion; light flag extended by breeze.	8-12	Twigs break off trees; walking generally difficult.	39-46
Dust or snow or leaves are raised; branches move.	13-18	Branches break off trees. High waves and tides.	47-54
Small trees in leaf sway; crested wavelets form on inland waters; tents flap.	19-24	Seldom experienced inland; trees uprooted.	55-63

TO READ THE WIND-CHILL TABLE: Estimate the wind velocity in miles per hour from the table above or other data, such as Weather Bureau forecasts. Read, estimate, or get probable lowest temperatures from forecasts. Locate wind speed in left-hand column and read right to column for thermometer reading or forecast temperature—number will indicate effective equivalent temperature.

WIND CHILL ON DRY BARE SKIN (Read as equivalent temperature at 0 mph.)

Estimated Wind Speed (mph)	Actual Thermometer Reading (° F.)									
	50	40	30	20	10	0	—10	—20	—30	—40
	EQUIVALENT TEMPERATURE (° F.)									
calm	50	40	30	20	10	0	—10	—20	—30	—40
5	48	37	27	16	6	—5	—15	—26	—36	—47
10	40	28	16	2	—9	—22	—31	—45	—58	—70
15	36	22	11	—6	—18	—33	—45	—60	—70	—85
20	32	18	3	—9	—24	—40	—52	—68	—81	—96
25	30	16	0	—15	—29	—45	—58	—75	—89	—104
30	28	13	—2	—18	—33	—49	—63	—78	—94	—109
35	27	11	—4	—20	—35	—52	—67	—83	—98	—113
40	26	10	—4	—22	—36	—54	—69	—87	—101	—116

(wind speeds greater than 40 mph have little additional effect.)

Little Danger (to properly clad person)   Increasing Danger   Great Danger

Danger of Freezing Exposed Flesh

HEALTH, SAFETY, AND FIRST AID

Hypothermia

This is the loss of body heat. When your body temperature drops more than 3 degrees below normal (98.6), it causes body changes that could lead to death.

When hypothermia is understood, and campers are prepared for it, there's no problem. Preparation just means having adequate protection—enough warm clothing, windbreaker, and rain gear—for weather extremes that

you might meet. Even then, a combination of cold, wetness, wind, and fatigue could produce the condition. A fall into a cold lake or stream, followed by cold wind on wet clothing could bring on hypothermia.

It is related to that TV-weatherman concept of the wind-chill factor. You've heard the expression many times, but do you really understand it, and what it can mean to you in the outdoors?

Your skin is a big radiator that your body uses to get rid of excess heat. If this radiator gives off heat faster than the body can generate it, eventually your body temperature will be lowered. Several things can cause this to happen—inadequate clothing for normally cold weather, inadequate clothing for low wind-chill conditions, and damp or wet clothing. Of these, the wind-chill factor is probably the least understood by most campers. They know that they are colder when the wind blows, but few realize by how much.

Here are two charts to help you know your location's wind-chill factor without having a TV weatherman tell you. The first chart will help you to estimate your wind

velocity in miles per hour. You need to know this to use the next chart, the wind-chill table.

Identification of Hypothermia and Treatment

The first stage is normal shivering, and is often overlooked. But as soon as you notice uncontrolled, violent shivering in yourself or a family member, suspect the onset of hypothermia. This may be accompanied by difficulty in speaking clearly.

If you see these signs, go into action. Get the victim warm and out of wet or damp clothing into dry clothes. Make a big fire and walk the victim around the heat of the fire.

If the victim is alert, offer hot liquids (sugary tea, chocolate, cocoa, fruit juices) if they don't cause nausea or vomiting. Under no circumstances should you give alcoholic beverages.

When the shivering is controlled, keep the victim as warm and comfortable as possible.

If the victim should become unconscious, put him on his back and tilt the head back to open the airways for breathing. Prompt hospital care is essential. Insulate the victim from further heat loss by completely wrapping him in a blanket or sleeping bag. Constantly monitor for breathing difficulty.

All of this treatment is designed to rebuild the body heat lost. Hypothermia is deadly serious. Victims can and do die from it!

Cuts and Scratches

Even a small cut or scratch can be dangerous. It lets germs get through your skin. Germs cause infection. Soap and water is your best defense against infection. Wash the cut. When the skin dries, put on an adhesive bandage. Don't touch the part of the bandage that will cover the cut.

Larger Cuts

Wash with soap and water. Put on a sterile dressing big enough to cover the cut. Hold it by the corners. Don't touch the part that will cover the cut. Hold the dressing in place with adhesive tape. If you don't have any, use a cloth bandage. Tie with a square knot.

Burns and Scalds

Burns are classified by degree. You've heard the expression, "a third-degree burn." Don't become confused trying to classify burns. Instead, learn what to do for the burn you see.

If the skin isn't broken, run cold water on the burned or scalded area. If you have ice, put it in water and keep the burned part in the cold water until it quits hurting. If the burn is on a part of the body that won't fit into a pan of cold water, hold ice directly on the burn. Remove it from time to time if it's too cold.

Don't break blisters if they appear. Don't apply grease or ointment, just cover the blisters with a gauze pad. Hold it in place with layers of bandage. Cover the bandage with aluminum foil, a plastic bag, or plastic wrap to keep out the air.

If there is charred flesh, don't apply grease or ointment. Wrap a clean cloth over the burn. Don't try to pick off anything that may be stuck to it, like burned clothing. Treat the victim for shock. Get to a hospital emergency room. This type burn is very serious.

Blisters

The most common blisters in camp are usually those caused by a shoe rubbing when hiking, or from too much chopping with an ax or hatchet, or a swing with a bowsaw.

Your best treatment for blisters is to stop them, before they start. Watch for soreness and redness. Cover the spot with an adhesive bandage before the blister forms. If one does form, wash the area with soap and water. When dry, cover with an adhesive bandage or sterile pad. If you think the blister might break, drain the liquid. Sterilize a needle in the flame of a match or lighter. When cool, push the needle through the skin at the side of the blister and up into it. Gently press out the liquid. Put on a sterile bandage. Repeat the removal of liquid if more develops.

If a blister has already broken, wash it gently and cover with a sterile bandage. Watch for signs of infection. If the reddish area gets bigger or becomes more painful, see a doctor.

Sprains and Fractures

Is it just a sprain, or is it a fracture? Only a doctor can tell for sure. Swelling can start immediately. If in doubt, treat it as if it's a fracture.

First, let the patient lie down right where he is with as little motion as possible. Make him comfortable with something under and over him. Call for an emergency vehicle. Treat for shock.

Sprains

If you are sure that it's a sprain and not a fracture, elevate the sprained area. Put cold, wet cloths on to ease the pain, and help reduce swelling.

Most common sprains in camp are of ankles. If this happens don't take off the shoe. Tie an ankle bandage around the ankle and shoe. Better see a doctor. It could still be a fracture and failure to treat properly could cause permanent lameness.

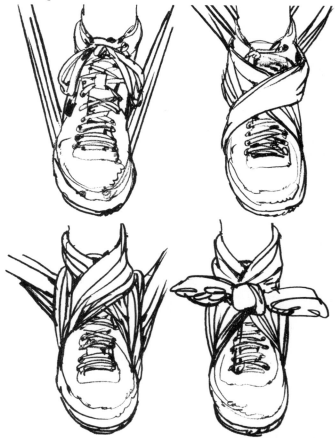

HEALTH, SAFETY, AND FIRST AID

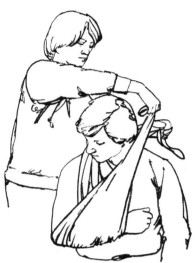

Bring ends around the patient's neck.

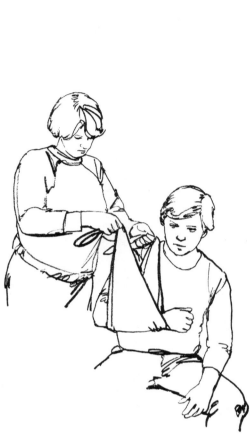

No splint is used for a collarbone fracture. Use a triangular bandage to make a sling to support the arm.

Tie ends with a square knot.

Put a second bandage over the injured arm and around the chest.

Fractures

When a patient has a broken bone and medical help (physician, ambulance service, paramedic or RN) is available, you should make the patient comfortable, treat for shock, and arrange for medical help. If the skin is broken around the fracture, keep the area clean and stop bleeding.

If, however, the victim of a fracture must be moved without prior attention by medical help, splinting is needed. The purpose of a splint is to keep the break from becoming worse while the patient is being moved. Splints can be made of padded sticks on both sides of the break and extending well above and below it. You can use a board, magazine, newspaper, heavy cardboard, or almost any rigid flat material. The splints should be tied securely in place with several ties to spread the support.

How to Make a Sling Using a Triangular Bandage

The patient should lie down. Tie an overhand knot in the point of a triangular bandage. This makes a cup for the elbow. Tie the ends of the triangle together with a square knot. Slip over the victim's head so the front of the sling comes around the neck on the side of the injured arm.

Slip the injured arm through the loop with the elbow in the pocket. When the patient stands up, adjust the knot behind the neck so the hand is a little higher than the elbow.

HEALTH, SAFETY, AND FIRST AID

Upper Arm Fracture

Use only one padded splint, slightly longer than the distance from the shoulder to the elbow. Fasten the splint on the outside of the arm with two bandages.

Put the forearm on a narrow sling and tie the ends behind the patient's neck with a square knot.

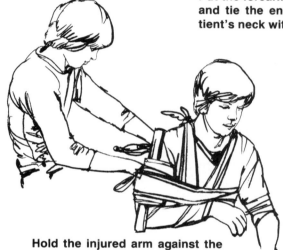

Hold the injured arm against the patient's body with a second narrow bandage tied in back.

Forearm or Wrist Fracture

Pad the splint and bind in place with two or more bandages. Be sure the splint reaches from fingertips to elbow.

Rest the splinted arm on a support and tie a sling around the neck.

Be sure the thumb is up and the hand supported a couple of inches higher than the elbow.

HEALTH, SAFETY, AND FIRST AID

Thigh or Leg Fracture

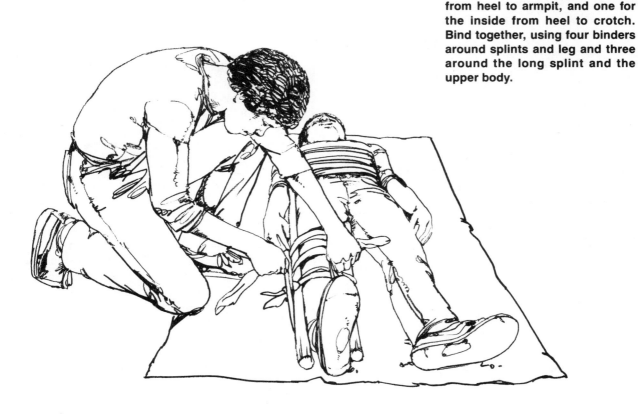

Use two padded splints, one for the outside of the leg reaching from heel to armpit, and one for the inside from heel to crotch. Bind together, using four binders around splints and leg and three around the long splint and the upper body.

For a lower leg fracture, you can eliminate the long outside splint. Use the short splint on the outside of the broken leg, and tie the splint and broken leg to the unbroken leg with four binders.

Moving the Injured

Generally, it's best not to move an injured person yourself. Where possible, get medical help to come to your location. In this day of well-equipped paramedic vehicles, including helicopters, seriously injured people can be evacuated from practically any location. Give specific directions to the victim's location, meet the ambulance, and show it the way.

Puncture Wounds

These are caused by things like nails, splinters, knife stabs, gunshots, and fishhooks. They are dangerous because they often are deep and don't bleed freely to help clean out the wound. And, the germs of tetanus (lockjaw) may have been carried into the wound.

A splinter will hurt until it comes out. Remove it with tweezers or a sterile needle. Wash with soap and water. Bandage.

If skin is snagged by a fishhook and the barb has gone into it, cut the line at the hook. Go to a doctor, hook and all. If it happens in the back country, push the hook so the barb comes out through the skin. Cut off the barb with wire cutters. Take out the shank. Wash and bandage.

After taking out the cause of the wound, squeeze gently around the hole to make it bleed and to clean out dirt. Wash with soap and water. Bandage. See a doctor. You may need tetanus antitoxin to prevent lockjaw. This especially may be needed for a fishhook wound because worms used in fishing often come from soil loaded with tetanus germs. Campers should be immunized with tetanus toxin every 10 years. Keep a family record.

Animal Bites

A bite should be treated like a puncture wound. Wash the bite under running water. Use soap if you have it. Be sure the animal's saliva is washed away. Cover the bite with a sterile gauze pad. Hold in place with a bandage, and get medical help.

Try to identify the animal that did the biting so it can be examined for a rabies check. This could avoid the necessity of painful rabies treatments.

Stomachache

You need to pay attention to little pains and aches in the abdomen. If someone has a stomachache and you know the person has overeaten, eaten an unusual combination of foods, or eaten foods that person doesn't eat very often, give ⅓ teaspoon of baking soda in a half glass of water. Don't give a laxative.

If you can't determine the cause of the pain, or if it lasts a long time, call a physician or take the patient to a hospital emergency room. It could be the beginning of appendicitis or a serious problem in another abdominal organ.

If it's appendicitis, the patient will almost always have a sharp pain, usually starting in the pit of the stomach and then slowly moving to the right lower part of the abdomen. The person will feel tired, won't want to eat, and might vomit.

Get the patient to lie down with knees drawn up slightly—over a pillow, for example. Don't give anything to eat or drink. Call a physician immediately.

Choking

This usually happens during a meal when someone chokes on food. If a person can't breathe, have him bend over so his head is lower than his chest. Give a series of hard whacks in the area between the shoulder blades with the heel of your hand.

If this doesn't dislodge the object, get behind the victim. Wrap your arms around his waist. Make a fist, and put it thumb side against the victim's abdomen below the rib cage and slightly above the navel. Grasp your fist with your other hand and press it into the victim's abdomen with a quick upward thrust.

Repeat until the airway is opened.

Choking

HEALTH, SAFETY, AND FIRST AID

Something in the Eye

Don't rub. Blink your eyes. Let the tears flow to flush out the object. For something under the upper lid, pull the lid down and out over the lower lid. The lower lashes may brush the object out.

If the object is under the lower lid, put your thumb just below the lid and move it down gently. Take out the speck with the corner of a clean handkerchief.

If these things fail, cover the eye with a sterile pad. Hold it in place with a bandage. Go to a physician. Your eyes are too precious to take chances with.

Nosebleed

Keep calm. It may look bad, but it's probably no big deal.

Pinch your nostrils together. A cold cloth on the nose will help. If bleeding is severe or doesn't stop, get medical help.

Cardiopulmonary Resuscitation (CPR)

This is a valuable adjunct to first-aid skills, but isn't something that can be learned from a book. At least one adult member of the family should have American Red Cross or American Heart Association CPR training.

Your First-Aid Kit

First-aid kits are available commercially in almost any size. For family use, this range is probably from too small to too big. But in between there may be just the one for you.

You can tailor-make your own first-aid kit by buying a plastic fishing tackle box, the kind with many compartments in assorted sizes. Here are things recommended for family camping:

_____Your family members' personal medications, if any

_____Aspirin or similar headache remedy

_____A non-prescription diarrhea remedy

_____Antacid tablets or liquid

_____Antihistamine

_____Rubbing alcohol

_____Adhesive bandages in assorted sizes

_____3 x 3-inch gauze pads

_____Butterfly strips for pulling sides of cuts together

_____A 2-inch roll of adhesive tape

_____Gauze roller bandages in assorted sizes

_____Triangular bandage

_____Roll of elastic bandage

_____Package of cotton-tipped swabs

_____Scissors

_____Tweezers

_____Safety pins

_____Needle

_____Razor, disposable type

_____Single-edge razor blades—not for use in the disposable razor

_____Oral fever thermometer

_____Snakebite kit if going into poisonous snake country

_____Small bar of soap

_____Sunscreen ointment (not just suntan oil)

_____Lip salve

_____Poisonous plant lotion (calamine)

_____Foot powder

_____Absorbent cotton

_____Water purification tablets for drinking water

_____Instant ice packs

_____Paper cups

_____Small flashlight with extra batteries and bulbs

_____A first aid book for memory refreshment.

Consider what a valuable resource your first-aid kit can be around your home when you're not camping. Just don't forget to pack it when you leave on your trips!

COOKING

"Bacon sizzles over a campfire; stew bubbles in a kettle; and biscuits turn golden brown in a Dutch oven—man, that's livin'."

Scout Handbook

No single item—planning, housing, campsite selection, equipment, or activities—will make family camping an exciting and successful event. But, a great outdoor meal comes mighty close.

The cooking methods and recipes you can use vary as widely as your equipment, which may range from an open campfire to a propane or electric stove with full oven in a self-contained trailer or motor home. Most suggestions in this chapter will apply to any situation. A few won't. You can't cook some things over a campfire that you could in a fancy oven, but you can do almost as much depending on the outdoor cooking gear you have. A Dutch oven and charcoal can cook almost anything that a full oven can handle.

It's up to you, the family camper, to look at what you have and use those recipes and menus that fit your situation, and disregard those that don't.

Planning

Planning is the secret of a successful cooking adventure. But before you can start your cooking planning, you have to know the type of camp you'll be making. Will it be a traveling camp, where you'll spend a night or two in one location, and then move on to a new spot?

Perhaps it will be a weekend camp in the same site for two or three days. Or, maybe a week-long or longer camp at the same campground where you can really settle in. Another kind, probably less common among family campers, is a backpack trip.

What's the difference?

For the weekend camp, you'll bring most food from home and count on a portable ice chest or refrigerator to keep perishables.

In the traveling camp, you'll probably bring most non-perishables with you, but stop at grocery stores enroute to pick up perishables for a day or two.

If you'll be in a permanent site for a week or longer, plan to travel to nearby stores for supplies, both perishable and non-perishable. You won't want to try to pack food for a week or more in your limited storage.

And, finally, you'll recognize the special conditions of a backpacking trip where everything must be carried from one site to the next.

Another factor influencing your menu planning relates to the amount of time you want to spend cooking that fantastic meal, versus the time left for other camp activities. One way to save time can be found on the shelves of your supermarket. There is a great variety of pre-packaged mixes, sauces, dehydrated, and pre-cooked foods available. Here are a few to stimulate your thinking:

Menus

How many days? _____

How many breakfasts? _____ lunches? _____ dinners? _____

Special dietary needs? _____

Family Camping Menu Planning Guide

Day # _____

MEAL	SOUP ETC.	MAIN COURSE	VEGETABLE	DRINK	DESSERT
Breakfast					
Lunch					
Dinner					

Biscuit mix
Gravy mix or canned gravy
Muffin mix
Pudding
Sloppy Joe sauce
Hollandaise sauce
Tartar Sauce
Sweet and sour sauce
Bottled dressings
Stuffing mix
Instant scalloped potatoes
Instant rice
Macaroni and cheese

Pancake mix
Cake mix
Cookie mix
Gelatin mix
Chili sauce
Taco sauce
Spaghetti sauce

White sauce
Instant mashed potatoes
Instant potatoes au gratin
Hot cereal
Instant soup packets
Soup and stew starter mixes

There are also backpacking specialty stores where you can buy packages with entire meals that are lightweight and easy to store. These are great for backpacking, but weigh the cost against the benefits for regular camp use.

HINT *Bread. Whole grain breads are more likely to stick to the pan than white bread, so pans must be oiled generously.*

You'll also save time on your first day away from home if you plan to eat a hearty breakfast before leaving. Another timesaver in camp is to fix your first meal at home. You can then eat it as a picnic lunch and save time on the road, or eat it before or after setting up camp when you get to the campsite.

Recipe Ingredient Lists

Your food lists will come from the recipes for the menus you wrote on your Family Camping Menu Guide. Just note each item and the quantity needed for each recipe. If an item is listed in more than one recipe, add the amount called for to the amount you already show for the item to get a total for the whole trip.

You probably have many of the food items at home — things like salt, pepper, spices, sugar, and flour.

In making your lists for the trip, set up columns as shown on page 65. You will use the last column only if your campsite or sites will be near a grocery store that has the items you need. These will be mainly perishables.

Food Buying

Once your food buying list is made out and you know your needs from the Buy and Take column, all you have to do is go to the store and buy it.

HINT *Nuts and seeds make a tasty (and nutritious) addition to salads, fruit cups, and vegetable dishes.*

Since this will be a family camp, the buying experience could be shared by all family members. Children, particularly, can learn a lot from this early experience in decision-making at the grocery store.

You might break up your list so each member of the family has a share—canned goods for one, fruits and vegetables for another, meat, fish, and chicken for another, and so on. At the checkout counter all carts would come together for the final tally.

If you plan to do a lot of family camping, you might consider keeping a collection of non-perishable items from

---

HINT *Seasonings. Caraway, dill, celery and mustard seeds make interesting substitutes for salt. There are also several commercial vegetable seasoning mixtures available. These seasonings offer a viable way to cut down on salt without losing flavor and are especially beneficial to people on low-salt diets.*

---

trip to trip. This saves having to buy small quantities each time. Here are a few items to consider:

Catsup
Steak sauce
Bouillon cubes
Pepper
Dry cereals
Instant cocoa
Packaged soups, sauces, etc.
Pancake syrup
Mustard
Worcestershire sauce
Vegetable oil

Spices
Cornstarch
Dry Milk
Soy sauce
Pickles, relish
Salt

Baking powder
Beverage mixes
Flour
Sugar

HINT *If a recipe specifies a certain ounce weight for a can of ingredients but you can't find the exact weight at your store, use one that is close to it, or use two smaller ones to total the amount called for, or close to it.*

Packing and Storage

Going in a trailer or motor home? You'll have few concerns about packing and storage. But if you don't have those convenient cupboards and shelves, or a gas or electric refrigerator, then this subject becomes important.

Sturdy rectangular baskets, either wire or plastic, are great for carrying canned goods, fruit, vegetables, and prepackaged foods not needing refrigeration.

Food Buying List

Item	Amount Needed	Already Have	Buy and Take	Buy at Campground

You'll want a cooler for perishables. Block ice is preferable to crushed because it lasts longer. Dry ice is fine, too, but keep food from coming in direct contact with it. There are also products that contain a liquid that can be frozen at home and then used in the cooler to keep food cool. These are OK for short trips.

Packing Tips

Where practical, transfer food from glass jars to plastic containers. They weigh less and aren't as apt to break.

Label everything that doesn't already have a label. The things you transferred to other containers probably looked familiar when you did it, but how will they look when you're ready to cook?

Use masking tape to seal closed all your already opened "easy-open" spouts on boxes of salt, rice, and similar items. Keep the tape in your kit so you can reseal before traveling again.

Put some rice in your salt shaker. It will absorb moisture and keep the salt free-flowing.

Put powdered and granulated sugar, salt, pepper, and other pourables in large salt shakers. Unscrew the lids before traveling, and cover each lid with plastic wrap. Then screw the lids back in place.

Don't store fruit or vegetables in plastic bags. They'll sweat, heat, and tend to rot quickly. An exception to this is with green bananas or avocados that you want to ripen. Put them in plastic bags. The gasses given off by the fruit will speed ripening.

A piece of apple inside a covered container of brown sugar will keep the sugar soft.

Buy butter or margarine in plastic tubs. The contents will be better protected than if in paper or cardboard.

Put bread in a shoebox or plastic container to keep it from being squashed.

Pack eggs by breaking them into a plastic juice container with sealable pouring spout. Keep refrigerated. Another way is to wrap each egg individually in newspaper, and then carry in a plastic container.

Your Camp Kitchen

In a trailer or motor home your kitchen is compact, organized, and has convenient storage and work space.

Your outdoor kitchen can, too.

Where possible, your work area should be at waist height and covered with a surface that can be easily cleaned. A piece of oilcloth clovering a table top fills the bill for this.

Your stove should also be at working height, but that's not always possible. Many campgrounds have a table at each site. In this case, put your portable gas stove on it. If you are using a charcoal grill it, too, could be on the table, or, if it has legs, it will be at working height without needing a table.

Some campgrounds have built-in fireplaces where you can build a wood or charcoal fire. If not, and you have to cook near the ground, raise your grill up on short legs or on rocks so a fire can be built underneath.

Your storage area should be near your work space. A chuck box can help with this. A surplus ammo belt hung around a tree near your cooking area can provide convenient storage for pots, pans, and kitchen implements. Hang them on "S" hooks from the belt.

You'll want your wood or charcoal handy so you can add fuel to your fire while cooking. Have a piece of 4-mil plastic to cover your fuel during rainy weather and at night when it might be damp.

Before you can cook in your outdoor kitchen, you need heat—heat from wood, charcoal, electricity, kerosene, gasoline, propane, or butane. A description of these stoves can be found in "Camping Gear" (Chap. 2).

There is potential danger in the careless use of any of these heat sources, but in the outdoors the danger of a fire spreading out of control is perhaps the greatest.

Fire Safety

Fire safety depends on three things: a safe spot for the fire, a safe fire, and complete extinction of the fire after use.

In most campgrounds you'll find fireplaces of stone, brick, cement block, or similar materials. These are designed to contain your fire safely.

But even where you have a prepared fireplace, make sure there are no flammable materials within at least 5 feet of the fire in every direction. These would be things like dry leaves and grass. Also be sure there are no flam-

crumple some newspaper loosely and put it under your kindling.

Kindling is the next size up. Small dead branches still on a tree make good kindling. Kindling must be dry and not green to do its intended job. There's a saying, "If you can't snap it, scrap it." If your kindling won't snap when you bend it, it's probably damp or green.

Fuel is the larger wood that gives you the flames or coals you need for cooking. Use deadwood near your camp, if avail-

HINT

Make an easy firestarter before leaving home by filling cups of a cardboard egg carton with lint from your dryer or with shredded paper. Then fill each cup half full of melted wax.

Break off a cup and put under your tinder. Light with a match.

Store firelighters in a sealable plastic bag.

mable materials above your fire area near enough to catch fire. This 10-foot circle rule is especially important where you have to build your own fire area from scratch using stones or other materials available at the site.

Firebuilding

To start your fire, you'll need tinder, kindling, fuel, and matches.

Tinder is stuff that flares when you touch it with a lighted match. Dry bark, dead weed tops, tiny twigs, or shavings from split dry wood all will work as tinder. But in camp, paper is the handiest and best tinder. Just

Tinder.

able. Saw it into 12-inch lengths, and split it lengthwise. Split wood lights and burns better than unsplit wood.

If there isn't any firewood available at your campsite, or you're staying at a campground where gathering firewood is prohibited, then plan to use charcoal or a camp stove.

HINT *Don't rule out softwood for camp use. Its hot flames will boil water fast, and are good for fast frying. Make a nice leaping campfire, too.*

You can start a charcoal fire by adding the charcoal to the bigger pieces of wood once they are going strong. Charcoal lighter fluid works well, too, *but never add the fluid to a fire that has already started.* There is also a quick lighting charcoal now on the market.

Your best cooking fire in the open is of glowing coals. Use hardwood or charcoal as the fuel to produce these. Softwoods give hot flames for a short time, but quickly die down to ashes instead of coals.

Specialty Cooking

Dutch Oven Cooking

The camp Dutch oven resembles those used in the home, but it has a different lid, and three short legs. The lid is flat and has a lip around the top to contain coals, which heat the interior from the top down. The legs make it possible to set the oven on a layer of charcoal without cutting off the air supply. The oven has a small metal ring in the center of the top. You use this ring to lift the hot lid with a hook or tongs.

One trick in using the Dutch oven is getting the heat just right for the job you want to do. How do you know if the pre-heated temperature of a Dutch oven conforms to recipe instructions such as "Bake in a slow oven," or "Pre-heat to 375 degrees"?

Put a teaspoon of flour on a pan or plate that will fit in the oven. The color of the flour after baking with the lid in place as shown will give you a pretty accurate measurement.

Light tan	in 5 minutes	Slow oven	About 250 degrees
Medium tan	in 5 minutes	Moderate	About 350 degrees
Dark brown	in 5 minutes	Hot	About 450 degrees
Dark brown	in 3 minutes	Very hot	About 550 degrees

You regulate heat by adding coals or taking some away. The tendency usually is to get the oven too hot, especially on the bottom. Remember, most cooking in a Dutch oven is from heat gained from the coals on the lid.

HINT *A quality 2-inch paintbrush is handy for spreading sauces, and for buttering pans and toast.*

You can check progress during cooking by sneaking a peek now and then. Lift the lid quickly with a hook or tongs, but don't look very long or you'll lose valuable heat.

Your Dutch oven needs to be "seasoned" before cooking with it the first time. This involves putting a generous amount of vegetable oil in the oven and heating it until it smokes. Use a brush to spread the oil up the inside of the oven from time to time. After a thorough heating, allow it to cool and then wipe out surplus oil with a paper towel.

Once your Dutch oven is broken in, never wash it with soap or detergents. Just wipe it out after use with a paper towel. The breaking-in process puts oil into the pores of the metal, allowing you to use the oven without the oil unless it's called for in a recipe. When a recipe calls for frying in oil, add the oil, but if it doesn't, as in a casserole recipe, put the ingredients right in the oven without any oil.

For baking things like potatoes or fruit, put the item on an inverted metal plate.

Very few recipes in this book can't be prepared as well in a Dutch oven as in a full oven such as you'll find in a travel trailer or motor home.

Aluminum Foil Cooking

Use heavy-duty foil in your foil cooking. It doesn't pay to try to get by with two layers of lightweight foil. The rough handling it might get in your fire is apt to puncture it. Then you lose the juices in the packet, and the meal burns.

Foil Wraps

There are three common ways to wrap a foil package: the Drugstore, the Bundle, and the Two-Handled wrap.

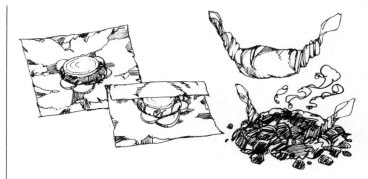

• The Drugstore Wrap

Put the food in the center of a square oblong piece of heavy-duty foil large enough to allow for folding at the top and sides.

Bring the two long edges together above the food. Fold down loosely in a series of locked folds allowing for heat expansion and circulation.

Fold the short ends up and over. Crimp to seal.

• The Bundle Wrap

Put food in the center of a square of heavy-duty foil large enough to permit adequate wrapping.

Bring the four corners up together in a pyramid shape. Twist the ends together to seal, but allow room for heat circulation and expansion.

• The Two-Handled Wrap

Follow directions for the Drugstore wrap to fasten the two long edges together.

Then, twist each of the ends together to seal and provide handles.

This wrap is especially handy when a recipe calls for burying the package in coals. You can leave the ends above the coals to make it easy to find and remove when cooking is done.

You can also use foil to make handy one-time utensils:

• Forked Stick Skillet

Mold a length of double thickness heavy-duty foil from one side of a forked stick to the other. Roll up the outer edge to make an enclosed flat center.

• Griddle

Cover grill or wire rack with a double thickness of heavy-duty foil.

• Saucepan

Mold a length of double thickness heavy-duty foil over the end of a stump or log to form desired shape and size. Leave extra foil on one side for a handle.

Fold down edges to make a rim. Twist the foil on the long side around a stick to make a handle.

• Serving Bowl

Mold a length of double thickness foil as with the saucepan, but don't leave extra foil. Remove foil and crimp down edges to make a rim.

• Baking Pan

Use double thickness heavy-duty foil large enough to make the size pan you need. Fold up the sides about 1½ to 2 inches. Miter the corners for strength.

• Cup

Mold a short length of double thickness heavy-duty foil around your fist. Remove and turn under the raw edges to form a smooth lip.

• **Strainer**

Follow directions for the cup. Punch small holes in the bottom of the cup.

Reflector Oven Baking

A reflector oven is usually made of shiny aluminum. It's designed so heat from a fire reflects on both the top and bottom of a shelf in the middle.

The fire for a reflector oven should have flames instead of the coals recommended for most cooking. Heat for a reflector oven is controlled by moving the oven nearer or farther from the flames. Check the distance with the back of your hand. Hold your hand in front of the oven with its back to the flames and slowly count to eight. If you can't keep your hand there that long, the fire is too hot. Longer means it is too cool. Move the reflector accordingly.

You can watch your food through the open front, and avoid scorching or burning.

Keep your oven bright and shiny so it will be efficient.

Baked foods can be made in this oven, especially biscuits, pies, and cakes.

Charcoal Cooking

Start your charcoal by using starter fluid or by putting the charcoal on an already burning fire. *Never add starter fluid to a fire that is already lighted.*

After lighting, wait to use the fire until the coals are covered with a thin layer of white ash.

Determine the height at which you want your grill above the coals by using your "hand thermometer." Hold your hand above the coals. The number of seconds you can bear to hold your hand over the fire is your guide.

HINT *Old-time blacksmiths knew the value of a bellows to fan the charcoal in their forges. You can use a bellows, too, if you have one, but it's easier to make a lung-operated blower. Just get a piece of ½-inch diameter plastic hose about 2 feet long, and a piece of metal tubing also ½ inch in diameter, about 8 inches long. Insert one end of the metal tube into one end of the plastic tube. Heat the plastic in hot water so it will be pliable for the insertion.*

To use the blower, hold it so the metal tube is aimed at the area of the charcoal you want to fan up, and blow in the open end of the plastic tube. The metal part keeps the plastic from overheating near the charcoal.

Raise or lower your hand to find the temperature you want according to the chart below. Put your grill at that height.

Hand removed	Temperature about	Heat
Between 4 and 5 seconds	300 degrees	Low
Between 3 and 4 seconds	350 degrees	Medium
In less than 3 seconds	400 degrees	High

HINT *Start a charcoal fire at least 20 minutes before you'll begin cooking to be sure you have hot coals.*

HINT *You can put out and reuse charcoal briquets after first use by extinguishing them in an airtight container or by dowsing with water (stay out of the hot steam) and spreading out in the sun to dry.*

The preceding discussion of charcoal cooking applies equally to the use of hardwood coals.

After the Meal

Dishwashing

HINT *Use paper cups, plates, and bowls, and plastic knives, forks, and spoons. End camp dishwashing except for pots, pans, and kitchen utensils.*

Dishwashing is important, and doing it properly is vital to a healthy camp. It's easy if done right. There are a few simple steps.

1. Rough clean. Wipe out your dishes with a paper towel, rubber scraper, or dish brush. Burn soiled towels when through.

2. Wash. Hot dishwater and soap or detergent are needed. Hold dishes and utensils with tongs and scrub with a dishmop or brush.

3. Rinse. Have another pot of very hot water. Hold plates with hot tongs in the almost boiling water. Dump utensils right into the hot water. This will heat everything so they'll dry by their own heat. You won't need a dishtowel.

4. Sanitize. You can be sure your rinse water will sterilize your eating gear by adding a chemical sanitizing agent to the water.

5. Dry. Spread out your utensils so they can air-dry. Then store under a dust and dirt protector such as plastic or oilcloth.

Garbage, Paper, and Tin-Can Disposal

Pollution controls aren't the same in each state. Check local laws about getting rid of trash and garbage by burning. Many campsites have garbage cans with regular pickup.

Where permitted, you can get rid of most paper and dry trash by burning. Turn it with a stick so it burns thoroughly.

Put empty tin cans in your fire to burn out scraps of food. Take the hot cans out with a stick. When cool, flatten by stepping on them.

Wash out empty glass jars. Put them with the flattened cans in your tote-litter bag. Get rid of them at the next trash can or at home. Be sure your tote-litter bag has a plastic liner.

Dispose of waste water in the campground's sewer, septic tank, or disposal sump. Most developed campground have these. If such facilities are not available, carry waste water to the edge of the campground. Scatter, don't pour the water on the ground.

Putting Out Your Fire

You built your fire in a safe place. You were with it from the moment you started it until you were ready to put it out. Putting out your fire is one of the most important parts of firebuilding and cooking.

Your fire must be COLD OUT—cool enough to touch with your bare hand.

If you have water, sprinkle it on your fire. Stir the wet embers with a stick. Sprinkle again and stir again until soaking wet ashes are the result. Turn half burned pieces of wood and drench all sides. Give everything the COLD OUT test with your hand.

If you don't have water, work soil into the ashes. Stir, stir, and stir again, until the last ember is out. Rub burned sticks against the ground until all sparks are out. Give everything the COLD OUT test with your hand.

Only when your fire passes the COLD OUT test can you leave.

Recipes

Cooking Terms

Many of these recipes use cooking terms familiar to experienced cooks, but to make sure others understand, here's an explanation.

Bake	To cook by dry heat as in conventional oven or Dutch oven, or in aluminum foil.
Baste	To moisten food while cooking, by spreading with melted fat, drippings, or special sauces.
Boil	To cook in water or other liquid hot enough to bubble (212 degrees F. at sea level, -2 degrees for each 1,000 feet of elevation; double given cooking time at 5,000 feet).

Braise	To cook meat tender by browning in hot fat, then cooking in covered pan, usually with added liquid.
Broil	To cook meat directly over or in front of an open fire.
Cut in	To blend cooking fat with flour to make dough, by pressing in with fork or cutting in fine chunks with a knife.
Deep Fry	To cook by immersion in very hot fat or oil.
Dredge	To coat meat with flour, often seasoned, before browning or frying.
Fry	To cook in open pan with small amount of fat or oil.
Marinate	To tenderize or flavor meat by covering with spiced vinegar and oil, salad dressing, or commercial marinade sauce.

HINT *Check recipes while making your shopping list and read them twice before starting to cook. They clue you on ingredients, utensils, fire techniques, and timing—all important. Don't improvise unless you must.*

Pan Broil	To cook meat in a very hot skillet with a minimum of fat. This method makes it possible to cook food by broiling over a gas or electric stove.
Poach	To cook just below the boiling point of (usually) water.
Roast	To cook meat and vegetables in hot air, as in covered pan in oven, or in aluminum foil covered by coals.
Scald	To heat to just below boiling point.
Sear	To seal surfaces of meat by exposing to intense heat so juices are contained.
Simmer	To cook in liquid just barely at boiling point.
Steep	To extract the value by soaking in hot water.
Saute	To fry quickly in a little fat.
Stew	To cook meat by searing, then simmering until tender, usually with vegetables added. Also to cook vegetables and fruit (often dried fruit).
Tenderize	To render meat easier to cook or chew by softening the tissues by pounding, with chemicals, or by marinating.

Cooking Measurements

There are three of you and the recipe says the quantity is for four, or six. Or there are six in your family, and all the recipes seem to be for four. Use the old ratio equation, which, translated for your purpose, says:

Multiply the quantity of an item stated in the recipe by
The number of servings you want
and
Divide by the number the recipe says it will serve.
The answer is the quantity of the food you need.

OR...

$$\frac{A}{B} \quad : \quad \frac{a}{X}$$

$$\frac{B \times a}{A} = X$$

Here are quantity equivalents:

Dash	= 6 or 7 drops
Pinch	= less than ⅛ teaspoon
¼ teaspoon	= 15 drops
1 teaspoon	= ⅓ tablespoon
1 tablespoon	= 3 teaspoons
2 tablespoons	= 1 fluid ounce
4 tablespoons	= ¼ cup or 2 fluid ounces
8 tablespoons	= ½ cup or 4 fluid ounces
16 tablespoons	= 1 cup
1 cup	= 8 fluid ounces
2 cups	= 1 pint
1 pint	= 16 fluid ounces
4 cups	= 1 quart
1 quart	= 32 fluid ounces
4 quarts	= 1 gallon (US)

Canadian cups, pints, quarts and gallons are 25 percent greater in volume than in the USA.

In each of the following recipes the number served by the recipe is shown. These numbers are averages. Obviously four hungry teenage boys will eat more than four small children. Look at the ingredients and adjust quantities according to the appetites in your family.

> **HINT** *Thicken soup, gravy, or other hot liquid with a mix of flour and water stirred with fork to smooth consistency, and then stirred into hot soup, gravy, or other liquid.*

Breakfasts

Corned Beef Hash and Eggs

4 servings

15-oz. can corned beef hash

1 or 2 eggs per person

Open both ends of corned beef hash can. Remove one end, but leave the other as a base to push against. Push from that end and slice ¼-inch slices from the other as the hash comes out. Cook on both sides in a lightly greased skillet until heated through, longer if you like it crisp.

> **HINT** *Since most camp lunches will be light and eaten cold, breakfasts should be more than toast and coffee or dry cereal with milk.*

Keep cooked hash patties warm while frying eggs to your liking—usually sunnyside up or over-easy with this recipe. Serve the eggs on top of the hash. Toast bread over your fire, if desired.

> **HINT** *Supplement breakfasts with fresh or canned fruit or fruit juice, and a hot beverage.*

Cinnamon Oatmeal

4 servings

1½ cups old-fashioned oatmeal

½ teaspoon cinnamon

¼ cup seedless raisins

1 apple, cored, peeled, and cut into ½-inch cubes

1 teaspoon salt

Combine all ingredients with 3 cups of cold water in a kettle. Bring to boil and simmer for 15 minutes. Serve with milk.

Pancakes

4 servings

2 cups biscuit mix

Liquid and eggs to make dough according to biscuit recipe

Margarine or butter to grease griddle and to put on cakes

Syrup, jam, or jelly

Mix the biscuit dough. Beat lightly until smooth. Bake on hot, lightly greased griddle. Turn when bubbles appear, and a few break. Serve with margarine or butter, and syrup, jam, and jelly.

> **HINT** *Check ahead to see whether your campground has 110-volt electrical outlets at your campsite. If so, bring along an electric fry pan with dome lid. It can handle innumerable cooking tasks.*

French Toast

4 servings

3 eggs

1 cup milk or ½ cup dry milk with water

½ teaspoon salt

2 tablespoons sugar

8 slices bread

Syrup, jam, jelly, confectioners sugar

Margarine or butter to grease griddle and put on toast

Break eggs in bowl and beat. Stir in milk, salt, and sugar.

Dip bread, slice by slice, in mix until both sides are coated. Fry on greased skillet or griddle until golden brown on both sides. Serve with syrup, jam, jelly, or confectioners sugar.

Quick Hot Cereal

Cook quick oats, cream of rice, farina, etc., according to instruction on the box. Serve with milk and your favorite fruit sliced on top.

Paul Bunyan Breakfast

4 servings

½-pound bacon

6 eggs

29-oz. can potatoes, diced in ½-inch pieces

½ teaspoon salt

Dash pepper

Cut bacon in 1-inch strips and fry until almost fully cooked. Drain most of grease, leaving enough to brown potatoes.

Add diced potatoes to bacon and brown them. Scramble the eggs in another pan, using some of the bacon grease. Add cooked eggs to potato and bacon mix and serve up Paul Bunyan-size portions.

Scrambled Eggs

Per person servings

1 or 2 eggs per person

Salt and pepper to taste

1 tablespoon milk per egg used

2 or 3 slices of bread per person

Break eggs into a bowl. Stir in salt, pepper, and milk. Beat until well mixed, and eggs are broken up. Pour into a greased skillet. Turn the mix frequently while cooking. When egg is in cooked chunks, it's done. Toast bread over fire and serve with eggs.

Soft Boiled Eggs

Per person servings

1 or 2 eggs per person

Salt and pepper to taste

2 or 3 slices of bread per person

Put eggs in small kettle. Cover with water. Bring water to a boil. Take kettle off fire. Let stand for 4 minutes.

Toast the bread while eggs are standing.

After 4 minutes, take the eggs out and use right away by carefully cracking open and spooning contents over toast.

Poached Eggs

Per person servings

1 or 2 eggs per person

Salt and pepper to taste

2 or 3 slices of bread

Bring about 2 inches of water in a pan to a boil. Reduce heat until water is simmering. Break eggs into a cup and then slide each egg into the hot water. Remove pan from heat and let stand for 4 minutes.

Toast bread over a fire while waiting for eggs.

Serve eggs on toast.

Lunches

Most campers don't like to break a day with a lot of time spent cooking lunch. Instead, they usually prepare simple lunches that can be served cold. Here's a typical camp lunch that's filling and tasty.

Assorted cold cuts

Sliced cheese

Rye or whole wheat bread

Deviled eggs (Hard boil eggs when cooking breakfast)

Butter, mustard, salt, and pepper

Cookies

Beverage

Deviled Eggs

Shell hard-boiled eggs. Cut in half lengthwise and remove yolks without damaging the whites. Crush yolks in bowl and moisten with a soft butter, lemon juice, and sugar mixture. Mix one of the following in the moistened egg yolks:

Anchovy paste	Deviled ham
Liver sausage paste	Grated Blue cheese

Put egg yolk filling back in the egg white halves.

Here are some lunch recipes:

Camp Pâté

4 servings

½-pound liverwurst

1 tablespoon sweet pickle relish

¼ cup mayonnaise

1 tablespoon catsup

1 teaspoon prepared mustard

Dash Worcestershire sauce

8 slices dark bread

Salt and pepper to taste

Remove casing from liverwurst. Put meat in bowl and mash with fork. Mix in remaining ingredients except bread. Spread on bread, making 4 sandwiches.

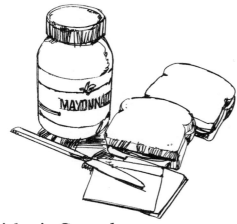

Sandwiches in General

Don't downgrade sandwiches. They're an excellent choice for camp lunches. Sure, the kids may moan about peanut butter and jelly again, but sandwiches can have variety. Here are few good sandwich fillings:

Mashed bananas	Sardines and cheese
Peanut butter and honey	Peanut butter and marshmallows
Tuna salad	Deviled ham
Cheese and raisins	Egg salad

Bacon, lettuce, and tomato (fry bacon at breakfast time)

Use different breads and spreads such as butter, mayonnaise, and mustard with these fillings and you'll have a great variety of sandwiches. Lettuce will add a little zip.

Serve with carrot sticks, pickles, potato or corn chips, and a beverage, and you'll have 'em calling for more tomorrow.

Soups

With all the excellent canned and dried soups available in grocery stores, it hardly seems worth the space to list any "made from scratch" recipes in this book. Hope you agree!

Dinners or Main Courses

Chicken

Fast Chicken Creole

4 servings

3 cups cooked rice (1 cup uncooked rice)

3 tablespoons butter or margarine

½ cup chopped green pepper

1 chopped medium onion or 2 tablespoons instant chopped onion

½ cup thinly sliced celery

10 ½-oz. can condensed chicken gumbo soup (undiluted)

16-oz. can tomatoes (drained)

3- or 4-oz. can sliced mushrooms (drained)

2 5-oz. cans boned chicken (diced)

¼ teaspoon crumbled leaf marjoram

⅛ teaspoon garlic powder

¼ teaspoon salt

4-oz. packaged shredded American cheese

Put cooked rice in a lightly greased 2-quart baking dish or regular Dutch oven.

Saute green pepper, onion, celery, and garlic in butter or margarine in a saucepan until tender. Stir in remaining ingredients except cheese.

Pour mixture over rice, spreading evenly. Sprinkle with the cheese. Cover.

Bake in moderate oven (350 degrees) until bubbly hot.

HINT *Keep cooking fires small and concentrated. They shouldn't be much bigger around than the bottom of the biggest kettle you'll be using.*

Chicken and Rice

4 servings

6 chicken legs (thighs included)

3 10½-oz. cans condensed chicken broth (undiluted)

1½ cups uncooked converted long grain rice (not instant)

½ teaspoon salt

In a tightly covered kettle or Dutch oven, simmer the chicken in the broth for 30 minutes.

Add the rice, making sure it's mixed in the broth.

Cook for 20 minutes over low heat until the rice is tender. All liquid should be absorbed by the rice and the chicken falling apart.

Chicken Breasts with Rice

4 servings

4 chicken breasts, preferably boned

10½-oz. can condensed cream of mushroom soup (undiluted)

⅔ cup instant rice

8 14-inch squares heavy-duty aluminum foil

Put each piece of chicken on a separate piece of double thickness foil.

Mix soup with instant rice. Spoon over the chicken breasts.

Seal packages using the Drugstore wrap and put them on a grill about 5 inches above hot coals. Turn once during cooking. Cook about 40 minutes. Check one packet for doneness before removing all four. Reseal and put back on grill if not done.

Salt and pepper to taste.

HINT *Cooking coals need monitoring. Campfires aren't like electric or gas stoves that give instant heat when turned on. It takes awhile for wood or charcoal added to a fire to come up to full heat. While this is happening, food that's cooking could drop below recommended cooking temperature.*

Brunswick Stew

4 servings

1 small chopped onion or 1 tablespoon instant chopped onion

8-oz. can whole kernel corn (drained)

8-oz. can green lima beans (drained)

6-oz. can chunked and ground chicken with broth (drained)

8-oz. can tomato sauce

½ teaspoon salt

4 squares heavy-duty aluminum foil (about 18-inches square)

Combine all ingredients and spoon equal parts into center of foil sheets.

Seal with the Bundle wrap.

Cook over medium-hot coals until very hot.

Chicken in Orange Sauce

6 servings

1 2- to 3-pound chicken, cut up

⅓ cup frozen orange juice concentrate

1 small onion, sliced thin

1 teaspoon salt

10 peppercorns

3 tablespoons all-purpose flour

¼ cup chopped cashew nuts

Put chicken in Dutch oven. Combine orange juice, onion, salt, and peppercorns. Pour over chicken. Cover and cook for about 1 hour with coals both under and on top of oven. Check from time to time to be sure fire isn't too hot. Remove some coals, if it is.

While cooking, mix flour with 3 tablespoons cold water to make a smooth paste.

Remove chicken. Take coals from top of oven and put underneath . Add the flour paste mixture to the juices in the oven and stir until mixture boils.

Pour the mixture over the chicken. Garnish each serving with cashew nuts.

Serve with rice or potatoes and a vegetable.

Quick Paella

4 servings

¼ cup margarine or butter

1⅓ cups instant rice (uncooked)

½ cup minced onion or 2 tablespoons instant chopped onion

⅓ cup minced green pepper

2 cloves minced garlic or ¼ teaspoon garlic powder

2 8-oz. cans tomato sauce

7-oz. can minced clams (drained)

5-oz. can cooked chicken

Heat margarine in large skillet and lightly brown rice, onion, green pepper, and garlic.

Add remaining ingredients along with 1½ cups water, and mix well.

Bring to a boil. Lower heat and simmer for 5 minutes.

Beef

Ground beef is the basic meat for many camp recipes. It is recommended that extra lean ground beef be used in outdoor cooking. You'll have less fat to drain off, and when cooking on a grill over coals there will be less flare-up from dripping grease.

HINT *Control flareups caused by fat dripping from meat on hot coals by avoiding fatty meats and trimming off all fat possible before putting on the grill. If you still have flareups, control them by squirting the base of the flames with water from a water pistol.*

Guess What Burgers

4 servings

1 pound ground beef

1 teaspoon salt

⅛ teaspoon ground pepper

8 hamburger buns or rolls, or 16 slices of bread

Filling (see below)

1 tablespoon instant chopped onion or 1 small onion (chopped)

Mix ground beef lightly with the salt, pepper, and onion. Shape in any of the following ways to fit the bread, rolls, or buns you have:

8 thin rounds to fit hamburger buns.

8 rectangles to fit hot dog rolls, club rolls, or 3-inch slices of French bread.

8 squares to fit sliced sandwich bread.

Put two patties together for each burger, sandwich style, with the filling of your choice from the following:

- Thinly sliced tomatoes sprinkled lightly with seasoned salt and grated Parmesan cheese
- Canned baked beans seasoned with crumpled crisp bacon and a dash of catsup
- Chili con carne spooned right from the can
- Canned French-fried onions, coarsely crushed
- Dry or canned chopped or sliced mushrooms
- Dill, sweet, or crisp cucumber pickles, sliced
- Crumbled or mashed blue cheese mixed with equal amounts of cream cheese
- Thinly sliced hot dogs topped with mustard
- Pickle relish blended with chopped celery, grated carrots, and a little mayonnaise or salad dressing.

After adding your filling to one patty, put the other on top. Press the edges together to seal.

Grill over hot coals or in a skillet, turning once until the meat is done the way you like it. Eat sandwich style with your choice of rolls, buns, or bread.

More and More Burgers

4 servings

Same ingredients as Guess What Burgers

Mix ingredients except bread; then add one of these special seasonings before shaping patties. These burgers do not have fillings. The seasonings are mixed right in.

- ¼ cup barbecue sauce (commercial bottled)
- 1 2- or 3-oz. can deviled ham, 1 teaspoon prepared mustard, and 1 tablespoon pickle relish
- ½ cup grated cheddar cheese and ¼ cup catsup
- ⅓ cup chopped walnuts, peanuts, or toasted almonds
- ¼ cup chopped stuffed green olives with pimiento or chopped ripe olives
- ½ cup cooked rice, 2 teaspoons soy sauce, and 1 teaspoon instant chopped onion
- ½ cup crushed cheese crackers or crushed plain or seasoned potato or corn chips.

Cook as described for Guess What Burgers, but for less time since patties are single, not sandwiched with filling.

Mulholland Burgers

4 servings

1 pound ground beef

½ envelope instant meat marinade

4 large poppy-seed rolls, split and toasted

Shape the ground beef into 4 patties about ¾-inch thick.

Mix the marinade and water following label directions. Pour over the patties. Turn to coat both sides. Grill over hot coals or in skillet, brushing several times with remaining marinade. Turn once during cooking. Cook until done the way you like them.

Serve in the toasted buns along with sweet pickles and potato or corn chips, if you like.

HINT *Add water-soaked hickory or mesquite chips to your fire to give that choice smoked flavor to meat cooking above it. Continue to add chips during cooking to keep up a dense smoke. Soak chips about ½ hour before using. If they catch fire, just remove them with tongs and soak again.*

One Pot Hamburger Meals

4 to 6 servings

Here are eight recipes in one. They all use the same basic ground beef base.

1½ pounds ground beef

1 medium chopped onion or 1 tablespoon instant chopped onion

½ green pepper, chopped

10 ¾-oz. can condensed tomato soup (undiluted)

Salt and pepper to taste

Ingredients as required for any of the combinations below

Brown ground beef. Add the other ingredients except those required for combinations below. Simmer until thoroughly heated.

Add to this base any of the following to make:

- Yum Yums. Mix in ½ teaspoon chili powder, serve on or in buns
- Campers' Spaghetti. 1 16-oz. can of spaghetti
- Spanish Rice. Small package of instant rice added while base is browning
- Macroni and Cheese. ½ pound of macaroni and cheese cooked separately
- Hunters' Stew. 2 10½-oz. cans condensed vegetable soup (undiluted)
- Chili. 1 16-oz. can red beans and chili powder to taste
- Squaw Corn. 1 16-oz. can whole-kernel corn and ½ pound of diced or shredded cheese
- Hungarian Hot Pot. 1 16-oz. can baked beans

Hurry Hash

4 servings

10½-oz. can condensed cream of mushroom, celery, or other creamed soup

8 biscuits, rusks, or Melba toast

2 sliced hard-boiled eggs

¼ cup milk

1 pound ground beef or sliced weiners

Brown the ground beef or hot dogs in a skillet.

Heat the soup slowly in a kettle, stirring, and adding milk gradually. When smooth and hot, add meat and eggs. Heat thoroughly. Season to taste.

Serve over biscuits, rusks, or Melba toast.

Quick Stew

4 servings

1 pound ground beef

2 10½-oz. cans condensed vegetable soup (undiluted)

¼ stick margarine or butter, or 4 tablespoons cooking oil

Form the ground beef into golf ball-size balls. Brown the meatballs in margarine, butter, or oil in a skillet. When well browned transfer to a kettle.

Pour the undiluted soup over them. Heat thoroughly. Season to taste.

Beefburger Supreme

4 to 6 servings

1½ pounds ground beef

¾ cup soft bread crumbs

⅓ cup milk

¼ cup catsup

1 finely chopped medium onion or 1 tablespoon instant chopped onion

1 tablespoon prepared mustard

2 teaspoons Worcestershire sauce

2 teaspoons horseradish

1½ teaspoons salt

Combine all ingredients. Mix lightly. Shape into 4 to 6 large patties. Grill 4 inches from hot coals about 7 minutes on each side. Serve on toasted hamburger buns.

Porcupine Balls

4 servings

1 pound ground beef

½ teaspoon salt

Dash pepper

⅔ cup uncooked instant rice

1 tablespoon cooking oil

¼ cup chopped onion or 1 tablespoon instant chopped onion

½ cup catsup

¼ cup grape or currant jelly

Mix ground beef, onion, salt, pepper, and uncooked instant rice. Lightly form into golf ball-size meatballs.

Heat oil in a skillet and brown the meatballs, turning so they brown all over.

Mix catsup, jelly, and ½ cup water. Pour over browned meatballs.

Cover and cook over low heat for 25 minutes.

Sloppy Joes

4 servings

1 pound ground beef

1 chopped green pepper

1 chopped small onion or 1 tablespoon instant chopped onion

1 stalk celery, chopped

Oil to saute vegetables

1 package Sloppy Joe Mix

4 sliced hamburger rolls

Saute the vegetables in oil until tender.

Break up the ground beef and add to the vegetables. Cook until brown.

Prepare the Sloppy Joe Mix according to package directions.

Pour excess fat off meat. Add Sloppy Joe Mix and stir well.

Simmer until ready to serve on open face rolls.

Burger Dogs

4 servings

½ pound ground beef

4 weiners split the long way

4-oz. can tomato sauce

Grease to brown ground beef

1 tablespoon instant chopped onion

4 sliced hot dog buns

Brown ground beef in a heavy skillet. Add weiners, tomato sauce, onion, and 1 tablespoon water. Cook about 15 minutes.

Toast buns face down on grill.

Serve mixture on open face warm buns.

Kaleidoscope Mix

4 servings

1 pound ground beef

16-oz. can French-cut green beans

10¾-oz. can condensed tomato soup (undiluted)

2 tablespoons instant chopped onion

½ teaspoon garlic powder

Instant mashed potatoes to make 4 servings

Ingredients called for on potato box for 4 servings

¼-oz. package shredded cheddar cheese

Grease to brown ground beef

Brown ground beef in heavy skillet. Stir in onion and garlic powder while browning. Drain off excess fat.

Stir in green beans and soup. Heat until bubbly.

While beef mixture is heating, prepare 4 servings of instant mashed potatoes following package directions. When finished, stir in cheese.

Spoon the beef topping over the potatoes.

HINT *When adding fuel to an existing cooking fire, add it at the edge of the fire. When it's going well, put it on the other coals with tongs. If you add unlighted fuel to the center of your fire, you reduce the temperature until the new fuel catches and burns hot.*

A Foil Meal

Per person

1 large peeled potato, sliced the long way into 4 pieces

1 medium onion, sliced

2 carrots, sliced

¼ pound ground beef

1 14-inch square of heavy-duty aluminum foil

Put half the vegetable slices flat in the center of the foil. Salt and pepper to taste.

Shape a hamburger patty and put on top of the vegetable slices.

Put the rest of the sliced vegetables flat on top of the patty. Salt and pepper again to taste.

Seal the foil package with the Two-Handled wrap.

Put the package on a bed of coals and cover with more coals, leaving the handles uncovered. Cook 15 minutes.

This can also be cooked on top of the coals. If you do, cook 10 minutes each side.

Beef Enchiladas

4 servings

Filling

10 to 12 corn tortillas

1 pound ground beef

¼ 8-oz. can tomato sauce

¼ 10-oz. can mild enchilada sauce

1 teaspoon salt

1 medium onion, chopped

½ cup seedless raisins

3 tablespoons chopped and peeled green chilies (canned)

4 oz. shredded cheddar cheese

Grease to brown ground beef

Sauce

¾ 8-oz. can tomato sauce

¾ 10-oz. can mild enchilada sauce

2 oz. shredded cheddar cheese

Brown beef in skillet and drain. Add ¼ can tomato and ¼ can enchilada sauce. Add salt. Simmer 3 to 4 minutes until thickens. Set aside until needed later.

Mix ¾ can tomato sauce and ¾ can enchilada sauce.

Put a few tablespoons of the meat mixture across the center of a tortilla. Sprinkle with onion, raisins, chilies, and cheese.

Roll the tortilla and put flap side down in a Dutch oven. Repeat with the rest of the tortillas. When you have a layer in the bottom of the oven, cover with sauce and continue adding enchiladas. Cover each layer with sauce.

When all enchiladas are in the oven, top with 2 ounces cheddar cheese.

Put lid on Dutch oven. Heat gently with a few coals on top and underneath. Cook until thoroughly heated through, about ½ to ¾ of an hour depending on your heat.

Tamale Pie

4 to 6 servings

1 pound ground beef

28-oz. can tomatoes

¾ cup yellow corn meal

1 tablespoon chili powder (more if you're from the Southwest

16-oz. can whole-kernel corn (drained)

4-oz. can chopped ripe olives

Grease to brown ground beef

Brown ground beef in skillet. Add tomatoes.

Mix cornmeal with ¾ cup cold water and add to skillet mixture, stirring constantly. Transfer to a large kettle.

Simmer uncovered 20 to 25 minutes, stirring occasionally. Add remaining ingredients. Salt and pepper to taste. Heat through.

Corned Beef Hash

4 servings

16-oz. can corned beef

Instant mashed potatoes to make 4 servings

¼ pound butter or margarine

1 cup milk

4 eggs

Mix corned beef, well broken up, with uncooked potatoes in large kettle. Melt butter or margarine and add with the milk, stirring well. Simmer for ½ hour. Stir from time to time.

Just before ready to take from fire, break in the eggs. Stir in and cook for another 4 minutes.

Campfire Pizza

4 servings

2 cups biscuit mix

1 bottle pizza topping sauce

3½-oz. package sliced pepperoni

8 oz. shredded Mozzarella cheese

4-oz. can sliced ripe olives (drained)

4-oz. can sliced mushrooms, stems and pieces (drained)

Heavy-duty foil to line and cover pie plates with three thicknesses

Prepare biscuit dough for pizza crust recipe on package. Divide dough into 4 pieces. On waxed paper or foil, roll each part into a thin circle.

Prepare metal pie plate by lining with heavy-duty foil. Oil foil. Put prepared pizza crust on each plate. Pour pizza sauce over crusts, spreading to edges.

Top with pepperoni, mushrooms, and olives. Sprinkle with shredded cheese to cover well. Cover with heavy-duty aluminum foil, crimped around edges of pan so it doesn't sag. Place on grill over coals. Lift a few coals from below with tongs and put on foil cover.

Grill over medium-hot coals 25 minutes or until crust is brown around edges and pizza sauce and cheese bubble lightly.

Belly Stretcher
(obviously named by a teenager)

4 servings

15-oz. can corned beef hash

10½-oz. can condensed cream of celery soup

1 cup milk

¾ pound elbow macaroni

4 oz. shredded process American cheese

2 tablespoons instant chopped onion

Cook macaroni as directed on package. Drain. Stir in all other ingredients. Heat over medium heat until bubbly, stirring occasionally.

Oven Pot Roast

4 servings

2 pound pot roast of beef

4 peeled potatoes, cut into 2-inch cubes

4 small onions

4 sliced carrots

Dredge roast in flour and brown on all sides in hot oil in Dutch oven or skillet. If in skillet, move to roasting pan. If in Dutch oven, leave there. Add water to a level of about ½ inch.

Cover Dutch oven and put coals underneath and on lid. Put roasting pan, if used, in a regular oven.

Simmer for 2 to 3 hours, adding water as needed. Replace coals on top of Dutch oven as the old ones burn up.

Add potatoes, onions, and carrots for last 45 minutes of cooking time.

Beef and Mushroom Delight

4 servings

1 pound stewing beef cut into ½-inch cubes

4 peeled baking potatoes

8-oz. carton sour cream

1 envelope onion soup mix

¼ cup milk

¼ teaspoon garlic salt

½ teaspoon salt

Dash pepper

4-oz. can sliced mushrooms (drained)

2 small onions cut in wedges

8 14-inch squares heavy-duty aluminum foil

Divide beef into 4 equal portions. Put each portion in center of a foil square. Sprinkle beef with seasonings. Evenly distribute mushroom slices and onion wedges among portions.

Seal with Bundle wrap. Set aside.

Slice potatoes and combine with remaining ingredients in a kettle or bowl. Spoon this mixture evenly in the center of each of the 4 remaining pieces of foil. Seal with Bundle wrap.

Put the potato packets on medium-hot coals and cook for 45 to 55 minutes or until potatoes are tender.

After the potato packets have cooked for about 15 minutes, put the beef mixture packets on the coals and cook until the potato packets are done.

Corned Beef and Cabbage

4 to 6 servings

2 pounds corned beef

1 head cabbage

¾ cup milk or 3 tablespoons dry milk

¼ teaspoon coarsely ground pepper

6 14-inch squares heavy-duty aluminum foil

Cut corned beef into 6 portions. Wash cabbage and cut into 6 wedges.

Put one portion of beef and one of cabbage on each foil square.

If using dry milk, add ¾ cup water and stir. Pour it or the regular milk between cabbage leaves in each portion. Sprinkle with pepper. Seal with the Drugstore wrap, leaving room for expansion.

Cook on medium-hot coals for 30 minutes, turning once.

Pork

Chili Dogs

8 servings

20-oz. can chili con carne

6-oz. can tomato paste

1 teaspoon prepared mustard

½ teaspoon salt

1 pound wieners

8 hot dog buns

Split and butter the buns. Mix chili, tomato paste, mustard, and salt in bowl. Put wieners on grill 4 inches above medium coals. Put chili mixture in pot on same grill. Cook 7 to 10 minutes, turning hot dogs and stirring chili frequently. During last couple of minutes, toast buns buttered side down on grill. Put a hot dog in each bun and cover with chili mixture.

Barbecue Hot Dogs and Kraut

4 servings

8 wieners

8-oz. can sauerkraut

Prepared mustard

Catsup

4 hot dog buns

4 12 by 18-inch pieces of heavy-duty aluminum foil

Split hot dogs lengthwise, not cutting all the way through. Spread mustard on 4 of the split hot dogs and catsup on the other 4. Put each mustard-spread dog on a piece of foil, cut side up.

Spoon ¼th of the sauerkraut on top of each mustard dog.

Top with the catsup dogs, split side down. Seal with Drugstore wrap. Cook directly on hot coals for 3 minutes each side.

Hot Dogs, Sauerkraut, and Dumplings

4 servings

27-oz. can sauerkraut

½ pound wieners

1 cup biscuit mix

Milk as called for in dumpling recipe on mix box

Drain sauerkraut. Rinse with clear water and drain. Put in large kettle and add ½ cup water.

Add hot dogs so they are distributed evenly through the kraut. You can slice the wieners if you like.

Simmer the wieners and kraut until heated through.

While heating, make the dumpling dough. Drop the dough by teaspoonfuls on top of the hot mix. Cover tightly and cook over medium heat for 20 minutes more.

Hot Dogs and Baked Beans

6 servings

1-pound package of wieners

2 16-oz. cans pork and beans

Put canned beans in kettle. Slice hot dogs to bite size and mix with beans. Heat through.

You can season with brown sugar and catsup if you like.

Jambalaya

4 servings

¾ cup instant or converted rice

8-oz. can tomatoes

1 medium onion, chopped, or 1 tablespoon instant chopped onion

2 slices bacon, cut in 1-inch lengths

1 tablespoon all-purpose flour

15-oz. can pork sausage hash

Prepare the rice according to package instructions. Keep warm.

Fry bacon until almost done. Add onion to bacon and fry until light yellow. Add flour and stir until smooth.

Add tomatoes undrained. Bring to a boil and add meat broken into small chunks. Add rice.

Simmer while stirring until well heated.

Old West Pork Chops

4 servings

4 ¾-inch thick pork chops

3 tablespoons vegetable oil

1 large onion cut into 4 slices

1 teaspoon chili powder

1 chopped green pepper

1 cup uncooked converted rice

8-oz. can tomato sauce

2 teaspoons salt

Brown chops well on both sides in oil in skillet. Remove.

Stir in chili powder and cook for 2 minutes. Add green pepper, rice, tomato sauce, 1¼ cups water, and salt.

Heat to boiling. Pour into a 2-quart baking dish or 12-inch Dutch oven. Arrange pork chops over the rice mixture. Put an onion slice on top of each chop. Cover and bake in a moderate oven for 1 hour or until liquid is absorbed.

If using a Dutch oven, put coals under oven and on the lid. Check by inspection to see when liquid is absorbed.

Barbecued Ribs in Foil

4 servings

3 pounds country style pork spareribs

1 cup bottled barbecue sauce

2 pieces heavy-duty aluminum foil to make a double thickness wrap

Salt and pepper to taste

Put the ribs in a single layer on the double foil. Season to taste with salt and pepper.

Fold foil and seal with the Drugstore wrap. Put on grill about 4 inches from hot coals and cook for 45 minutes, turning once during cooking.

Remove packet from grill, and open carefully without burning fingers or tearing foil. Spoon barbecue sauce on each piece. Broil in open packet for 5 minutes more. Turn ribs and spoon sauce on other side. Broil another 5 minutes.

Serve with fried or baked potatoes and a vegetable.

William Tell Pork Chops

4 servings

4 pork chops about 1-inch thick

¾ cup apple juice

Dash Worcestershire sauce

Salt and pepper to taste

8 slices of lemon

Make three ¼-inch cuts in fat edges of each chop to stop curling during cooking. Heat the skillet and grease lightly with the fatty edge of a chop.

Brown chops on both sides. Sprinkle with salt and pepper. Add apple juice, Worcestershire sauce, and four of the lemon slices. Cover and simmer for 30 to 40 minutes or until chops are done.

Serve each chop with a lemon slice and spoonful of pan gravy over all.

Serve with rice or potatoes, and a vegetable.

Fish

Tip-Top Tuna

4 to 6 servings

2 10½-oz. cans condensed cream of celery soup (undiluted)

1 pound noodles or macaroni

¼ stick margarine

2 7-oz. cans tuna (drained)

16-oz. can peas (drained)

Cook noodles or macaroni as directed on package. Drain and add margarine to coat pasta.

Heat soup and add peas.

Spread tuna over the noodles. Pour heated soup and peas over tuna. Cover and heat on low fire until bubbly.

California Tuna Bake

4 servings

8 oz. macaroni

6-oz. can tuna (drained and flaked)

16-oz. can peas (drained)

¼ cup pimiento-stuffed green olives

2 tablespoons instant chopped onion

½ teaspoon salt

¼ teaspoon pepper

10½-oz. can condensed cream of mushroom soup (undiluted)

4-oz. package cream cheese, cubed

Cook macaroni according to package directions. Drain and combine with tuna, peas, olives, and onion in a large bowl.

Toss lightly to mix well. Salt and pepper. Toss again. Stir in soup until everything is evenly coated. Fold in cheese cubes.

Spoon mixture into a 2-quart baking dish or 12-inch Dutch oven. Cover and bake in moderate oven or in Dutch oven with coals under oven and on lid for about 30 minutes or until bubbly hot.

Tuna Puff

4 servings

Instant mashed potato mix to make 4 servings

Ingredients called for on potato box

13-oz. can tuna, flaked (drained)

4 eggs

⅓ cup grated Parmesan cheese

2 tablespoons fine dry bread crumbs

1 envelope white sauce mix

Butter to grease baking dish

1 tablespoon lemon juice

Dash of seafood seasoning (optional)

Prepare potatoes and combine with tuna, beaten eggs, and cheese in a large bowl. Mix well.

Butter a 2-quart baking dish and sprinkle with crumbs. This can also be done with a Dutch oven.

Put potato mixture in baking dish or Dutch oven.

Bake in moderate oven for 1 hour or until puffy and brown. If using Dutch oven, put coals under oven and on lid and cook for 1 hour or until puffy and brown.

Prepare white sauce in bowl following label directions. Add lemon juice and seafood seasoning, blending well. Serve separate to spoon over individual servings of the tuna puff.

Clam Chowder Potato Scallop

4 servings

7½-oz. can minced clams

1 package scalloped potato mix

Liquids to make potatoes according to box directions

Drain clams, saving liquid. Empty potato mix into skillet and mix according to box directions, adding clam juice liquid. Heat to boiling. Cover and simmer 30 to 35 minutes. Stir in clams and heat through.

Fish Chowder

4 servings

4 strips bacon

1 cup chopped onions

3 medium diced potatoes

1 pound fish filets

½ cup diced celery

1 tomato cut into wedges

½ can canned milk

Cook bacon until crisp. Remove from pan, crumble, and save for later. Put bacon grease in soup kettle.

Add chopped onions and brown in bacon grease. Add 3 cups water and potatoes. Cook until tender. Cut fish filets into small squares. Add to mixture along with diced celery, tomato wedges, and canned milk.

Heat below boiling point until very hot. Season to taste.

Fish in Foil

2 or 3 servings for each pound of fish

1 whole fish (1 to 3 pounds, dressed)

Butter

1 medium or large sliced onion, depending on weight of fish

Salt and pepper

Tarragon, parsley, dill, rosemary, and thyme

Tartar sauce

Sheet of heavy-duty aluminum foil large enough to wrap fish

Spread butter in center of sheet of foil. Top the butter with half the onion slices. Sprinkle cavity and outside of fish with salt and pepper. Put the fish on the onions on the foil. Top fish with remaining onion slices. Sprinkle with herbs. Dot with butter.

Seal package with Drugstore wrap. Put on grill over medium-hot coals. Cook a 1-pound fish for 15 minutes, a 2-pound fish for 25 minutes, and a 3-pound fish for 35 minutes. Regardless of weight, turn fish 2 or 3 times during cooking.

Serve with tartar sauce, either from jar, or made from tartar sauce mix and mayonnaise according to package label.

Serve with macaroni and cheese or hush puppies and a vegetable.

Pan Fried Fish

Number served according to amount of fish

Freshly caught fish

Cooking oil

Seasoned flour

Scale fish if required. Wipe to dry. Remove head, tail, and fins after gutting. Heat ⅛ inch oil in skillet. Coat the fish in seasoned flour and fry until golden brown. Rock the pan from time to time to prevent sticking. Turn once during cooking.

Serve with rice, potatoes, or macaroni and cheese; hush puppies; and a vegetable.

Salmon Fluff

4 servings

4 servings of instant mashed potatoes

Ingredients to prepare potatoes as shown on box

16-oz. can salmon

1½ teaspoons salt in addition to that needed for potatoes

⅛ teaspoon pepper

1 tablespoon instant chopped onion

Prepare mashed potatoes. Mix salmon, salmon liquid, and hot mashed potatoes. Stir in seasonings and onion. Cook in covered pot until heated through.

Miscellaneous

Stew and Dumplings

4 servings

2 16-oz. cans beef, chicken, veal, or lamb stew

1 medium chopped onion

1 cup biscuit mix

Liquid to make dumplings according to recipe on mix box

1 teaspoon parsley flakes

Heat stew to boiling in large kettle. While heating, mix the dumpling dough, adding the parsley flakes.

Drop teaspoonfuls of dough into the boiling stew. Cook uncovered for 10 minutes. Cover and cook 10 minutes longer.

Macaroni and Cheese

4 servings

¾ pound uncooked macaroni

2 tablespoons butter or margarine

2 tablespoons all-purpose flour

¾ cup milk

8 oz. American cheese

½ teaspoon Worcestershire sauce

Cook the macaroni according to package directions.

Make a sauce by melting butter or margarine, adding flour, and stirring with fork until smooth. Add milk to the heated mixture. Cook until it boils, stirring during cooking.

Melt the cheese. Add it and the Worcestershire sauce to the sauce. Pour over the cooked and drained macaroni.

HINT *Put a little vegetable oil in the water when cooking spaghetti, macaroni, or other pasta. It helps keep the pieces from sticking together.*

Squaw Corn

4 servings

4 slices bacon

1 chopped medium green pepper

1 small chopped onion or 1 tablespoon instant chopped onion

2 16-oz. cans cream-style corn

1 teaspoon salt

⅛ teaspoon pepper

4 eggs, beaten

Fry bacon until crisp. Drain on paper towel. Drain all but about 3 tablespoons bacon fat from skillet. Brown the green pepper and onion while stirring until onion is tender. This is not necessary if using instant onion.

Add remaining ingredients. Cook and stir until eggs are thickened but still moist. Crumble bacon over mixture.

Corn Chowder

4 servings

4 slices bacon cut in 1-inch lengths

1 small chopped onion

2 cups milk

2 16-oz. cans whole-kernel corn

3 medium potatoes

½ teaspoon salt

Peel and dice potatoes in ¾-inch cubes. Boil with a tablespoon of the chopped onion in salted water. Meanwhile, fry bacon until light brown. Remove from skillet and save. Fry rest of onion in bacon fat until tender. Pour off all but 1 cup of potato water when potatoes are cooked.

Add bacon, onion, corn, and milk to potato pot. Put back on fire until heated through.

Serve over biscuits or on bread slices.

All-Purpose Fried Rice

4 servings

2 slices bacon cut in 1-inch lengths

¾ cups uncooked, converted rice

10½-oz. can condensed beef or chicken broth (undiluted)

1 small diced onion

Fry the bacon until light brown in large skillet. Add rice to the hot fat and stir until it is thoroughly browned, but not scorched.

Add onion and continue to cook and stir until onion is light yellow.

HINT *Use flat-bottomed pans that are steady, even when empty.*

Use with your choice of the following:
1 12-oz. can corned beef; ¾ pound browned ground beef; or 1 6½ oz. can tuna, salmon, shrimp, or boned chicken; and 1 8-oz. can tomatoes.

If using beef, add beef broth to the basic mix. If using chicken, fish, or seafood, add chicken broth to mix. Cover the pan and cook over medium heat, stirring occasionally for about 5 minutes. Add your choice of meat, chicken, or seafoods, and the tomatoes. Mix well and heat uncovered until entire mixture is bubbly.

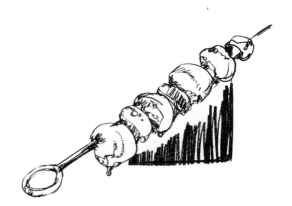

Kabobs

4 servings

1 pound beef, lamb, or combination of the two, cut into chunks

1 large onion, cut into wedges

1 green pepper, cut into wedges

8 cherry tomatoes

16 fresh mushroom caps (from the store—never eat mushrooms found growing in the wild!)

16 pineapple slices

4 commercial Kabob skewers or make your own from straight green sticks about as big around as a pencil and 14 to 18 inches long. Sharpen one end of each to a fine point.

String ingredients on skewers or sticks, alternating ingredients.

Cook over hot coals for about 15 minutes. Turn sticks once during cooking so both sides are evenly cooked. Season to taste.

It is traditional to remove the cooked Kabob from the stick and put on a bed of cooked rice.

Vegetables

Baked Potatoes in Foil

Per person

1 large baking potato

Vegetable oil

1 14-inch square of aluminum foil

Scrub potatoes and rub with oil. Poke a few holes in each with a fork to let steam escape. Seal in foil using the Two-Handled wrap.

Roast on medium coals for about 50 minutes, turning frequently, or bury in coals with handles sticking out, and cook for 35 to 40 minutes. Check for doneness by spearing with a wood splinter. It should enter to the center easily and come out with mealy crumbs sticking to it, if potato is done.

HINT *Yogurt makes a good substitute for sour cream, although it is not recommended in cases when prolonged cooking is required. Yogurt has more protein and less fat than sour cream and is actually a valuable aid to digestion.*

Dutch Oven Baked Potatoes

Per person

1 baking potato per person

Vegetable oil

1 14-inch square of aluminum foil

Poke holes in potato with fork and wrap in foil using Bundle wrap. Put three small pebbles or soda bottle caps with cork removed in bottom of Dutch oven to support a metal rack off the bottom. Put potato packets on metal rack and place in the pre-heated oven. Cover, and add coals to the lid.

Bake about 40 minutes and check for doneness with splinter. (See Baked Potatoes in Foil recipe.)

Potatoes can be cooked in foil the same way in a conventional oven.

Other Ways with Spuds

- Boiled. Scrub, don't peel new potatoes. You can peel baking potatoes and boil them, too. Boil in salted water in a covered pot for 20 to 30 minutes for new potatoes, and 30 to 40 minutes for quartered baking potatoes.

- Home Fries. Slice peeled, cold boiled potatoes into enough hot fat to keep them from sticking to the skillet. Add sliced onions for zing. Fry until brown and salt to taste.

- Scalloped. You can cook these from scratch if you want, but the packaged scalloped potatoes are so easy to prepare and so tasty that it's hard to justify the time taken from other activities to cook these from scratch.

- Au Gratin. Same as for Scalloped.

Corn Roasted in Foil

4 servings

8 ears sweet corn

8 pieces 12 by 14-inch heavy-duty aluminum foil

Butter or margarine

Salt to taste

Remove large outer husks. Turn back inner husks and remove silk. Spread corn with soft butter or margarine. Pull inner husks back over ear. Place in foil.

Seal with Two-Handled wrap. Roast corn directly on medium coals for about 12 minutes, turning once. Check one ear to be sure it is done. Reseal and cook longer, if necessary.

HINT *Vegetables. Save the cooking water from vegetables to use in making stocks, soups, and sauces. Organically grown vegetables don't have to be peeled; a good scrubbing should be sufficient. Much of the nutrient value of such vegetables as carrots and potatoes lies just beneath their skins and is easily lost when they are peeled before cooking. If you grow some of your own vegetables, you can be sure they are free of pesticide residues and chemical fertilizers.*

Some vitamins (B-complex and C) are water soluble and can leach out of vegetables during prolonged submersion in water. Never soak your vegetables; instead, wash them quickly and chop or slice them right before cooking. Washing vegetables after they are chopped will also remove water soluble vitamins. Exposure to air also depletes vitamins, and vegetables should not be allowed to stand uncovered before cooking and serving. It's a good idea to salt vegetables after, not before cooking, because salt tends to draw out the natural juices.

Instead of reheating leftover vegetables, serve them in salads. Reheating destroys much of the nutrient value remaining in cooked vegetables. Try chopping up leftover beans, carrots, broccoli, cauliflower, and other vegetables and adding them to tossed salads or finger salads.

Roasted Onions

4 servings

4 large Bermuda onions about the same size

Wash onions and put on low coals or on grill 3 inches from medium coals. Cook 30 minutes, turning occasionally. Check for tenderness with wood skewer.

Serve by squeezing the tender center from the blackened crust.

Mushrooms in Foil

4 servings

1 pound fresh mushrooms (store-bought)

4 squares of 12 by 12-inch heavy-duty aluminum foil

3 tablespoons butter or margarine

Put ¼th of mushrooms on each piece of foil. Dot with butter or margarine. Seal with Two-Handled wrap. Cook for 20 minutes about 3 inches above hot coals. Turn often using handles to turn.

Serve with grilled steak.

Vegetables in General

- **Canned.** It's only necessary to heat canned vegetables in their own juice. Simplest way is to open a can and set it on coals. Remove from fire when heated, drain, and add butter or margarine.

- **Fried.** Canned potatoes can be cut into home fry size and fried as shown for the Home Fries recipe. Okra, onions, and zucchini are also good battered and pan fried.

- **Boiled Fresh.** Clean thoroughly. Peel or pare if the vegetable needs it. The general rule is to boil vegetables in as little water as possible over a medium fire. Exceptions to this rule are onions, beets, greens, and cabbage and its cousins. These should be covered with water and boiled in an open pot over low heat. Cooking times are as follows: quartered cabbage, 15 minutes; cauliflower, 20 minutes; broccoli, 10 minutes; beets, ½ to 1 hour depending on size; and greens, 20 minutes. Among those vegetables that follow the general rule and are cooked in a minimum of water, times are: corn on the cob, 5 to 10 minutes; carrots, 25 minutes; okra, 10 minutes; peas, 15 minutes; lima beans, 35 minutes; and pared sweet potatoes, 15 minutes.

- **Steamed.** Use a small amount of boiling water to cook vegetables in steam, adding more water during the steaming process if necessary. Consult the following chart for cooking times. The best guide until you gain experience with steaming vegetables is to be aware of the qualities of properly cooked vegetables and to keep checking the vegetables you are steaming until you see they are ready. After a few experiments you'll be able to estimate steaming times more accurately.

Vegetable	To Clean	Steam For
Asparagus	Break off tough ends of stalks; check carefully for dirt under scales	5-10 minutes
Beans, lima	Shell beans and rinse thoroughly	15-20 minutes
Beans, snap	Wash; snap off ends; break into inch-long pieces	15-20 minutes
Beets	Remove tops, leaving about 2 inches of stem; wash thoroughly; do not peel or cut off roots and stem until after cooking	30-40 minutes
Beet greens	Remove tough stems; wash well	5-10 minutes
Broccoli	Cut off tough ends of stalks; do not peel; wash well	7-10 minutes
Brussels sprouts	Remove any discolored outer leaves; wash	5-10 minutes
Cabbage	Remove outer leaves only if damaged; wash whole head; cut in quarters and remove core; shred or cut in wedges	10-15 minutes 5 minutes if shredded
Carrots	Cut off tops; scrub well; do not peel if organically grown; cut to desired size	10-15 minutes
Cauliflower	Remove outer leaves and stalk; separate into florets and wash	7-10 minutes
Celery	Scrub well; cut off tough ends of stalks and any spoiled leaves	10-15 minutes
Chard	Discard tough stems; wash well	10-20 minutes
Collards	Remove leaves from tough stems; wash well	10-20 minutes
Corn	Husk; remove silk; rinse quickly	5-8 minutes
Eggplant	Wash; peel and slice	7-12 minutes
Kale	Wash well; remove leaves from tough stems before cooking	10-20 minutes
Mustard greens	Wash well; discard tough stems	10-20 minutes
Okra	Wash; remove stem ends	7-12 minutes
Parsnips	Wash; peel and cut to desired size	10-15 minutes
Peas	Shell; rinse thoroughly	10-15 minutes
Potatoes	Scrub well; remove eyes; leave skins on whenever possible	20-40 minutes
Pumpkin	Wash; cut in half and scoop out seeds and fibers; peel; cut in pieces	10-15 minutes
Rutabagas	Wash; peel; cut in pieces	10-25 minutes
Spinach	Wash carefully; cut off any tough stem ends	5-7 minutes
Squash, summer	Wash; trim off stem ends; slice or cut as desired	8-15 minutes
Squash, winter	Wash; cut in half and scoop out seeds and fibers; peel; cut to desired size	10-20 minutes
Sweet potatoes	Scrub well; cook in skins	15-30 minutes
Turnips	Cut off tops; wash; peel; cut as desired	8-12 minutes

Supplement	Supplies	Add to
Bran	dietary fiber	cereals casseroles breads bread crumb mixtures white flour dessert toppings
Brewer's yeast	B vitamins protein minerals	soups casseroles breads beverages
Kelp or other powdered seaweed (as a partial salt substitute)	iodide	soups sandwiches casseroles meat dishes
Rice polish	B vitamins	white rice breads cookies
Soy powder or soy grits	protein	stews meat loaf breads cookies

Beverages

You'll probably want to stick to a few simple drinks in your family camp, such as:

Fresh milk	Reconstituted dry milk
Powdered fruit bases	Hot gelatin*
Lemonade	Hot and cold cocoa and chocolate
Coffee	Decaffeinated coffee
Tea	Sodas

*Hot gelatin is simply a gelatin mix made just as if you were making the finished product, but used as a hot beverage before it begins to set up. Great when it's rainy or cold.

HINT *UHT (Ultra High Temperature) long-life, shelf-stable milk is a great innovation for campers. When unopened, the milk keeps for up to 6 months without refrigeration. Quart cartons have an expiration date stamped on them.*

This milk may be labeled "Sterilized" instead of "UHT" on some brands. It is usually found in the powdered milk section of your market, but don't let this fool you. It is fluid milk and tastes like regular pasteurized milk.

Breads

The easiest and quickest bread for camp is the store loaf. But if you have time, you might want to add that extra something to a meal—camp baked pastry.

Dutch Oven Biscuits

Hard to say how many of these you'll need, especially with butter and honey. There's something about a Dutch oven biscuit that's special.

Start with 2 cups biscuit mix

Mix dough as described on the box. Use water recipe. Roll out dough and cut into 2-inch circles with cookie cutter or empty soup can, cleaned and with both ends removed.

Preheat your Dutch oven, both oven and lid. Put about ⅛ inch of vegetable oil in the oven. Put each round of dough into the hot oil, and turn over so that it has oil on both sides. Fill the bottom of the oven with a single layer of dough circles. Continue pre-heating the lid while filling the oven.

Put on the lid; add a few coals on top. If the oven was well pre-heated, you probably won't have to put it on more than two or three coals.

Check progress by lifting the lid with a hook or tongs. When biscuits are golden brown, they're ready to eat with butter and honey. Put on another batch while eating the first.

Dutch Oven Biscuit Variation

All ingredients called for in Dutch Oven Biscuit recipe
¼ cup dry onion soup mix

Mix onion soup and biscuit mix while still dry, and then proceed to mix dough and make biscuits as in regular recipe.

HINT *Keep biscuit dough from sticking to your hands by sprinkling dry mix on the damp dough before handling or rolling.*

Hush Puppies

Makes about 24

2¼ cups yellow cornmeal

1 teaspoon salt

2 teaspoons instant chopped onion

¾ teaspoon baking soda

1½ cups buttermilk

Oil

Butter or margarine

Mix the cornmeal, salt, onion, and baking soda in a bowl. Add buttermilk and mix well. Drop by spoonfuls into hot oil (about 1 inch deep) in deep skillet or Dutch oven. Cook until well browned, about 2 minutes. Serve immediately with butter or margarine.

Hush puppies are traditionally served with grilled or fried chicken, fish, or shellfish.

Cinnamon Rolls

Makes about 12

2 cups biscuit mix

¼ cup sugar

1 teaspoon cinnamon

Mix dough, roll out, and cut as described in Dutch Oven Biscuits recipe. Mix sugar and cinnamon and roll each circle of dough in mix to coat both sides.

Cook as described in Dutch Oven Biscuits recipe.

Bannock

4 servings

2 cups biscuit mix

Mix the dough as directed on the box. Use the recipe that calls for water. Flatten out into 1-inch thick loaves big enough to fit in your ungreased skillet.

Bake over slow coals for 7 or 8 minutes to brown the bottom.

Hold pan on edge near side of coals to brown the top.

Test for doneness by sticking a dry stem of grass into the center. When it comes out clean, Bannock is done.

Desserts

Deep Dish Dutch Oven Pie

8 servings (Don't try to make less. It'll keep to next meal.)
2 cups biscuit mix

2 21-oz. cans prepared pie filling—blueberry, cherry, apple, etc.

Mix dough using water recipe on box. Divide into two parts, ⅔ for crust and ⅓ for top. Roll out bottom dough about ⅛-inch thick and about 8 inches wider than the oven, e.g., 20 inches for a 12-inch Dutch oven. Fold in half with loose biscuit mix between to keep from sticking. Put in Dutch oven and shape to bottom and sides without stretching the dough. Put oven over coals, put on lid, and add coals to top. Check after about 10 minutes. Shell should be firm, but not done.

Lightly rub the inside of the crust with oil. Add the prepared fruit filling up to the rim of the crust. Be careful not to break the crust or the filling will leak through and burn.

Roll out the rest of the dough and cut in strips to fit across top of filling like a lattice. Cut each piece about an inch longer than needed for its place in the lattice.

Put pieces in place. Moisten ends slightly with water and seal to original crust. Leave some slack for shrinkage.

Replace hot lid and bake until top of pie is brown. Add more coals to top, if needed. Prepared fillings don't have to be cooked, just heated through.

You can also make a closed top crust, but you'll have to make some slits in the top crust to vent steam. With closed top crust, both top and bottom with filling in place are cooked at the same time.

Dutch Oven Cobbler

8 servings

2 cups biscuit mix

¼ cup sugar

2 16-oz. cans fruit—peaches, cherries, blueberries, etc.

Pre-heat the oven and lid. Prepare the biscuit dough using water recipe on box while oven is heating. Roll out and shape to size of Dutch oven.

Pour the fruit, juice and all, into the Dutch oven. Put the dough on top of the fruit. Sprinkle sugar on top of dough.

Put on the lid and add coals on top. If the oven was thoroughly pre-heated you don't need coals underneath. The canned filling only needs to be heated through.

Check progress by lifting lid. When dough is golden brown, the cobbler is done. Serve hot.

Apple Dumplings

4 servings

1 cup biscuit mix

Milk to make dumplings according to recipe on box

27-oz. can applesauce

¼ cup sugar

Heat-applesauce in kettle, adding ½ cup water and stirring until applesauce has consistency of thick soup.

While applesauce is heating, mix dumpling dough with sugar added to the mix.

When applesauce comes to a boil, drop dough by teaspoonfuls into applesauce, covering the top. Cover kettle and simmer until dumplings swell up.

You can brown dumplings by covering your kettle lid with heavy-duty aluminum foil to protect it, and putting a few coals on top.

Apple Betty

4 servings

1 box cornflakes

16-oz. can applesauce

½ cup sugar

Cinnamon

Put ¼-inch layer of applesauce in deep pan or kettle. Add ¼-inch layer of cornflakes. Then another layer of applesauce. Continue alternating cornflake and applesauce layers until all applesauce is used.

Sprinkle sugar and cinnamon on each layer of applesauce.

This can be eaten without cooking, but if you want it hot, dot the top with butter or margarine and heat through in an oven or over low heat on grill.

Crunchy Bananas

4 servings

4 bananas

2 cups cornflakes, crushed

1 beaten egg

2 tablespoons brown sugar

½ teaspoon salt

¼ cup melted butter or margarine

1 12 x 18-inch piece heavy-duty aluminum foil

Mix egg, sugar, and salt. Peel bananas. Dip in egg mix and roll in flakes.

Put in center of foil and grill unsealed about 3 inches above hot coals. Cook 10 minutes, turning once and basting often with butter or margarine.

Fruit on Rice

4 servings

16-oz. can peach halves

1 cup uncooked instant rice

¼ teaspoon salt

¼ teaspoon allspice

½ cup diced dates

6 maraschino cherries (optional for color)

8-inch aluminum foil pan (optional—can use metal equivalent)

12 x 12-inch piece heavy-duty aluminum foil

Drain peaches and save ½ cup syrup. Mix saved peach syrup, rice, salt, allspice, and ½ cup water in foil pan. Sprinkle dates over mixture. Top with peach halves, cavity side up. Put a cherry in each cavity.

Cover pan with foil and seal around edges. Grill 4 inches above medium coals for 30 minutes.

HINT *Two 8-inch aluminum foil pie pans can be used to bake quick breads from packaged mixes. To use, lightly grease each pan. Pour mix into one pan and invert the second on top of the first. Clip together with paper clips, or add a piece of foil over top and around openings between plates to seal.*

S'mores

Per serving

4 squares milk chocolate candy bar

2 graham cracker squares (not rectangles that have 2 squares)

1 toasting size marshmallow

Put 4 squares chocolate on graham cracker. Toast marshmallow on skewer—try not to flame it. Put on top of chocolate and cover with other graham cracker square.

Magic Lemon Pudding

4 servings

1 can sweetened condensed milk

2 tablespoons lemon juice

Crushed graham crackers, chocolate wafers, vanilla wafers, etc.

Mix condensed milk and lemon juice. Mix in a few handfuls of the crushed cookies. Don't cook, it's not necessary.

Coffee Cake Ala Orange

4 servings

2 large navel oranges

7-oz. package muffin mix

1 egg

⅓ cup light brown sugar

½ teaspoon cinnamon

1 tablespoon melted butter or margarine

4 12-inch squares heavy-duty aluminum foil

Cut orange in half horizontally. Remove fruit from peels, keeping peels intact.

Stir together muffin mix, egg, and ⅓ cup water until just blended.

Fill orange-peel "cups" ⅔ full with muffin batter. Combine cinnamon, brown sugar, and butter or margarine and sprinkle on muffin batter in each orange.

Put each "cup" in center of a piece of foil. Seal with Bundle wrap, leaving room for muffins to rise. Cook on hot coals 10 to 15 minutes.

Serve orange slices with the hot muffins.

Chocolate Dumplings

6 to 8 servings

1 cup packed brown sugar

2⅓ cups biscuit mix

6-oz. package semisweet chocolate pieces

2 tablespoons dry milk

¼ cup granulated sugar

½ teaspoon cinnamon

Stir together brown sugar and ⅓ cup biscuit mix in large skillet. Gradually stir in 3 cups water. Add chocolate pieces and cook over low heat, stirring constantly until chocolate melts and the mixture thickens slightly.

Mix remaining 2 cups biscuit mix, dry milk, granulated sugar, cinnamon, and ½ cup water into a stiff batter.

Drop batter by tablespoonfuls into simmering chocolate mixture. Cook 10 minutes uncovered. Cover and cook 10 minutes more.

To serve, spoon chocolate mixture over dumplings.

Cakes

Cakes can be baked in a Dutch oven, Bendonn oven, or a conventional oven, using prepared cake mixes. Frost with prepared frosting mixes.

Nosebags

Know what a nosebag is? When horses used to be worked all day they needed food during that time. A nosebag was simply a bag of oats or other grain, hung over the nose and mouth of the horse and secured by a loop or strap over the horse's neck. The horse could then eat while in harness.

Campers picked up this term, and applied it to quick snacks that can be carried on the trail to give quick energy when needed.

For best results, nosebags snacks are eaten slowly over a period of time.

Honey Bars

4 servings, more or less

Make at home and store for later use.

¼ pound seedless raisins

¼ pound dry figs

¼ pound dry apricots

¼ pound roasted and chopped peanuts or almonds

1 teaspoon lemon juice

Honey to give proper consistency

Put fruit through grinder or food processor. Mix in chopped nuts and lemon juice. Add honey to make a stiff dough, well mixed. Form into candy bar-size chunks, Wrap in aluminum foil. No ingredients need refrigeration, so bars can be stored for future use.

Hiker's Mix

Per person

¼ pound seedless raisins

¼ pound favorite cheese

¼ pound sweet or semisweet chocolate

1 apple

Put in plastic bag and eat when needed.

Walking Salad

Per person

1 large apple

Chunky peanut butter

Seedless raisins

Cut off top of apple. Core out center almost to bottom. Fill the hole with mixture of peanut butter and raisins. Replace top of apple. Put in self-sealing plastic bag

Birdseed

Make as much as you want

1 part sugar-coated cereal

1 part candy-coated chocolate

1 part roasted peanuts

Put in self-sealing plastic bag. Mix and munch when needed.

Death Valley Special

Makes a lot. Store extra. Use on next trip.

6 cups rolled oats

2 cups chopped walnuts

2 cups seedless raisins

½ cup chopped pitted dates

Package candy-coated chocolates

Toast rolled oats in oven preheated to 250 degrees. Spread out oats and walnuts in a roasting pan. Bake 1 hour, mixing from time to time. Cool, and mix with raisins, chopped dates, and chocolates. Spoon quantity needed in self-sealing plastic bags and store remainder in covered containers for future use.

Nuts and Bolts

Number served depends on appetite

¼ pound raisins

¼ pound peanuts

¼ pound chocolate bits

Broken up graham crakers

Mix and put in self-sealing plastic bags to carry.

PLANNING THE TRIP CHAPTER V

"It isn't the fellow who's catching lots of fish and shooting plenty of game that's having a good time; it's the chap who's getting ready to do it."

Camping and Woodcraft, Kephart, 1916

A wise camper once suggested you should start planning the next trip before you get back from the one you're on. Ridiculous if you only make a trip or two a year? Not when you consider Kephart's quotation. Why waste all the fun of anticipation?

Many aspects of planning required for the first few trips become routine with experience. Selection of your camping gear, for example, takes a lot of planning, but once you have it your only consideration will be for minor additions and making sure it's in good condition, and packed to go.

There's a logical sequence to planning. You can't set a budget until you know where you're going and how long you'll be away. And, it's no use planning a cross-country trip for a one-week vacation.

Planning related to things like camping gear, safety, first aid, activities, menus, and food buying are covered in detail in other chapters of this book.

Where? How Long?

The average working man or woman can count on regular two-day weekends off, up to a half-dozen long weekends, and an annual vacation of one to four weeks depending on tenure with the same company.

Driving Time

Experienced safety people recommend that driving be limited to 300 or 350 miles a day, depending on road conditions. You can safely use the 350-mile limit if you're freeway driving, which avoids lots of stop-and-go. For most other driving, use the 300-mile maximum.

Plan to leave your campsite before 8 in the morning if driving the daily maximum. This allows time for rest and lunch stops, and will get you into your next campsite well before dark.

Plan for longer driving time on peak travel days, too. Long weekends with holidays cram the highways with the most cars. Your miles per hour will be less than middle of the week, non-holiday driving.

Destinations

To have any time at your camping destination, a one-week vacation trip should probably not be taken to a site more than 600 or 700 miles from home. Two days to get there and two days back leave only three days at your campsite.

You could use the same seven days in another way and you'll drive about the same distance, but camp in a variety of sites. Plan a circular route of about 1200 miles. The first day, drive 300 to 350 miles, set up camp, and spend the next day. On the third day drive again, and camp for another day. You've now used up four days. Drive the fifth day in a direction toward home, camp on the sixth day, and then drive on home on the seventh.

Another plan might be at a site within 300 miles of home. You'd have five days at a campsite and only two on the road.

Vacations lasting two or more weeks don't pose the same time problem, but careful planning is still called for.

Long 3-day and regular 2-day weekends are probably best planned with a short drive to a campsite near home, allowing time to enjoy the camping without spending a lot of time on the road.

Whole Family Involvement

The time frame depends on when the working members of your family can arrange vacations, and when school will be out for the kids. There's not much anyone can do about these factors. But, the next step is deciding where to go, and everyone can share in this planning.

Maps

You'll want a road atlas with a map of the nation plus detailed maps of each state. It will also be helpful if the atlas has maps showing mileage and estimated driving time between major centers.

Campground Guides

A few of the better known commercial campground books are Woodall's Campground Directory (national, western and eastern editions); Mobil Travel Guide (sectional); and Rand McNally's National Campground and Trailer Park Guide (national and western), National Park Guide, and National Forest Guide. The American Automobile Association also has a campground guide available for members.

Some of these guides show campground rates for the previous season, and so can help in comparing one against

Many gasoline companies have travel clubs you can join for a small fee. These clubs provide small campground guides. When so requested, they will recommend a route to your destination and mark it on a map. All you have to do is tell the travel club where you want to go, and any in-between stops you want to make.

Boy Scout camps are another source of sites. Their use is restricted to people who are registered members of the Boy Scouts of America. These camps aren't listed in the campground guides, but the BSA produces a Scouting Family Camping Directory, BSA No. 3680, that lists the Scout camps across America offering facilities for family camping. This directory is available through your local Scout council service center.

Not all Scout camps are open to family camping, but more and more are added each year. Remember, the main purpose of a Scout camp is to provide camping facilities for Scout troops of the council. Family use is incidental to this prime purpose. This means that many Scout camps only open their facilities to families during the "off-season."

HINT *If you are in an active Scouting position in your council, district, or unit, don't overlook the great family camping offered at Philmont Scout Ranch near Cimarron, New Mexico. You can combine a Scout training conference with a week's vacation for your family. Your council has details.*

If there's no listing for your council, give the office a call. Your camp may have been added since the directory was printed.

The directory carries information on eligibility for use, how to make reservations by phone or mail, and BSA camp rules. These camps are open to all registered members even though their registration may not be in the council running the camp in which they are interested.

To give you an idea of what is offered in the directory, one page is reproduced on the next page.

another. For accurate budget planning, however, ask for the campsite fee when making reservations.

A few guidebooks rate campgrounds on the quality of facilities and recreation available. These ratings are based on both personal inspection and reports from campers. These are helpful when making a choice from the campgrounds in an area.

Campground Classifications

Public campgrounds are those owned and operated by city, county, state, and federal governments. Most national campgrounds are listed in the campground guides. Many state and some county and city campgrounds also are listed, but not all. Write directly to city, county, or state

Western Region MAP NUMBER & CAMP NAME	NUMBER OF FAMILY SITES	TENT SITES	CABINS	TABLES	FIREPLACES	FLUSH TOILETS	HOT SHOWERS	ELECTRICITY	WATER (TRAILER HOOK UP)	TENTS	COTS	BOATS	CANOES	CANOE TRAILER	SWIM	HIKE	BOAT	FISH	OTHER	SIGHT-SEEING NEARBY	CAMP STORE NEARBY	CAMP OPEN S-SUMMER F-FALL W-WINTER SP-SPRING	COUNCIL ADDRESS & PHONE (CAMP ADDRESS & PHONE)
CALIFORNIA																							
4 Wolverton	6			X			X									X				X	X	6/30 to Labor Day	Great Western BSA, Box 3198, Van Nuys, CA 91407 213-786-9500 (PO Box B, Sequoia National Park, CA 93262)
5 Chawanakee	20	11		X		X	X	X	4	X	X				X	X		X				June to Oct.	Sequoia BSA, 1095 N. Van Ness, Fresno, CA 93728 209-268-4781 (Shaver Lake, CA 93664 209-841-2117)
6 Wente Scout Ranch	13			X		X	X	X	X	X	X	X			X	X	X	X	Sailing Horseback	X	X	Apr to Nov.	San Francisco Bay Area BSA, 8480 Enterprise Way, Oakland, CA 94621 415-638-3600 (PO Box 453, Willits, CA 95490)
7 Oljato	10	X		X	X	X	X	X		Fall use	Fall use	Fall use			X	X	X	X		X	X	S 8 week	Stanford Area BSA, 1305 Middlefield Rd., Palo Alto, CA 94301 415-327-5900 (Box 217, Lakeshore, CA 93634)
8 Lake Arrowhead	14	4	10	X		X	X	X	X		X				X	X				X	X	S	Los Angeles Area BSA, 2333 Scout Way, Los Angeles, CA 90026 213-413-4400 (Cedar Glen, CA 92321 213-413-4400)
9 Silverado	5	X				X		X							X	X	X	X		X	X	Contact Council	Silverado Area BSA, Box 392, Vallejo, CA 94590 707-644-0427 (Kit Carson, CA 95644)
10 Lost Valley Scout Ranch	24	X		X	X	X	X	X	10	Fall use	Fall use	Fall use			X	X	X	X	Horseback Riding	X	X	Mar. to Nov.	Orange County BSA, PO Box 5515, Santa Ana, CA 92704 714-546-4990 (Box 336, Star Rt.2, Aguanga, CA 92302)
11 Ahwahnee				X		X	X	X	X						X	X				X	X	July 9 to Aug.	Same as 10 (Green Valley Lake, CA 92391)
12 Rancho Las Flores				X		X														X		Labor Day to Memorial Day	Same as 10
13 Trask Scout Ranch				X	X					X	X					X				X	X	Year Round	San Gabriel Valley BSA, 540 Rosemead Blvd, Pasadena, CA 91107 213-351-8815 (1100 N. Canyon Dr, Monrovia, CA 91016 213-351-8815)
14 Masonite–Navarro	12	X	Tent			X		X							X	X	X	X		X		S	Sonoma-Mendocino Area BSA, 840 Western Ave., Petaluma, CA 94952 707-762-2405 (Navarro, CA 95463 707-895-3181)
15 Emerson	5		5	X		X	X	X				X			X	X	X				X	Year Round	California Inland Empire BSA, 470 E. Highland, Redlands, CA 92373 714-793-2463 (PO Box 639, Idyllwild, CA 92349 714-659-2690)
16 Helendale			5	X		X	X	X				X			X	X	X				X	Year Round	Same as 15 (PO Box 236, Running Springs, CA 92382 714-867-2480)
17 Whitsett				X								X	X		X	X	X	X			X	7/1 to Labor Day	Great Western BSA, PO Box 3198, Van Nuys, CA 91407 213-786-9500 (PO Box 35, Johnsdale, CA 93236 714-376-6469)
18 Jubilee Scout Ranch	8			X	X		X								X	X				X	X	Year Round	Same as 17 (PO Box 69, Pinon Hills, CA 92372 714-249-3877)
19 Forty-Niner		X		X	X	X	X	X				X	X		X	X	X	X		X	X	Year Round	Forty-Niner BSA, Box 1017, Stockton, CA 95201 209-465-0261 (PO Box 206, Avery, CA 95224)
20 Mirimichi	17	X	8	X		X	X	X				X		X	X	X	X	X		X	X	6/1-7/10 8/20-Labor Day	Mount Whitney BSA, 221 N. Encina, Visalia, CA 93277 209-732-3424
21 Stuart				X	X										X	X				X	X	Year Round	Santa Clara County BSA, Box 28547, San Jose, CA 95159 408-249-6060 (16191 Bohlman Rd., Saratoga, CA 95070 408-867-3629)
IDAHO																							
22 Bradley	12	X	6	X	X	X	X		X	X		X			X	X	X	X	Rifle Snowmobiling	X		Year Round	Snake River Area BSA, 3118 Falls Ave., East, Rt.3, Twin Falls, ID 83301 208-733-2067 (Stanley, ID 83278)
NEVADA																							
23 Fleischmann	4		X			X		X							X	X	X	X		X		Contact Council	Nevada Area BSA, PO Box 2310, Reno, NV 89505 702-329-2508

that many campgrounds don't allow pets. The National Park Service has banned pets from its campgrounds. Some campgrounds have special sites where you must camp if you have a pet.

A barking dog is a real headache in a campground. Even a little noise after hours is too much. Sites are close together, and many campers need to get up early for one reason or another, and so object to anything that keeps them awake after normal hours. If you've had any complaints about your dog at home, you'll get many more in camp.

Cats are poor travelers. They are notorious for getting lost in camp situations.

It is possible to get a poison plant skin rash from your pet. If it goes through a patch of poison ivy the oil may get on its coat, and contact with that oil by you or your children can bring on a painful rash.

On the other hand, a pet can be a great companion if it is well behaved, and trained. Children should be ready to share in its care by walking it on a leash regularly. If you decide to bring a pet, it shouldn't be allowed to roam loose, but should be on a leash the whole time—no exceptions. You should have a pooper scoop so that excrement from your dog can be picked up immediately and disposed of in your garbage can. It's not a pleasant thought, but you wouldn't want your children playing in an area where they might get into droppings.

If you do decide to take your dog or cat, bring along its shot records. You might need to show them if the pet bites someone.

tourist offices for information on those not listed.

Private campgrounds include farmers' fields and woodlots, independent campgrounds with facilities, franchise campgrounds representing a chain, and Scout camps. Most independents and franchise facilities are listed in the campground guides, but Scout camps and, of course, farmers' properties are not. Word of mouth or knowledge of the country is probably the only way to learn of the latter.

There may be restrictions at all of these pertaining to such things as vehicle length, tent camping, vehicle use, adults only, no pets, or members only. There may also be seasonal limitations. Many campgrounds in the colder climes don't operate in the winter months.

State Travel Brochures

Supplement whatever campground guide you choose with information available from state travel bureaus in those states you might visit. Write early for this material so you'll have it when your family gets down to the nitty-gritty of planning.

Family members could be given areas to research in your public library, things like National parks and monuments; scenic spots; special events like fairs, festivals, sporting events, etc.

Pets

A family decision may have to be made on whether to take a dog, cat, or other pet on the trip. Keep in mind

Campsite Courtesy

Your planning will give you a good chance to discuss this important subject with your children. You might talk about the Golden Rule and how it applies to campsite behavior.

Most campgrounds give you a set of rules when you check in. These usually set times when electronic sound devices must be shut off. Even when it's OK to have your radio, tape deck, or phonograph playing, be considerate, and keep the volume down. If your children must have full volume to appreciate their music, better get earphones to confine the noise to those who want to hear it.

If you have a separate generator in your RV to run 110-volt appliances, the rules will probably ask you to turn it off when it gets dark. This doesn't apply to the electrical generator that charges your battery off the campground's 110-volt supply. These generators aren't run by gasoline motors. Their hum is hardly noticeable.

Other noisemakers—chain-saws, motor cycles, and scooters—may not be used at all, even during the day, in some campgrounds.

Mention has been made of the early risers. There will also be late risers in camp. They like to sleep in the morning, so think of them, too, especially when you get up for that early morning bird hike, or to get an early start for your next campground.

Your children should be told that a person's tent or RV should be as private as his home. When they visit other people's homes, they don't go in unless invited. This is as true in camp as in town.

Bright, hissing gas lanterns can be objectionable when used out of doors after hours. They ruin one's night vision, and the sound of them running carries in the still night air. If you must use them late, keep them indoors.

Log Books

Just as advance planning is part of the fun of a camping trip, so, too, are the memories that you have when it's over. Your children might like to be responsible for keeping a log of the trip. Daily entries should be made, telling about major things that happened, the weather, food likes and dislikes for the day, etc. One person could be responsible, or a different one each day, or even all the kids could share in writing up the log.

The logbook probably will be a collection of items that can be put together after you get home. This will allow pictures taken on the trip to become part of the log, along with the daily report, campsite receipts, amusement ticket stubs, park entry receipts, and the like.

Such a logbook will bring back precious memories as the years go by and the children grow up.

Here are a few things that could be part of your log book:

- **Maps with routes and stops marked**
- **Mileage and fuel consumption record**
- **A copy of the trip menu**
- **Section for photographs and picture postcards**
- **Souvenir sight-seeing folders**
- **Receipts, admission stubs, permits, and licenses**
- **Travel papers, insurance, etc.**
- **A daily diary**

Car Sickness

You may already know whether any of your children become carsick on trips. Even if none has in the past, it will pay to be ready, especially if you'll be driving on crooked mountain roads. Here are a few suggestions to avoid or reduce the problem:

Eat lightly. If nothing else, it cuts the mess.

Don't permit reading or coloring, or anything else that keeps the eyes down.

If you're playing games, one like Distance Estimating as described in "Getting There" (Chap. 6) is better than the State License Plate game. It keeps eyes focused on the horizon instead of on speeding cars up close.

Even if it's cold, open the car windows and let lots of fresh air blow through at the first sign of nausea. Wearing jackets to keep warm is a lot better than nursing a carsick child.

Check with your doctor before leaving. Ask that motion sickness pills be personally prescribed for each member of the family. Dosages vary according to size of children and adults.

Budgets

Your children will have a better understanding of what it takes to travel if you let them share in the budget process. They'll know why you don't eat all your meals in restaurants. Major budget items include:

Vehicle expense based on total mileage (not just site to site mileage, but trips from the site as well), your vehicle's miles per gallon, and cost of gasoline or diesel. Remember, you will probably be buying fuel at highway off-ramp service stations where you'll pay from 10 to 40 cents a gallon more than if you take time to shop around. This is hard to do in unfamiliar territory, so prepare for the pain.

> **HINT** *You can avoid having to carry a lot of cash and the hassle of personal check-cashing by planning to use travelers' checks and personal credit cards for most large purchases.*

Figure the cost of an oil change and lube job prorated to mileage driven. Don't forget tire replacement. A 5,000-mile trip will use a fixed percentage of your total tire life. You may not need new tires during or even shortly after the trip, but sometime those 5,000 miles have to be accounted for. Theoretically, you should charge off depreciation on the old buggy, too, but that's carrying the commercial side of a vacation trip a bit far. You aren't calculating these expenses for the IRS.

Allow a contingency item in your budget to cover possible car repairs enroute. To be safe with your budget planning, use campground fees as quoted to you by phone or mail at the time of making reservations.

Food costs can be based on your home food budget plus a little extra for camp store buying instead of your local supermarket. Also allow for a few meals out from

Budget Planning Sheet

Estimated total miles _____

Estimated miles per gallon of fuel _____

Total miles divided by miles
  per gallon = total fuel _____

Estimated average price of fuel per gallon _____

Total fuel x price
  per gallon = budgeted fuel amount _____

Oil, oil change and lube, proportionate cost _____

Repair contingency _____

Food (to be prepared in camp) _____

Meals eaten out _____

Campground fees _____

Highway, bridge, and ferry tolls _____

Recreation _____

   Equipment rentals _____

   Entrance fees _____

   Souvenirs, postcards, film, etc. _____

Propane, ice, misc. _____

Subtotal _____

5% of subtotal for contingencies _____

TOTAL BUDGET _____

time to time and for those expensive candy bars and sodas at rest stops.

There will be costs for film, equipment rental, and admissions to parks and attractions.

Golden Eagle Passport

If you will be visiting any federal outdoor recreation area that charges an entrance fee, you can save money by buying a Golden Eagle Passport for $10. This permits entry without additional charge to national parks, monuments, historic and memorial parks, and seashores.

It does not cover "use fees" such as campsite rental or boat launching equipment.

You can get your passport from the National Park Service at its Washington, D.C. headquarters or any of 10 regional offices, but perhaps the easiest way is to get one at the first National Park you enter.

The passport is good for the current calendar year, isn't transferable, and the fee isn't refundable if you don't use it.

Golden Age Passport

If any member of your family is 62 or older, the Golden Age Passport can be obtained at any National recreational area that charges a fee. It gives free lifetime admission to that area and any others. The fee exemption extends to the permit-holder in a private vehicle and all accompanying him. To get this passport, proof of age

HINT *To operate on an economy budget, take advantage of attractions like National parks and monuments that can be entered without charge using your Golden entry card.*

must be provided. A driver's license, birth certificate, or signed affidavit attesting to one's age is considered to be proof.

Golden Access Card

This card is issued without charge to handicapped persons and carries the same entry privileges to National facilities as the Golden Eagle and Golden Age passports.

Travel in Other Countries

Canada

U.S. citizens don't need passports to enter Canada. Vehicle registration certificates must be carried. This

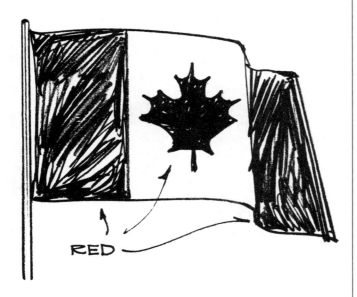

RED

When returning to the United States, you must prove your right to enter the country if asked to by customs' officials. Proof could be a birth, baptismal, or voter certificate. Naturalized citizens will need their naturalization certificates. Aliens living in the U.S. need their Alien Registration Receipt card.

Each person in your party may bring back up to $300 worth of articles after a 48-hour stay or longer, provided you haven't used the exemption within the last 30 days.

To be sure of customs regulations for entry into Canada and return to the U.S., write to Bureau of Customs, Department of the Treasury, P.O. Box 7118, Washington, D.C. 20044 for the booklet, "Know Before You Go" (50 cents), and to Customs and Excise, Sussex Drive, Ottawa, Ontario, K1A OL5, Canada, for their customs regulations.

For many years liquid measure in Canada was based on the Imperial gallon, which is about 1/4th larger than a U.S. gallon. Canada has now gone on the metric system and liquid measure is now based on liters. You will pump gasoline by the liter, buy groceries by the kilogram, and follow road signs in kilometers.

Better check the currency exchange rate shortly before you leave. This can vary over a period of time. You'll do better if you exchange your money at the nearest bank or money exchange after you cross the border into Canada, and again in Canada before returning to the USA.

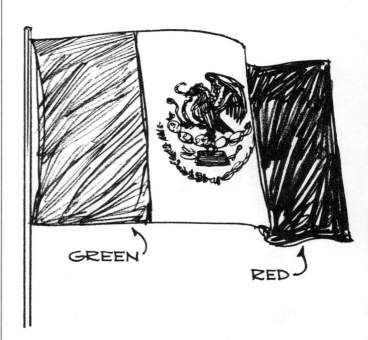

GREEN

RED

includes the certificate for your trailer, too. If your vehicle is a rental, or belongs to someone other than a family member, you should carry a letter of authorization from the registered owner.

Dogs can come with you if you have a certificate of rabies vaccination that's less than 12 months old. Your dog's description must appear on the certificate to assure customs' officers that the certificate is for the dog that's with you.

If you plan to fish in Canada, you'll need a non-resident fishing permit for the Province where you'll fish.

You should get a Canadian Non-Resident Interprovince Motor Vehicle Liability Insurance card from your insurance company before leaving on the trip. A photocopy of the section of your policy that states it is valid in Canada will suffice.

You can have a CB radio in your vehicle, but use is prohibited unless you have a U.S. license and a Canadian permit. You can get a permit by writing to Director of Operations, Department of Communications, Ottawa, Ontario, Canada K1A OC8. Send a photocopy of your U.S. license with your request. Allow 60 days for a reply.

HINT *You can get information on Canadian travel highlights by writing to the Canadian Government Offices of Tourism, 235 Queen Street, Ottawa, Ontario, Canada K1A OH6.*

Mexico

A passport or Tourist Card isn't needed to visit a narrow band of border towns fronting on the United States.

If you go deeper into Mexico, you'll need a Mexico Tourist Card. You can get one with considerable delay at the border when you cross, or by writing ahead for it to any Mexican Consulate or from the Mexican Tourist Council in Washington, D.C. These cards are dated for periods ranging from 30 to 180 days. Ask for a permit for the maximum time you plan to spend in Mexico. You must provide proof of U.S. citizenship with your request.

A Vehicle Permit is also required if you are traveling farther than the border area of Mexico. This is issued at the port of entry. Your Tourist Card, vehicle registration, title, and notarized authorization to use a vehicle belonging to someone else must be tendered to obtain the vehicle permit. A car and trailer are considered to be one vehicle, but a motor home towing a car is considered as two vehicles and must have papers and permits for both.

Be prepared to give a tip to the customs agent preparing your papers at the border. This is a way of life in these border stations. Don't fight it. It will just delay your entry into the country.

A word about the water. You've heard stories about diarrhea, dysentery, and other disease contracted by drinking impure water in Mexico. While most large hotels and restaurants advertise "safe" water, it's best to be sure. Bottled water is safe, if you are the person to open the bottle. Few campgrounds can guarantee a safe water supply, so plan to boil or sterilize your water as explained in "Health, Safety, and First Aid" (chap. 3). If you have a holding tank in your RV, fill it before leaving the United States and keep it filled with "safe" water when you can be sure. If you're not sure of the water, add a carefully measured ounce of liquid laundry bleach to each 20 gallons. You won't like the taste, but a faucet filter will remove most of it. And even without a filter, it's better than the misery of diarrhea.

Most highway signs are written in Spanish, so a little advance study will smooth your trip. Many highways use international pictographs, but there will be areas where knowledge of words commonly used on highway warning signs will avoid confusion.

Your return to the USA can be frustrating, depending on traffic volume and number of customs booths open to handle the load. The "Know Before You Go" pamphlet mentioned in the Canada Section will advise you on what you can bring back "duty free" to the U.S.

Your regular insurance policy won't cover you in Mexico, so stop at one of the many border companies with big "Mexican Insurance" signs to draw you in. They offer collision and liability coverage on a daily basis for the time you'll be in the country.

Europe

A camping trip overseas may sound like a dream, but don't automatically write it off. The major expense, of

course, will be the round-trip air fare, but once you're there camping can be cheaper than in this country, and surely cheaper than staying in hotels and eating meals in restaurants. Campgrounds are scattered throughout Europe. They commonly have only water and electricity hookups available for RV's, but most have adequate shower and toilet facilities, making up for the lack of sewer hookups.

Rental RV's (called caravans) and camping gear are available, so you don't have to haul a lot of gear with you on the plane.

Europe is so small compared with the U.S. that you can travel from one country to another as easily as you go from one state to another over here.

An Example of a Trip Plan

A trip from Oceanside, California, to Salt Lake City and return.

Objective—To visit Grand Canyon, Zion, and Bryce National Parks, Salt Lake City, and Las Vegas.

Departure July 1.

Day 1

Oceanside to Kingman, Arizona
350 miles, 7½ hours

Campground—Kingman KOA, page 17

Features—Cooler climate than any available earlier stops

Day 2

Kingman to Grand Canyon National Park, Arizona
169 miles, 4 hours

Campground—Grand Canyon Village Campground, page 16

Features—Grand Canyon National Park

Day 3

Full day at Grand Canyon

Day 4

Grand Canyon to Springdale, Utah
275 miles, 7 hours

Campground, Zion Canyon Campground, page 438

Features—Glen Canyon Dam enroute, Zion Canyon National Park

Day 5

Full day at Zion

Day 6

Springdale to Salt Lake City, Utah
320 miles, 7½ hours

Campground—Salt Lake City KOA, page 436

Features—Mormon Temple, Tabernacle, swimming in Great Salt Lake

Day 7

Full day in Salt Lake City

Day 8

Salt Lake City to Panguitch, Utah
320 miles, 7½ hours

Campground—Panguitch KOA, page 434

Features—Bryce Canyon National Park

Day 9

Full day at Bryce Canyon

Day 10

Panguitch to Las Vegas, Nevada
220 miles, 5 hours

Campground—Circusland, page 258

Features—Campground located in heart of Las Vegas strip

Day 11

Full day in Las Vegas

Day 12

Full day in Las Vegas

Day 13

Las Vegas to Oceanside, California
339 miles, 8 hours

Campground—Home

Features—Home

Planning Analysis

All routes were marked on a detailed map with a highlighter pen, making it easy to follow the route. Campsite selections were made from a current western edition of a campground directory. The page references for the campgrounds relate to the page in the directory containing the listing. This will make it easy to find the campground when approaching the town in which it is located.

Reservations were made for those campsites where use fell on a weekend or a holiday, and for popular locations such as the National Parks.

Most campgrounds will hold reservations without a deposit up to 6 p.m. If arriving after that time, paid reservations are advised.

Many travel planners suggest having alternate stops for each night out. This is probably a good idea, but if you carry a campground directory with you it's easy to pick alternate sites while driving, and you can phone ahead for a reservation while gassing up on the road. The alternate sites come into play when you have trouble on the road, or stay longer than planned for sightseeing.

"You ought to have some time to sit and dream. A campsite with a view of a beautiful lake, mountain, waterfall, or forest helps a camper to appreciate the wonders of God's great plan. Sit with your back against a stump and look across the land. Watch cloud shadows playing tag as they race across hills and valleys. You'll see things and think thoughts you didn't have time for before."

Fieldbook, BSA

When you have finished planning, that's it. You and your family are almost ready to go. You have the food, equipment, and a vehicle to take you there.

Now it's up to you and your crew to put it all together. You'll pack, travel—enjoyably because getting there is part of the fun of camping—and set up your home away from home for the next few days or weeks.

Preparing To Leave

There are several things to do before leaving on a camping trip—lots if you'll be gone for a week, but still some important things even for a weekend.

Your car, pickup, or motor home needs to be in perfect shape. Your car probably will be doing heavier work than usual. There'll be more weight to carry, and longer distances to cover. If it needs a tuneup, get it done before the trip. If it needs an oil change and lube, get it done before the trip. Check all motor belts and hoses. Replace any that are suspect, before the trip. Check your battery water level, and, if necessary, add distilled water before the trip. If you're going where the temperature will be below freezing, make sure your antifreeze is strong enough to protect your radiator and engine before the trip. If traction conditions might be bad anyplace enroute or in camp, check your chains before the trip. Check your tire pressure. Bring it to that recommended by the tire manufacturer, before the trip. Too much "before the trip"? Much better before than during or after the trip.

> **HINT** *Make sure your car insurance is up to date before leaving home. Pay premiums ahead if any will fall due while you're away.*

If you'll be gone for more than a weekend, here are a few things to take care of:

1. Notify the post office to hold your mail.

2. Have your paper carrier stop delivery.

3. Leave a key to the house with friendly neighbors, and ask that they pick up junk deliveries that might tell a potential thief that you're gone.

4. Notify the police that you'll be away, and give them the name, address, and phone number of the neighbor who has your key.

5. Advise the neighbor with your key, and if possible relatives, where you can be reached in an emergency—name of campground for each night and phone number if it has one. If it doesn't have a phone, give name of nearest town where police could be contacted to reach you.

6. Arrange for someone to water and mow your lawn, and care for shrubs and other plantings so things don't die, or get so bedraggled that it will advertise your absence.

7. If you have indoor plants that will need watering while you're away, see whether your neighbor with the key might be willing to come in and water them. If not, you might set them out in the shade, possibly on the north side of the house, and have the person who is to care for

your lawn and outside plants, water them. The third alternative is to put about 2 inches of water in bathtubs and sinks. Set your plants in this water. It will hold them for a week or so without further attention.

8. Get rid of perishables that will spoil while you're away. This includes perishables in your refrigerator.

9. Put a couple of house lights on timers, one in the living room to come on at dusk and go off at the same time a second light goes on in the bedroom. That light can go off about 15 minutes later. It's also smart to put a radio on a timer so it goes on during the day, and off at about the same time the bedroom light goes off. Burglars are very leery of homes that have both lights and sound.

10. Before leaving, take an inspection trip around your home to make sure all appliances are off. It might be wise to unplug those that can be disconnected. Then you won't start worrying, "Did we shut off the coffee pot, or the burner on the stove?" when you're 40 miles down the road.

11. Make sure you have all drivers' licenses, vehicle registrations, spare keys, credit cards, travelers' checks, and an extra pair of eyeglasses.

12. Arrange to board your pet, or take its vaccination records if it will accompany you.

13. Lock all doors (including the garage) and windows.

For a weekend trip, steps 1-8 can be skipped, but 9 through 13 should be done.

Packing

Tent Campers

The weight and bulk of your equipment can so overload and fill your car that it's down on the axle and has no comfortable room for passengers. If bulk and not weight is your problem, it can be overcome with a cartop carrier

> **HINT** *Use every bit of space when packing. An empty bucket or camp stove is wasted space that should be used.*

to make room for everyone. There are two main types of carriers.

The cheapest is a portable rack that fastens securely to the rain gutters on your car. This rack has a strong frame with a grid of supports to hold your gear off the roof of the car. With this carrier, you'll need a tarp and rope or shock cord to tie over and under things in case of wet weather. A tarp with grommets to tie to will help you keep those annoying ends from flapping in the breeze.

The second kind is a little more expensive, but worth

every penny if you'll be doing much camping with a carrier. It's a closed carrier that looks like a big stream-lined box or pod on top of the car. The storage pod fastens to the car's rain gutter like the frame carrier. Usually made of plastic, it has a lid hinged at both sides. The hinge pins can be pulled on either side, making it possible to open the side most convenient for loading and unloading. It has hasps so padlocks can be attached to

protect your gear when you leave the car in town or camp. These storage pod carriers are light and totally waterproof.

If weight is your problem, the answer probably is a small cargo trailer. There are single- and two-wheel jobs depending on the weight and bulk you want to get out of the car. You might consider renting a trailer, at least for

a few times until you learn what you need. Rental is easier than ownership—just reserve your trailer, drive over, and pick it up. The rental people will provide you with all connections between trailer and car. The trailer will already be licensed.

If you'll use either a carrier or a trailer, you'll want to decide which items should be readily available in your car, and which might go in the supplemental space. Raingear, fun boxes for the kids, and lunches should be kept where you can get them easily. Other things could be stowed in the car, but not unless they'll be needed enroute or there's no room in the carrier.

Packing procedure is important if you're going to pack everything in your car. Put things you know you won't need enroute in the hardest-to-reach part of the car. Leave things you'll need enroute either on the floor in the back seat, or on top of the other things in your trunk.

You probably can't keep your spare tire and tools totally free, but it's a good idea to have a few easily removable things in front of them. Then you only have to move those things if you have a flat tire. Don't be one of those cars up on a jack along the highway with one wheel in the air, and piles of gear on the ground around.

RV's

The secret to packing an RV is to put everything in its place and secure it there, either with foam rubber padding or shock cord. Anything loose will jiggle around enroute. If it isn't damaged, it will damage something else as it vibrates, falls, or bounces around.

It is recommended that heavy items be put on lower shelves to keep the center of gravity low, but unless there is a great difference in weight, it isn't important enough to move things out of their accustomed places.

Balance fore and aft is important in loading a trailer.

You can overload the tongue, or have trailer tilt that puts lift on the rear wheels of your car. Both conditions are bad.

Be sure you don't overload your rig. You'll usually find a plate on the side of the unit giving its unloaded weight, and maximum allowable weight with cargo aboard. If you exceed this maximum you'll be living dangerously.

One way to be sure is to weigh each item before putting it aboard. Then add up to get total weight. An easier way is to load normally, drive to a trucking company, and have the whole thing weighed at once. You should only have to do that once, because from then on you'll have an idea of how much more can be added, or how much needs to be removed.

With a vehicle in which passengers can legally ride, don't forget to add their weight if they weren't in it when you weighed it.

Enroute

You gassed up the night before, you've packed all the gear, and you've made your inspection rounds of the house. Everyone piles in the vehicle and you're off on the great adventure.

Things are great for the first half hour. If there are new things to see, and great scenery, fine, but pretty soon you'll get the familiar question, "How much longer

until we get there?" Then, "I have to go to the bathroom." Riding for long periods with nothing to do and no new things to see can be boring for active children—it's even boring for adult passengers. So, in-car activities are important to keep children occupied with things to do instead of fighting.

GETTING THERE AND MAKING CAMP

Things To Do Enroute

It's easier to travel with children in a motor home, van, or camper than in a car or car with trailer. In larger vehicles, children have room to move around and can sit at a table to do their coloring books and play board games or cards. It is legal in all states to carry people in the living section of motor homes and vans, but illegal in a trailer or 5th wheeler in all but one state.

No matter how you travel, it's smart to have planned activities to keep the kids busy. It'll be fun for them and cut down on that "How much longer?" question.

Here are some ideas:

- Assemble a traveling fun box (cardboard will do). Contents:

  Paper, coloring books, and crayons or felt marking pens

  Magic Slate

  Board games — checkers, chess, backgammon, Chinese checkers.

  Card games — Uno, Old Maid, Rook, Pit, bridge cards

  Cribbage board and cards

  Puzzles — wooden block, wire, Mastermind (jigsaw, if there's a table)

  Dice games — Kismet, Yahtzee

  Word games — Scrabble, Speak and Spell, Mind Boggle

  Hand computer games — baseball, football, soccer, basketball

- Play Tic-Tac-Toe, Bingo, State License Plate Identification, Sink the Ship, and Can You Follow Directions?

(These games are described on the following pages.)

There are times when adults should take part in these car games, and times when they should stay out. When children are engrossed in their own activities, it's a good idea for parents to leave them alone.

There are things for the single child to do alone, but whenever it takes two to play, the non-driving parent should join in.

Other occasions for parent participation are when a referee, judge, or scorekeeper is needed, and in full involvement games like 20 Questions or Distance Guessing.

Here are a few good car games:

20 Questions

This is a game for two or more. Someone starts by thinking of something he or she sees in the car or along the road. The others take turns asking questions which can be answered "yes" or "no". This is called 20 Questions because in the original game questions were counted, and if no one guessed at the end of 20 the answerer was considered a winner, and someone else picked a thing for the next game. It seems to be more fun for children to forget about counting questions and keep going until the object is identified. The person who identifies the object wins, and can pick the next thing.

A variation that will make the game more difficult after players become good is to not restrict items to things seen in the car or along the road. Items could be people as well as things.

Name Making

When you go through a town, or on the highway see an exit with a town named, write down the name of the town. See how many words each person can form from the letter in the town name before coming to the next town or exit with a town name.

Distance Estimating (best suited to wide-open spaces)

The driver picks a prominent object in the distance ahead (water tower, butte, grain elevator, town, pass between hills, windmill, or lights at night, for example). Each person guesses the mileage to the object named by writing it down. When all have written their guesses, they tell what they were. Writing down the number keep them from guessing a little above or below someone else.

The reading on the car's odometer should be noted as soon as the object is picked. When the car is finally parallel to the object, the new reading is checked. The first reading subtracted from the second gives the correct distance. Closest guesser wins.

Right Side, Left Side

This is a game for two individuals or two teams. One is designated right side, and the other left side. A point system is set up. In a typical game you might pick animals. One point would be given for each animal seen on that team's side of the road. Fun can be added by putting five bonus points on something rare, like a white horse, or a flying duck, or what have you. Set a mileage limit to end the game—10 miles or any you choose. When the set mileage is reached the team with the most points wins.

HINT *Car games shouldn't be used just to keep children quiet. Many stimulate powers of observation, and reasoning. The more the kids see, the more they'll enjoy the trip.*

Other objects could be picked for other games—silos, barns, weather vanes, mail boxes, tractors. Be sure to put a bonus on one of the items to add spice.

This game can be played on divided highways if the center divider doesn't block the left side view, or if oncoming traffic isn't too heavy.

I See

There are three variations of this game, all for two or more people. The first two variations use the first letter of things you see along the road to run through the alphabet; for example, A for automobile, B for bus, C for chimney, and so on through the alphabet.

Variation #1. The first player starts by looking for an object starting with A. The next then looks for B, and so on.

Variation #2. The first player to see an object with an A gets that object and starts looking for a B. The other players must keep looking for an A until they find it. Each player progresses through the alphabet at his own speed. Whoever sees a zebra or a zoo after running through all the rest of the letters will probably win, unless a competitor sees a zig-zag first.

Variation #3. Look for letters of the alphabet in signs along the road. Play according to rules of either #1 or #2.

State License Plate Identification

This is a game that can continue from departure to return. Make a photocopy of this list of states if you don't want to mark up the one in this book. Pick a scorekeeper who will be responsible for checking the state squares as each state is seen. This can happen on the highway, at rest stops, in campgrounds, and parking lots.

Tic-Tac-Toe

This is a game for two players. One uses the X symbol, the other the O. Players take turns marking their symbols in squares trying to get three in a row across, down, or diagonally. The first player to do this wins, and the other player gets to mark first for the next game.

License Plate Addition

Find double, triple, or more consecutive numbers in license plates. For example, 611 would score 11 points for the first person to spot it. 133378 would score 333 points. One person should be scorekeeper. Set a limit for each game such as 200 points, and then start over with a new scorekeeper.

It is suggested that only license plates on cars going in the same direction as you be used—cars you pass, or those that pass you. Cars coming toward you will pass too quickly to verify. You'll save a lot of arguments doing it this way.

Car Bingo

Each player needs a Bingo sheet. Since each sheet must be different, and only one is shown here for each game, make two photocopies of the original. Cut one copy into vertical strips. Discard the center strip, which we'll call number three.

To make different sheets for each player, tape cut column one over old column two, and cut column two over old column one. Photocopy and you have a new sheet. To make other different copies, switch columns one and four, and one and five. For more, change two and four or two and five. Another can be made by switching four and five. This gives seven different Bingo sheets counting the original. Even more variations can be made by cutting strips horizontally and exchanging.

Rules for the first three Bingo games described here are the same since all players have the same objects or symbols. Whenever an item in the game being played is spotted, all players mark the item on their sheets. First player to get five items in a column down, across, or diagonally, or gets four corners, wins.

The difference for Game 4 is the ease of making the sheets, and the need for a scorekeeper, preferable a non-playing adult.

State License Plate Identification

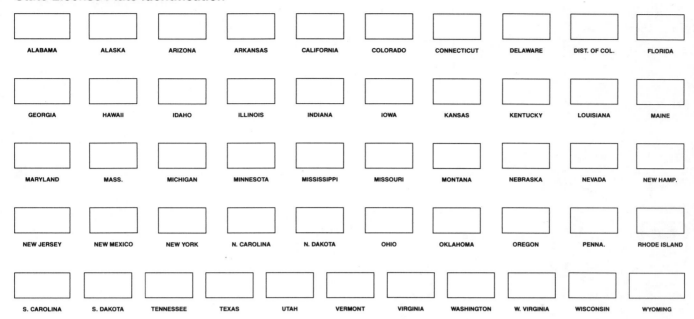

ALABAMA	ALASKA	ARIZONA	ARKANSAS	CALIFORNIA	COLORADO	CONNECTICUT	DELAWARE	DIST. OF COL.	FLORIDA
GEORGIA	HAWAII	IDAHO	ILLINOIS	INDIANA	IOWA	KANSAS	KENTUCKY	LOUISIANA	MAINE
MARYLAND	MASS.	MICHIGAN	MINNESOTA	MISSISSIPPI	MISSOURI	MONTANA	NEBRASKA	NEVADA	NEW HAMP.
NEW JERSEY	NEW MEXICO	NEW YORK	N. CAROLINA	N. DAKOTA	OHIO	OKLAHOMA	OREGON	PENNA.	RHODE ISLAND
S. CAROLINA	S. DAKOTA	TENNESSEE	TEXAS	UTAH	VERMONT	VIRGINIA	WASHINGTON	W. VIRGINIA	WISCONSIN	WYOMING

Car Bingo

Game 1. Play on undivided highways.

school	dog	open car	motel	horse
police car	bridge	curve sign	windmill	cow
boat	river	FREE	truck	stop sign
church	bicycle	trailer	barn	school bus
stop light	motor home	plane	cartop carrier	van

Game 2. Play on divided highways.

Game 3. Sign Signal Bingo

GETTING THERE AND MAKING CAMP

Game 4. License Number Bingo

Make this game by ruling paper into squares, five across and five down. Mark the center square FREE. Fill in the remaining squares with random numbers from 10 to 99 with no repeats. Make different sheets for different players by putting different numbers in the boxes.

The game is played by watching for the first two numbers of license plates on cars going in the same direction you are. When one is spotted that matches any number a player has, it is called out, and a score-keeper verifies and writes the two numbers used on a master sheet so when someone get Bingo, the numbers can be checked.

34	13	52	27	17
43	22	19	38	74
88	93	FREE	42	21
16	78	67	65	30
45	59	18	56	77

Cities and Towns

Any number can play. One player starts by naming any U.S. city. The next player names another city that begins with the last letter of the first city. The third player names a city beginning with the last letter of the second city, and so on.

For example, Boston could be answered with Nashville, and Nashville with Easton. If a player can't answer in turn, he or she is out of the game. The last player left wins.

Reading Aloud

This is an activity that has almost died out with the advent of television. Before reliance on the tube for entertainment, many parents read to their children. It's an especially good activity for younger children. They'll sit entranced while you read from Hans Christian Andersen, *Grimm's Fairy Tales,* or *Mother Goose.* Check with your library for books rated for the age level of your children, and take some with you on the trip.

Stories on Cassettes

If you don't want to read to the children, or if reading in a moving car makes you ill, you can buy pre-recorded cassettes to play on your car's or a portable cassette player. Check with stores selling pre-recorded tapes for titles and cost.

Storytelling

This is an activity you can do with a little practice. Don't try to make up you own stories, at least at first. Read adventure, mystery, or history stories in books or magazines. Then tell them in your own words.

To tell an interesting story, the places where the story happens should be as clear to you as your backyard. See in your mind every detail of each scene you'll tell about.

You need to know your characters. Get to know the people in your stories as well as you know your friends. Then you can describe them when you tell your story.

When you know your story, scenes, and people so well you can see them, just describe them. Be a reporter telling what you saw when covering a news story.

And, know what? Your kids will love it.

Funny Adjectives

Write a simple story telling of things that happen around home, but leave out all adjectives. Wherever a noun appears in the story, leave a blank space just ahead of it. For example, your story might start out like this: "One _____ morning when _____ Dad came into the _____ kitchen to eat his _____ breakfast..." and so on. Write the story at home before the trip, making sure you include names of children and their friends.

To introduce the game, ask passengers to think of adjectives. Give then a few suggestions such as dirty, sloppy, rotten, etc. After they have had time to think of a few, ask each person in turn to give an adjective. As they are given, write them in the blank spaces you have left in your story. Continue with passengers supplying adjectives until all blanks are filled. Then read the story.

Imagine the fun when the story you wrote turns out as this example might have: "One *dirty* morning when *smelly* Dad came into the *beautiful* kitchen to eat his *sloppy* breakfast..."

Can You Follow Directions?

Photocopy as many copies as there will be players. Don't let any player see a copy before the game starts.

Can You Follow Directions?

This is a time test—you have only 5 minutes.

1. Read everything carefully before doing anything.

2. Smile, then sit back comfortably for as long as you choose.

3. Circle the word "everything" in instruction No. 1.

4. Brush away an imaginary fly. Blink 12 times.

5. Sign your name after instruction No. 1.

6. Mentally subtract 19 from 26 and extend as many fingers as there are digits in the answer.

7. If 9 is divisible by 3, touch your head while you count silently to 11.

8. Draw a rectangle around the word "doing" in instruction 1.

9. Loudly call out your name when you get this far along.

10. On the reverse side of this paper add 8,950 and 9,805.

11. Put a circle around your answer for number 10.

12. If you think you have followed directions carefully to this point, call out loudly, "I HAVE."

13. Cross your left ankle over your right ankle. Then uncross your ankles and slap your right heel.

14. In your normal speaking voice, count from 10 to 1, backward.

15. Punch three holes in the top of this paper with your pencil.

16. If you are the first person to reach this point call out loudly: "I AM THE LEADER IN FOLLOWING DIRECTIONS."

17. Grasp your throat with both hands and open your mouth.

18. Underline all even numbers on the left side of this paper.

19. Say clearly: "I AM NEARLY FINISHED. I HAVE FOLLOWED DIRECTIONS."

20. Now that you have finished reading everything carefully, do only instructions 1 and 2.

Group Singing
Reprinted from the Boy Scout Songbook

She'll Be Comin' 'Round the Mountain

Novelty arrangement in italics

She'll be com-ing 'round the moun-tain when she comes —. She'll be

com-ing 'round the moun-tain when she comes —. She'll be com-ing 'round

the moun-tain, She'll be com-ing 'round the moun-tain, She'll be

com-ing round the moun-tain when she comes.

Sing each stanza and make appropriate gestures three times. Following the last singing of each stanza, repeat sounds and gestures of all preceding stanzas.

For example: At the end of the sixth stanza you say Scratch, scratch!; Yum, yum!; Hack, hack!; Hi, Babe!; Whoa, back!; Woo, hoo! and go through all the motions.

She'll be comin' 'round the mountain
When she comes, "Whoo, hoo!"
Pull down on imaginary whistle cord twice.

She'll be drivin' six white horses
When she comes, "Whoa, back!"
Pull back on reins.

This Land Is Your Land

Woody Guthrie   Gospel Tune

This land is your land,—this land is my land,—
From Cal-i-for-nia—to the New York Is-land,
From the red-wood for-est—to the Gulf Stream wa-ters,
This land was made for you and me.——

As I went walking that ribbon of highway
I saw above me that endless skyway,
I saw below me that golden valley,
This land was made for you and me.

I roamed and rambled, and I followed my footsteps,
To the sparkling sands of her diamond deserts,
All around me a voice was sounding,
This land was made for you and me.

When the sun came shining, than I was strolling,
And the wheat fields waving, and the dust clouds rolling,
A voice was chanting as the fog was lifting,
This land was made for you and me.

Shenandoah

Slowly   Traditional

Oh, Shen-an-doah,   I long to hear you. Way, hey, you roll-ing

river! Oh, Shen - an - doah, I long to hear you, Way,

hey, we're bound a-way 'Cross the wide Mis - sour - i.

Oh, Shenandoah, I love your daughter,
Way, hey, you rolling river!
Oh, Shenandoah, I love your daughter,
Way, hey, we're bound away 'cross the wide Missouri.

Oh, Shenandoah, I'm bound to leave you,
Way, hey, you rolling river!
Oh, Shenandoah, I'll not deceive you,
Way, hey, we're bound away 'cross the wide Missouri.

SINK THE SHIP

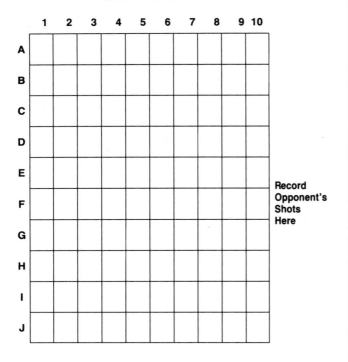

Record
Opponent's
Shots
Here

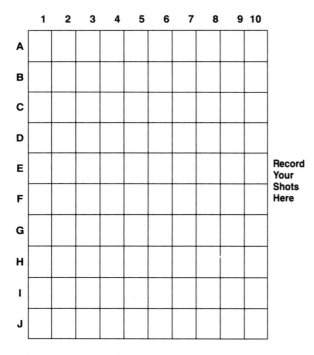

Record
Your
Shots
Here

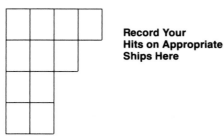

**Record Your
Hits on Appropriate
Ships Here**

Sink the Ship

This is a game for two. Prepare a sheet for each player. Rule, letter, and number as shown, or make photocopies. (You'll probably want to make many photocopies so the game can be played many times.)

Give each player one sheet. Have them sit so they can't see one another's paper. Each player marks the top diagram by outlining four squares in a line, which could be horizontal, vertical, or diagonal. The four squares represent a battleship. Each then marks three squares for a cruiser, and two sets of two squares each for destroyers.

The first player fires four shots by giving coordinates (B-6, D-5, F-1, and H-10, for example), pausing between each shot. The shooter records each shot on the bottom diagram, and the second player records the shots on the top diagram where his or her ships are located. After each round's shots are recorded, the player shot at must report the number of hits on type of ship, but not which shots scored. The second player then gets to shoot four shots. Players alternate shooting until a ship is sunk by hitting all outlined squares.

The loss of a ship reduces the holder of that sheet to three shots. A second ship sunk cuts the shots to two, etc. Continue until all of one player's ships are sunk.

Rest Stops

If you planned properly, you allowed time for rest stops. And not just when you need gas, or when someone needs to go to the bathroom.

Watch for rest stop signs along the highway. These areas usually have toilets, tables, and shade. There's room for the kids to let off some excess energy. A frisbie or ball and a couple of mitts would come in handy at these stops.

At gas stops you'll probably find refreshments for sale — soft drinks, candy bars, ice cream bars and cones, and similar food. Carry some premoistened towelettes with you for wiping sticky fingers and faces after eating.

Arrival

Try to arrive at your campground by mid-afternoon to allow time to set up, unpack, get firewood, and find your water source before dark. You'll also want to locate toilets, showers, the laundry, and the camp store while it's still daylight.

At most campgrounds, when you arrive you'll find an office near the entrance. You'll be asked to register, pay required fees, and be assigned to a campsite. You probably won't have any choice in the selection of your campsite unless it's in the off season. There may be exceptions for tent campers using facilities without site hookups such as water or electricity. The camp management may just say, "Follow this map to our tent camping area and pick an open site."

You'll probably be given a copy of the rules of the camp along with a map showing location of rest rooms and showers, laundry facilities, and garbage disposal sites. Careful reading of these rules and suggestions can save trouble later.

If you're not using a regular public or private campground, but are going to take your chances on finding a suitable camping area on some side road, then advice related to regular campgrounds won't apply. This kind of camping is becoming rare. Some suggestions for this kind of camping are given at the end of this chapter.

Setting Up

Your RV

Setting up is quite simple for RV campers. You back into your spot or pull into a drive-through site, disconnect the car from the trailer, if trailering, and hook up

to water, electricity, and sewer. You'll want to level your rig, a rather easy job if you have a side and front level attached to your RV. If you don't, you can get stick-on levels at most RV supply stores. They are well worth their cost.

Most campground sites today are quite level, and only need small adjustments. These can be accomplished fore and aft on a trailer by raising or lowering the tongue support. Right to left leveling can be done with built-in or separate leveling jacks. If there is a lot of side to side leveling needed, you'll want to drive your wheels up onto leveling chocks. These can be made of four pieces of 2 x 4-inch pine boards. Two of them should be 14 inches long, and the other two 8 inches long.

Most levels that attach to RV's show the number of inches needed to level out. If leveling is called for, pull ahead and put one long board behind the wheels on the low side. The amount of lift will vary if you have tandem wheels on a trailer, or front and rear wheels on a motor home or camper.

With tandem wheels on a trailer, one board under one wheel will raise your rig 1 inch when you back onto it; under both wheels, 2 inches. The shorter board on top of the first in a step position to make backing onto it easier, will raise your trailer 3 inches if used under one wheel, and 4 inches if used under both.

For a motor home or camper, one block front and back will raise the side 1 inch, and two blocks will raise it 2 inches. If you want more elevation, carry additional blocks.

Don't try to raise one side of any vehicle more than 4

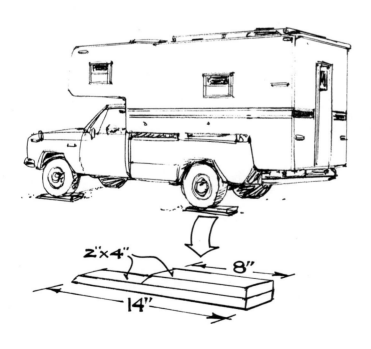

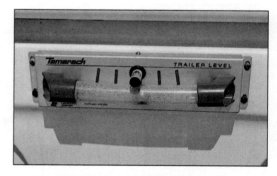

inches. If that's necessary, you'd better try to get a better site or settle for living on a slant. But remember, too much slant could make your refrigerator inoperative.

Once the vehicle is level, chock the wheels in front of and behind the tires. Then use your stabilizing jacks to ensure your vehicle's stability. With a trailer, the tongue jack will provide another stabilizer.

You'll probably want to check out the campground store to get an idea of what groceries and RV gear it carries, and how the prices compare with your home store. Don't expect them to be as cheap. Camp stores don't have the volume. They are a convenience. You'll have to balance their higher prices against the cost of driving to a store in town.

Setting Up Your Tent Camp

The *Fieldbook* of the Boy Scouts of America says, "The ideal site has trees, water, grass-covered ground, gently sloping terrain, protection from severe weather, and a view." It adds this hard reality, "The possibility of finding all these in one campsite is quite remote, but the more of them you can get in one site, the better it will be. Avoid natural hazards . . . What's ideal in fair weather can be dangerous in a thunderstorm. Don't pitch tents directly under trees. Nearby trees afford wind protection,

---

HINT *Children have a right to help in all camp chores, including setting up camp. Put that way, it's fun. If assigned as a chore, it's a drag.*

---

wood, shade, and cover for wildlife; but trees overhead will continue to drip water long after a rain, and heavy branches or whole trees can come down in windstorm.

"On knolls or gentle slopes, rainwater drains away from, instead of through the tent. Be sure the slant of the ground isn't too steep because, if you camp there, you'll wake up in the morning outside your tent."

This is still good advice if you have a choice in your site selection. Grassy slopes do have less rain runoff than bare ground. Nearby trees are a boon, but overhead they are a nuisance and can be dangerous. And, as stated so well in the introductory quotation to this chapter, a view is an asset.

Your Tent or Tents

It is recommended that the first thing you do after reaching the site is to decide where the kitchen and dining area will be. This decision is easy if there is a table and fireplace. You do this first because, if you have a dining fly, it should be the first thing set up. It gives a place where you can unload your gear, protected from the weather.

HINT *Unless guy lines are permanently attached to your tent, tie your taut-line hitch at the end of the line nearest the tent rather than at the stake.*

Lay out your dining fly and put all four pegs out from corners in a direct line from the opposite corner. On two opposing sides, put pegs at right angles to the sides and out from the middle.

While the fly is still down, fasten poles at each corner, and one along each side in the middle to match tent peg locations. The clove hitch is an excellent knot for this purpose. The knot section of this chapter shows how to tie it.

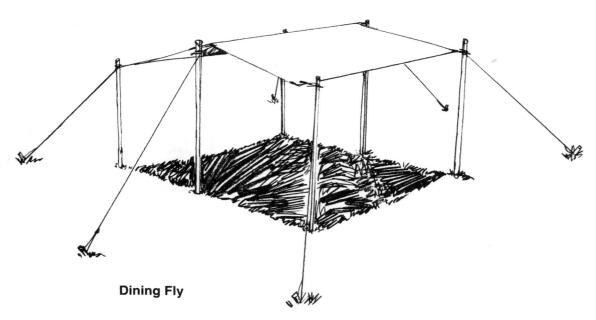

Dining Fly

Tie the guy line from the top of each pole to its corresponding peg, leaving plenty of slack to allow for raising the pole. Now raise two opposing corner poles and tighten the guy lines to hold. Then raise the other two poles and tighten. Raise the two side poles and tighten.

The purpose of the two side poles is to raise the center so that in a rain the fly will drain. If it doesn't, you'll end up with a great pool of water over your head. The two side poles should be about 6 inches higher than the corner poles. If the poles aren't already longer, compensate by sinking the corner poles in the ground, or by putting blocks under the side poles.

> **HINT** *Another way to make rain run off your dining fly is to put a pole, longer than the corner poles, in the middle of the fly. Protect the material by putting layers of cloth between it and the pole.*

Now you have time to decide where to put your tent. Check the location carefully to be sure you won't be in a bed of poison ivy, or on an exposed root, rock outcropping, or some other hard-to-remove obstruction. Pitching your tent on an anthill doesn't make for comfort, either.

Follow the manufacturer's directions for pitching your tent. Methods vary for different kinds of construction. Common practice with the old style tent with interior poles is to tie the door shut first. Clear away any loose sticks, pine cones, rocks, or other things that might puncture the floor or groundcloth. Spread the tent out flat in the position it will occupy. Stake down the corners, making sure the canvas is pulled tight between the tent pegs.

> **HINT** *Use ball-and-wire grommets to fasten ropes to canvas where there isn't a grommet to loop through.*

Put tent pegs out for whatever guy lines are needed. In most soils drive the pegs at a right angle to the pull of the line. Fasten the guy lines to the pegs at ground level, but leave plenty of slack in the lines. Then raise the tent pole, lifting the tent into position. Then, if it's a two pole tent, raise the second pole.

> **HINT** *In soft ground, strengthen the hold of tent pins by overlapping two of them.*

Retie the guy lines or reset the pegs to give proper shape and support. Use taut-line hitches to fasten lines to pegs so lines can be loosened at night or before rain when ropes will shrink and either pull out pegs or tear the tent. See the section on knots to learn how to tie the

> **HINT** *If your tent doesn't have a floor, you can take tension off your tent ropes by digging a small hole in the ground beside the base of your tent pole. When it rains, put the pole into the hole, lowering the tent to slacken ropes.*

taut-line hitch, a valuable camper's knot.

The final step is to put in the pegs around the base of the tent between the corners.

If your tent doesn't have a floor, this is the time to put in your groundcloth. If there is a sodcloth, put your

> **HINT** *If you have to sleep on the ground without air mattress or foam pad, you can sleep more comfortably by putting thicknesses of clothing under your head, the small of your back, and middle thighs.*

groundcloth on top of the sodcloth. This keeps out drafts and crawling things.

Put in your air mattressses, pads, or cot, and lay out your bedroll. Now you're ready to take care of all the other things that need doing, like setting up the kitchen, getting water, and collecting or buying firewood for an evening campfire, if permitted.

> **HINT** *Put your first aid kit in your kitchen area and make sure everyone in the family knows where it is.*

Campcraft Skills

There are a few skills you need to have an enjoyable camping experience. Two are firebuilding and cooking. They are covered in "Cooking" (Chap. 4). Some others that are valuable include knot tying, lashings, and tool sharpening.

> **HINT** *You can seal the cut ends of nylon rope by holding both ends in an open flame to melt the strands into one another. Watch out for hot dripping melted nylon. Don't do this over your gas stove, or any material that could be damaged by the hot stuff.*

• Knot Tying

Rope is essential to many camping activities. Tying knots that won't slip and are easy to untie can take many frustrations out of rope use. The basic knots shown here are ones that will be used, not just in camp, but around your home in daily living.

WHIPPING ENDS. Whenever a rope is cut, the ends start to unravel. In a short time a lot of rope will be unusable and wasted. You can stop this by dipping the cut ends in contact cement, or by whipping.

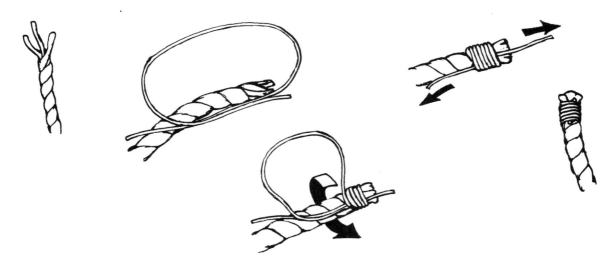

Use about 2 feet of thread, preferably waxed linen. Make a loop and hold at end of rope to be whipped. Wrap the thread tightly around the rope, working from the end of the rope back. Make turns until the whipping is as wide as the rope is thick. Then pull on both ends hard enough to tighten the whipping.

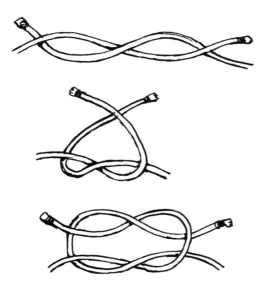

THE SHEET BEND. Greatest value of this knot is for joining two ropes of different sizes. Other knots slip when ropes aren't the same size.

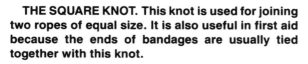

THE SQUARE KNOT. This knot is used for joining two ropes of equal size. It is also useful in first aid because the ends of bandages are usually tied together with this knot.

GETTING THERE AND MAKING CAMP

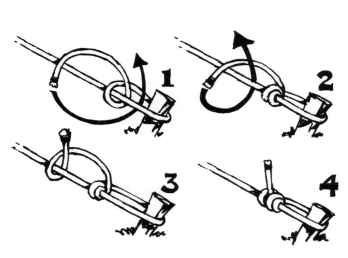

THE TAUT-LINE HITCH. This hitch can be used on all lines between tent and tent pegs. It holds tight under tension, but can be easily slipped when tension is eased.

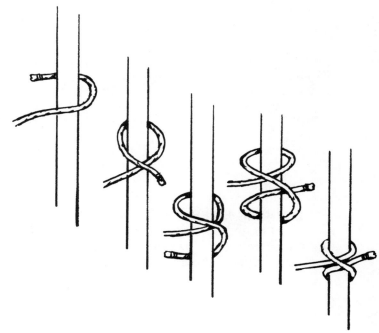

THE CLOVE HITCH. Used to start most lashings. It is also useful for tying a rope to a tree, or a guy line to the top of a tent pole.

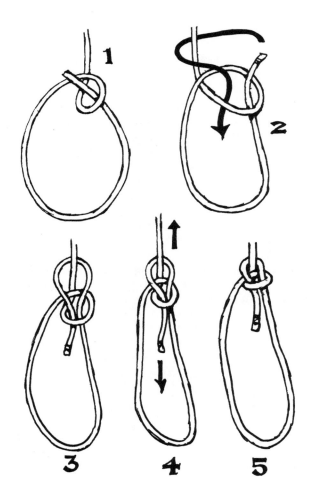

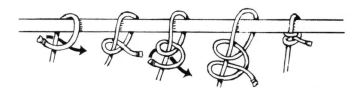

TWO HALF HITCHES. Use this for fastening a rope to a post or ring.

THE BOWLINE. —This is the best knot for forming a loop that won't slip and is easy to untie.

GETTING THERE AND MAKING CAMP

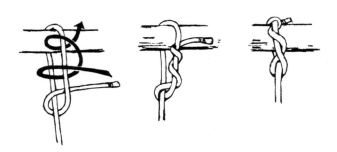

THE TIMBER HITCH. Used when two timbers need to be "sprung" together. It is also fine for raising logs, for dragging them over land, or for pulling them through water.

• Lashings

Knowing how to lash two pieces of wood together securely and at the proper angle gives you a real advantage in camp. You can make things for convenience and to meet emergencies.

When lashing timbers together with rope, it's important to use ropes of correct thickness and length. For staves and spars up to 1¼ inches in diameter, use tough twisted or braided line. For spars up to 3 inches in diameter, use ¼-inch line or rope. For length, allow one yard of rope for each inch of the combined diameters of the spars. For example, in lashing a 1-inch brace to a 2-inch leg, add 1 and 2 to make 3 inches. Thus, you need 3 yards or 9 feet of rope for lashing.

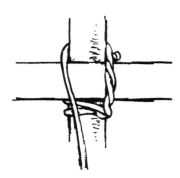

Twist the end of the rope into the working part, then wrap the rope around crosspiece and upright, binding them together.

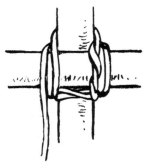

In wrapping, rope goes on outside of previous turn around upright.

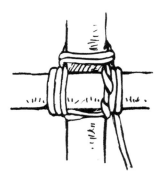

After three or four wrapping turns, make two or three "frapping" turns between the timbers. Strain them tightly.

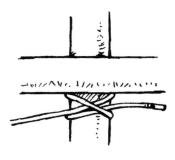

THE SQUARE LASHING. Start with a clove hitch around the upright, just below the spot where the crosspiece is to be.

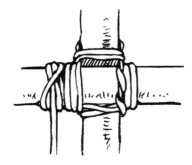

Finish with clove hitch around end of crosspiece. Remember: "Start with clove; wrap thrice; frap twice; end with clove."

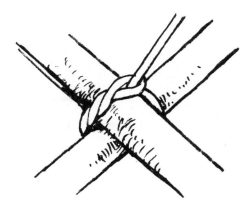

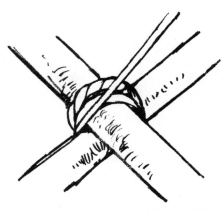

DIAGONAL LASHING. Begin with a timber hitch around the two timbers at the point of crossing, springing, or binding together.

Take three turns around both timbers, alongside the timber hitch. Put turns beside each other, not on top of each other.

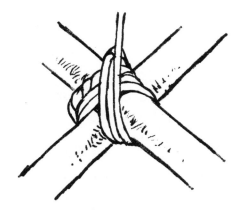

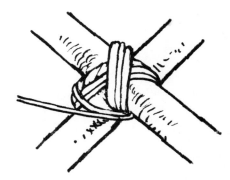

Take three more turns, this time crosswise to the previous turns. Strain each turn to be sure lashing is taut.

Make a couple of frapping turns between the timbers around the diagonal lashing turns. Pull them as tight as you can.

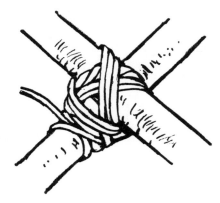

ALL lashings finish with a clove hitch. In the diagonal hitch it can go around the most convenient timber.

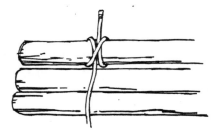

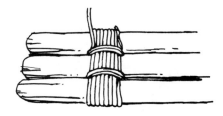

TRIPOD LASHING. Place three timbers next to one another. Attach rope to outside timber with clove hitch at proper place.

Bind poles with seven or eight loose wrapping turns and two frapping turns between the poles to form the hinge pivots.

Finish off lashing with clove hitch on the other outside leg. Spread the legs into proper position for use.

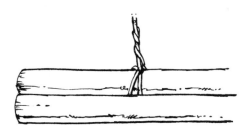

SHEAR LASHING. Place two timbers next to each other. Tie clove hitch around one of them, at right place.

Bend the two timbers together by laying seven or eight turns of the rope around them, loosely, one turn beside the other.

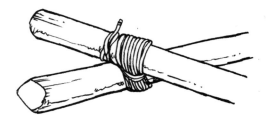

Make two frapping turns around the lashing turns between the timbers. Fasten rope with clove hitch around either timber.

GETTING THERE AND MAKING CAMP

• Woods Tools

An ax or hatchet, saw, and knife are the most common tools used to gather and prepare wood for camp use. These all can be dangerous tools when improperly used.

Hatchet or Ax. The safest way to cut or split wood with a hatchet is the contact method. Before starting to cut or split, get a chopping block. This can be any solid piece of wood—a tree stump or the thickest piece of downed wood you can find.

When using the contact method, keep the sharp bit of the tool in contact with the wood throughout each stroke, bringing both of them down against the chopping block at the same time.

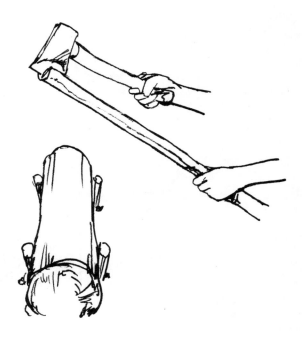

For chopping a stick by this method, set the ax bit on about a 45 degree angle to the stick. Raise the stick and the ax together...

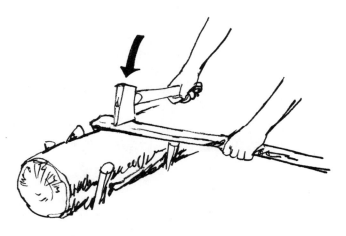

...then bring them down onto the chopping block still together. A stick should cut through in one cut; a branch may take more depending on its thickness.

In splitting, put the bit parallel to the grain and at the end of the stick, in a crack if there is one. Lift the stick and ax together...

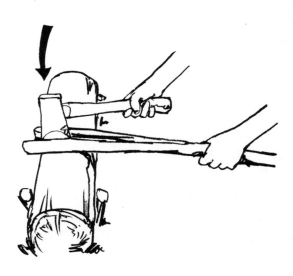

...bring the stick and ax down on the chopping block together. Just as they hit, twist the ax slightly. This will tend to break the wood pieces apart.

The ax, as differentiated from a hatchet, is used to lop or limb down trees, and to cut larger pieces into chunks for splitting.

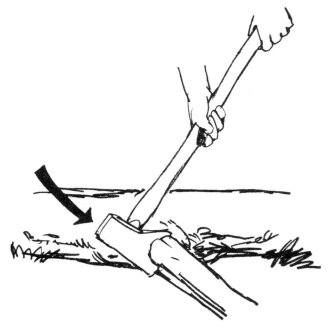

LOPPING OR LIMBING is the process of removing branches from a downed tree. Always chop from the butt towards the top of the tree. Stand on the side of the trunk opposite the branches being cut.

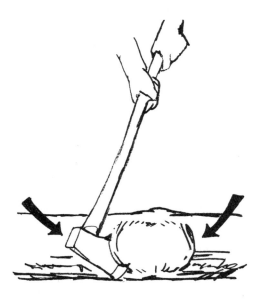

LOGGING OR BUCKING is done with two flying cuts, each as wide as the tree is thick. Make the first of these two cuts to the center of the tree . . .

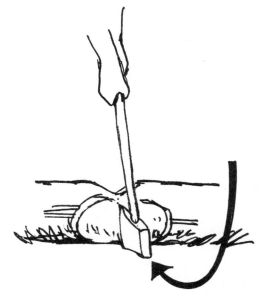

. . . then make a similar flying cut from the other side of the tree. If your log is heavy, make the cut with a series of three strokes at the top, bottom, and in the middle. Done this way, your ax won't stick.

GETTING THERE AND MAKING CAMP

Expert loggers often stand on top of the tree, and cut between their feet. This is risky business, only for a pro. Stay safe.

Ax Sharpening. Use an 8-inch mill file. Work toward the blade from the back. When one side is bright, turn the ax or hatchet over and do the other side. Finish the job with a sharpening stone.

Knife Sharpening. Lay the blade on a sharpening stone. Raise the back of the blade slightly and push across the stone with a cutting motion. Repeat, making sure every bit of the blade is sharpened. After working one side of the blade, do the same on the other side. Keep changing sides until the blade is sharp. Be sure to keep fingers holding the stone below its edge.

Making Camp in an Undeveloped Area

Before you leave home, check fire danger conditions where you're planning to go. Your campsite could be in a high danger area where no campfires are allowed. If the danger is extreme, you might not even be permitted to camp. If no fires are allowed, you can still cook on a gas stove.

Although this kind of camping is rare for a family, it's still rather common among those rugged individuals who are willing to put up with some inconvenience and discomfort for the peace and quiet of being alone. If you decide on this route, fine, but be sure the whole family is ready for it.

Arrival at your campsite will be quite different than at a formal campground. There's no check-in or registration, and no assignment to a campsite. Unless you have already visited the camping area and checked it out for suitable sites, allow time to make the best of your opportunities.

You either brought your water supply with you, or know that water is available in some form. You'll want to camp fairly near the source of water so you don't have to spend a lot of time hauling it. The water will probably

be from a lake and stream, so count on sterilizing it before use.

If you didn't bring a stove or fuel, wood gathering is another task to be taken care of. Remember, cut no green wood. It doesn't burn very well, anyway. Best firewood comes from lower dead branches of trees.

You'll want to stack a woodpile with enough wood for a couple of days, perhaps more if staying more than a weekend. The woodpile should be near your kitchen, and wood in it should be sorted by size, and cut into usable lengths. The size should range from twigs to larger split pieces for fuel. Cover your wood supply with a piece of plastic to keep it dry.

Digging isn't necessary if you come to this type of campsite prepared. Digging often is the start of an erosion problem. Bring your own chemical toilet and don't dig a latrine. Don't even consider burying garbage or cans. Take trash with you when you leave.

But if you don't have a chemical toilet, you'll have to make your own latrine. Simplest is probably a straddle trench. Dig a trench about 8 inches wide, 3 feet long, and 18 inches deep. If you are digging a sodded area, set the sod you remove from the trench and keep the grass alive by watering while you're at the site. Then put it back in place when you leave. Pile the topsoil at either end of the trench. Put the subsoil on a plastic sheet so it can be carried to your fire area to make a dirt hearth.

Use the subsoil to build up your fireplace. This protects the topsoil underneath from being damaged by the heat of your fire. It also makes a good base on which to position rocks to support any size kettle or pan in your camp kitchen. Be sure to take the dirt back and fill in the latrine trench with it before breaking camp.

Make privacy for the latrine, if it isn't already screened by nature. Shape a tarp screen or cut some brush and stick in the ground. Put toilet paper on a stick within reach. Cover it with a plastic bag to protect it from rain and night dampness. It's a good idea to hang a low intensity lantern near the latrine to mark its location in the dark.

This is called a straddle trench latrine because that's how it's used. After each use, cover excrement with a light layer of dirt from either end of the trench. Provide a scoop or paddle for this purpose.

You'll have to dispose of your garbage, including cans. Don't bury it. After you leave, animals will dig it up looking for food, and the campsite will become a mess. Plan to burn out your empty cans in the fire, flatten them by stepping on them when they cool off, and bring them home, or drop them off in the first trash container you see.

Wet garbage can be burned by putting it at the edge of your fire, and pushing the heat-dried materials into the coals and flames while more is drying. You can use plastic trash bags to take wet garbage home with you, too, if you don't want to burn it. Paper can be burned directly in the fire.

Dishwater and other waste water should be carried to the edge of your campground and scattered, not poured, on the ground. Animals and birds will soon eat the food scraps from the dishwater.

GETTING THERE AND MAKING CAMP

ACTIVITIES

"Have you never seen buffaloes roaming in Kensington Gardens? And can't you see the smoke from the Sioux lodges under the shadow of the Albert Memorial? I have seen them there these many years."

Aids to Scoutmastership, Baden-Powell

When the founder of Scouting wrote these words in 1920, he was telling leaders that imagination is important when working with youth.

Your mind can take you anyplace and you can be anyone. The imagination of a child makes these fantasies even more real than for an adult. Well planned activities at the right time in the right place can stimulate and supplement that imagination.

The right balance of activities adds to the value of your camping trip, balance meaning not too many, and not too few.

A review of the ideas that follow might lead you to think your family camp should be one big activity after another. Not so! These are like a smorgasbord, and as with any smorgasbord you can fill your plate with so much food that nothing tastes good when you've finished eating.

There will be times when you don't need any planned

activity. You can sit in the shade reading a good book, or lie in the sun and drowse. During these lulls, your children can do those kinds of things so important to them—things like building fantastic sand castles, or great highways for their toy cars, or playing with newfound friends from a neighboring campsite. Unstructured time, time for play is valuable.

But there are other times when you'll want some good activities up your sleeve. Times when you'll want to stimu-

late your children's minds, and in the process get to know them better, and let them get to know you in an environment different from the one at home.

Look over these suggestions. Match them with the camping you'll be doing. Mark those that seem to fit your family and your campsite. Then you'll be ready when an activity is needed.

HINT *For occasional use, things like boats, canoes, bicycles, and sports gear are cheaper to rent than to buy and maintain.*

At the Site

Campground Provided Recreation

During your trip planning you probably checked out the major features of campsites in your area of travel. You learned their special activity features, especially those of the sites finally picked for use.

You found campgrounds with swimming pools. Others had lakes for swimming, boating, canoeing, and fishing. Some offered native trails, horseback riding, recreation rooms, bike rentals, and playgrounds with horseshoes, volleyball, shuffleboard, croquet, badminton, and children's equipment like swings and teeter-totters. Obviously all of these aren't available at each site, but your campground directory told you what each campground offered.

Cub Scout Achievements

If you have a Cub Scout son, the family camp is a great place for him to pass many of the outdoor achievements. Use his Wolf, Bear, or Webelos book to see what he might accomplish while in camp. Many of the activities suggested here use the skills of achievements, electives, and Webelos activity badges.

HINT *Give your Cub Scout credit when he takes part in achievement-related camp activities. Sign his accomplishments in his Cub Scout book. That's your right and privilege as a parent.*

Scout Advancement

Unlike Cub Scout achievement work, the requirements for Scout advancement are the responsibility of the Scoutmaster and other designated adult and boy leaders of the Scout's own troop. The family camp, therefore, isn't a place where a Scout can pass his Scout requirements. It can, though, be a great place to gain and practice the skills needed to pass them.

Many items of Scout advancement have already been covered in other chapters of this book, things like knot tying, tent pitching, ground beds, camp safety, and sanitation. Other skills explained include cooking, firebuilding, knife and ax safety and use, and first aid.

This chapter on camp activities has references to using maps and compasses, and measuring distances. Since these are basic skills of the outdoors, and not covered in other sections of the book, they'll be briefly explained here.

ACTIVITIES

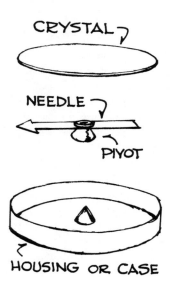

CRYSTAL

NEEDLE

PIVOT

HOUSING OR CASE

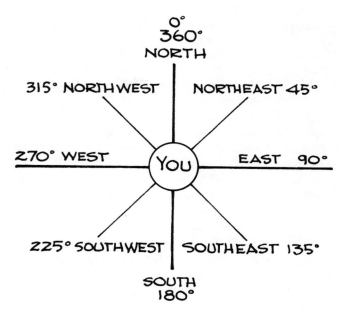

0°
360°
NORTH

315° NORTHWEST   NORTHEAST 45°

270° WEST   YOU   EAST 90°

225° SOUTHWEST   SOUTHEAST 135°

SOUTH
180°

The Compass

The earth acts like a gigantic magnet with a plus and minus pole. One of these is called the north magnetic pole. It attracts the north end of the compass needle.

The needle is the only movable part of the standard compass. Directions are shown on the face.

Suppose you had to walk northeast. Hold the compass still and level. When the needle stops swinging it will point to the north magnetic pole. Hold the compass in both hands with your index fingers together at 45 degrees on the dial. That's northeast. Hold the compass against your chest. Keep it steady and watch the needle as you turn. Stop when the needle points to N on the dial. Without turning your head, look up. Northeast is as far as you can see straight ahead. Any other direction or degree reading can be found the same way.

There are more complicated and sophisticated compasses, but all are based on a needle or compass card with needle attached. Each of these compasses has its own directions for use. They are provided by the manufacturer with the compass. Follow these instructions in a step-by-step fashion, and you'll soon master the use of your compass.

Directions

No matter where you are there are four main directions: north, east, south, and west. Between them are northeast, southeast, southwest, and northwest.

Using numbers, there are 360 directions, called degrees. A small circle near the upper side of the number means degrees. North is both 0° and 360°. Northeast is 45°; East, 90°; Southeast, 135°; South, 180°; Southwest, 225°; West, 270°; and Northwest, 315°.

Distance

You can measure distance by counting your steps and converting the number of steps into feet. Measure a course exactly 100 feet with a tape measure. Walk this measured course. Walk naturally and count the steps it takes to cover the distance. Walk it again to be sure your count is accurate.

If your count was close to 50, each step is about 2 feet long. You can count by twos each time a foot hits the ground. If your count was nearer 46 than 50, try to change your step length to make it come out to 50 on the measured course. Practice until it does.

If your count was near 40, each step is about 2½ feet. You can count by fives each time the same foot hits the ground, which foot depending on how you stepped off. If your count was 44, try to lengthen your step slightly to make it come out to 40 on the measured course. Practice until it does. If you're a little less than 40, shorten your step.

Some men with a long stride will find their count to be somewhere between 30 and 35. If they adjust their step to 33 to the 100 foot course, they can count by threes every time a foot hits the ground and be quite accurate.

Maps

A map is a picture of the land. The top of the map is usually north and the bottom is south. The left side is west and the right is east.

Most maps (all topographic maps) have two north arrows. One points to the north magnetic pole, and the other to true north. Only along a line from the Keweenaw Peninsula of Michigan to the southern tip of Florida do the two arrows match up. In other sections of the United States, the difference between the arrows varies from a few degrees to an extreme of 35 degrees in Alaska. The number of degrees of difference will be shown by a number between the two arrows.

You can orient a map (turn it so it matches the terrain) by sight or by compass. With a detailed topographic map, first find your location. Then look around for prominent features of the landscape that also are shown on the map. These could be lakes, rivers, high points, a church steeple, or the like. Put your map on a flat surface and turn it so that a line from your location on the map across the map symbol for your selected prominent point continues on to the real things. Your map will then be oriented, and all other things on the map will be in accurate relationship to the terrain.

To orient a map using a compass, put it just below the two north arrows on the map. Turn the map so the north arrow on the compass is on a direct line with the magnetic north arrow on the map. While the angle between the arrows isn't as exact as the degree reading between the arrows, it will be accurate enough for any use except surveying.

Your map also will have a scale showing how many feet or miles there are to an inch. Lay a slip of paper on the map with one edge on a line from where you want to start measuring to where you want to finish. Make a mark on the paper edge opposite the point where you want to start measuring and another where you want to end up. Now, lay the marked slip below the scale with the starting point at 0. Read the distance to the second mark. If the distance is greater than the scale is long, make marks at appropriate places and move the paper back so the new mark is at 0. Keep track of the times you move.

If there are turns along the trail, mark from the start to the first turn, turn the paper, keeping the mark at the turn, and make another mark at the next turn, and so on until you reach your destination.

Nature Projects

Plaster Casting Tracks

You'll need some plaster of paris, water, strips of cardboard, and some bird or animal tracks. Check for tracks near a watering place where animals might come to drink.

If you don't find tracks, set up an area where you can bring them in and get their tracks. Someplace away from the main traffic of your campground, find an area of bare ground. Put two paper plates in the center of the area. Fasten them down by driving a small twig through an edge of each into the ground. Put water in one plate, and food in the other. Attract birds with seed, bread crumbs, or small pieces of fruit. For other animals, scraps from your supper should do the trick.

Put your lure in place in the evening before dark. Smooth the dirt around it with a branch or brush. Then sprinkle the ground with water without stepping into the muddy area. Tracks hold more firmly in damp ground. Check your baited area the first thing next morning. If tracks have been made, plaster casting can begin.

Shell and Rock Collections

Protect your collections in empty egg cartons. They will keep shells from breaking, and rocks from scratching shelves. When your collection is small, use the bottom half of a carton. When that's full, use the top, too. Start a new carton when the first one is full.

Label all items. One value of a collection comes from the knowledge gained in making it. Labeling is part of learning.

Leaf Collections

Collect real leaves or exact ink renderings of them.

Real Leaves

Cut newspapers to fit in a heavy looseleaf notebook. Carefully put a leaf of a tree or shrub between the sheets of newspaper. Write down the kind of tree, date, and where collected. Use a good tree or shrub identification book to help. Put this note between the pages with the leaf. Repeat, using leaves from different trees.

Use a belt or strap to hold the notebook securely shut until the leaves dry. Put a heavy weight on it when you get home.

When the leaf is dry, attach it to unlined looseleaf notebook paper with clear tape or glue. If leaves are small, you can put more than one on a page. Attach a label near each leaf. It should give the information you wrote when collecting. Clear plastic, available by the yard in hardward or department stores, can be used to cover each page to make it permanent.

Use the same process for a wildflower collection.

Plaster Casting Tracks

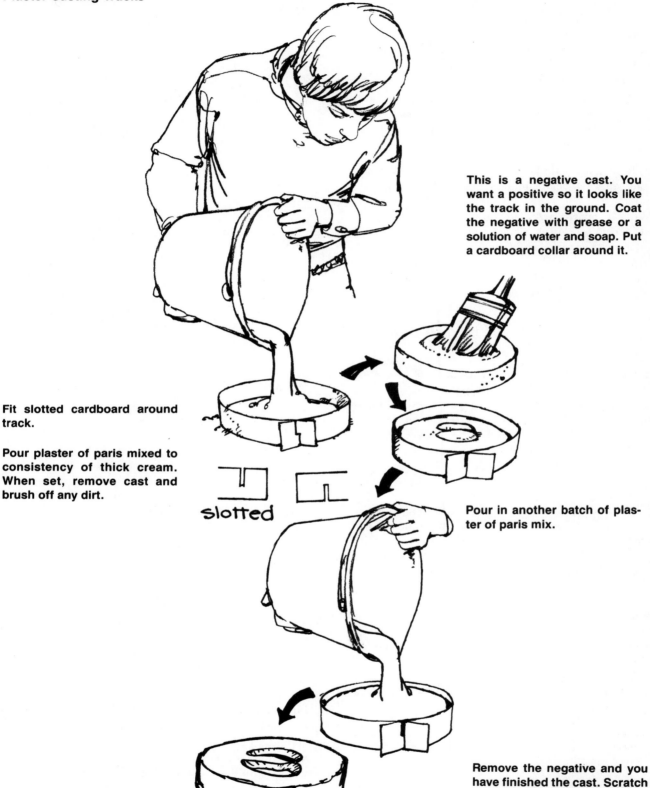

This is a negative cast. You want a positive so it looks like the track in the ground. Coat the negative with grease or a solution of water and soap. Put a cardboard collar around it.

Fit slotted cardboard around track.

Pour plaster of paris mixed to consistency of thick cream. When set, remove cast and brush off any dirt.

slotted

Pour in another batch of plaster of paris mix.

Remove the negative and you have finished the cast. Scratch the name of the bird or animal that made the track on the cast.

Insect Collections

Make a collecting net by shaping a piece of bent wire as shown and taping it in notches in the sides of the end of broomstick. Attach cheesecloth to the metal ring by wrapping with heavy thread, using a needle to push through the cloth.

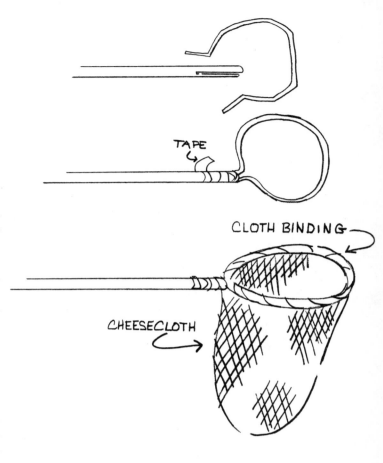

You'll need a killing jar so that a captured insect can be killed quickly before it damages itself struggling to get out.

Mounting boards are made from soft wood or cardboard. Strips of cardboard with pins at each end will hold the wings in place while the insect dries.

When the insect dries, remove from the mounting board and pin through the body to a clean piece of cardboard. Identify and label each insect.

Leaf Prints

Carbon Paper. Put a green leaf on a piece of carbon paper, vein side down. Lay a newspaper over the leaf and the carbon paper and rub the newspaper several times with your hand to get a good carbon deposit on the leaf. Then put the leaf, vein side down, on a sheet of white paper. Put another piece of clean paper over the leaf and rub again to force the carbon on the leaf to print on the paper.

Crayon Prints. Put a few layers of newspaper on a table or other solid surface. Put a leaf on the newspaper with the vein side up. Put a sheet of white paper over the leaf. Rub a point flattened crayon across the paper with all strokes going in the same direction. The design of the leaf will show through on the crayon side of the paper.

Spatter Printing. Pin a leaf to a piece of white paper, making sure the pins don't slant out beyond the edges of the leaf. Hold a piece of wire screen about 8 inches above the paper. Dip an old toothbrush in India ink or show card color. Scratch the brush across the screen so a spray falls on the leaf and paper. When dry, unpin the leaf, remove, and label.

HINT *Sketch in leaf veins on leaf prints where they don't show. Use ink and spray with clear lacquer for permanence.*

Printer's Ink Prints. You'll need more elaborate materials for this. Get a small amount of printer's ink, a rubber roller, a pane of glass bigger than the roller in each dimension, some pieces of newspaper, and unlined white paper, preferably punched for a 3-ring binder.

Put a small amount of the ink on the glass and roll it out with the roller until the roller is evenly inked. Put the leaf on a piece of newspaper with the vein side up. Roll the inked roller over the leaf. Put the leaf with the inked side down on a piece of white paper. Cover with another piece of newspaper. Roll over the newspaper to press the inked leaf firmly against the white paper. Be careful not to let the leaf move while rolling.

Lift off the newspaper, and then the leaf. When the ink dries, label the sheet with information about the leaf, and put it in a 3-ring binder with the rest of your leaf collection.

Plot Study

Introduce your children to a whole community right under their feet. Not a town of living people, but a community of living creatures. It's exciting to study, to look at in detail, to see the different kinds of insects and other small animals and watch what they're doing.

Start by having your children check the plants in an area about 3 feet by 3 feet. Help them to think small for this. How many different kinds are there? Then look for living creatures. Use a magnifying glass to look for smaller ones. What are they doing?

Use a shovel and carefully remove the sod from an area about 1 foot square. Dig up the dirt in that space and let your children check it out for more living things. Put the dirt and sod back when the children are through.

Scavenger Hunt

Before conducting the hunt, walk around the campground, writing down items of nature that could be collected by your children—things like leaves, flowers, weeds, seeds, pebbles, and similar items.

List the things on separate but identical sheets of paper for each child. Pass them out with instructions to collect as many as they can identify, and decide on a signal to mark the end of the hunt—like two quick honks of the car horn. Explain that items won't count unless the child can identify each one.

If you don't think your children will be able to identify the things on your list, take a nature hike with them before giving out the lists. Point out each thing on your list, and give its name, but don't tell them they'll be collecting.

License Plate Game Variation

Remember the State License Plate Identification game in "Getting There" (Chap. 6)? The one where the family tried to spot a license plate from every state?

You can play a variation of this using nature guidebooks for your area. Pick one that looks like fun for the area where you'll be traveling and camping.

Let's say you choose birds. The object of the game will be for your family to spot and check off as many different birds as are common to the area, using a guidebook to the birds of that area. This is an activity that could continue for many trips by trying to add new birds to the list of those identified. The same game could be played using one or more of the other guidebooks written for the areas you visit.

Star Study

Stars have an unbelievable brightness when seen for the first time on a moonless night in camp. There are no

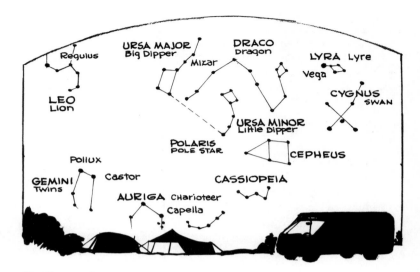

Northern sky.

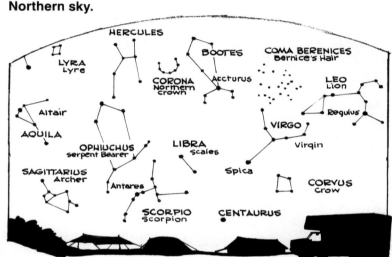

Southern sky.

city lights to dim their brilliance, and no air pollution.

For thousands of years people have grouped the stars together into figures called "constellations." Legends and myths have grown up around the constellations. It's fun to learn and tell your children these legends while pointing out the star clusters in the sky. Before going to camp, ask your librarian for a book about legends of the constellations.

To start your children on a fascinating "tour" of the constellations, locate the Big Dipper. You'll find it in the northern sky. Four stars make up the bowl of the dipper, and three bright ones seem to make up the handle. Actually, the middle point in the handle is composed of two stars. Look closely. Maybe you can see both of them. Indians called these two stars the squaw and the papoose. They used them to test the eyesight of their young braves.

The two stars in the bowl farthest from the handle are called the pointers because, if you follow the line, they take you to the North Star. This star is almost in a direct line with the axis of the earth, and so doesn't seem to move as the earth turns. All other stars seem to rotate around the North Star.

Using the Big Dipper, the North Star, and a star chart, you'll see that the North Star is the first star in the handle of the Little Dipper. Follow the handle stars down to the bowl to see the whole constellation. If you follow a line across the North Star from the middle star in the handle of the Big Dipper, you'll see five stars making a big "W." Legend has it that this is Cassiopeia, the lady in the chair.

It will be helpful to have a flashlight with a powerful beam. When you see a constellation, point it out with the flashlight beam. And when your children see one, let them point to it with the flashlight.

Finding Directions Without a Compass

Shadow Stick. You can find directions without a compass using a shadow stick.

On a sunny day, drive a stick into a section of flat ground so that it makes no shadow, by slanting it directly at the sun. Within 15 or 20 minutes a shadow will appear at the base of the stick. The shadow will point to the east. A line at right angles to the shadow will be a north-south line.

Don't take the stick out. Come back from time to time during the day to check the shadow. It will get longer and longer, but will always be pointing east in the summer.

The shadow stick is most accurate in the summer when the sun is high overhead, and least accurate in winter when the sun is low in the southern sky. Check how the east-west shadow line changes direction during the day in winter.

Watch Method. Hold a watch flat. Put a match or straw upright along the edge of the watch. Turn the watch until the shadow of the straw falls directly along the hour hand, meaning the hour hand is pointing directly at the sun. Between the hours of 6 a.m. and 6 p.m. (standard time), a line from the center of the watch dividing the small angle between the hour hand and the figure 12 will point true South. Between 6 p.m. and 6 a.m. while the sun is still up, divide the large angle to find South. If you're on daylight savings time on your watch, turn it back one hour. No digital watches, please.

Conservation Projects

For the camper, conservation often means not doing something: not ditching tents, not digging holes, not burying garbage, not overusing a campsite. Not hacking or carving trees may mean healthy trees for years to come.

It's hard for kids to become enthusiastic about not doing something, so concentrate on doing things for the environment, at the same time helping them to learn what not to do.

Conservation means doing things correctly, too. Before you try to undo damage to the environment, be sure you won't just exchange one kind of harm for another. Nature's balances are very delicate and easily disturbed.

Professional conservationists will be glad to advise you on needs in the area of your campsite, and to point out steps to be taken to do worthwhile things.

Projects children seem to enjoy include stream improvement, erosion control, and tree planting. Be sure you know what you're doing.

The Outdoor Code

The Boy Scouts of America has developed an Outdoor Code as a guide for its members. This code can be your code, too. Read it to your children, and explain to them in your own words what it means.

Campsite Improvement

This is more practical in a wilderness type campsite than in a developed campground. There will be a greater need for gadgets, and more dead wood to use in making them.

You'll find the lashings taught in "Setting Up Camp" (Chap. 6) helpful in making your camp more efficient and comfortable.

Camp Gadgets

Tripods. The basic tripod is made by lashing three poles together with—what else?—the tripod lashing. For a tripod to hang your pots over your fire, the poles must be long enough that the base will be out of the fire danger zone. Lash a crosspiece between two of the legs. Center the crosspiece above your fire and high enough to hang your pots from S hooks made from coat hanger wire. Cut the hook off a coat hanger with wire cutters.

THE OUTDOOR CODE

AS AN AMERICAN, I WILL DO MY BEST TO—BE CLEAN IN MY OUTDOOR MANNERS

I will treat the outdoors as a heritage to be improved for our greater enjoyment. I will keep my trash and garbage out of America's waters, fields, woods, and roadways.

BE CAREFUL WITH FIRE

I will prevent wildfire. I will build my fire in a safe place and be sure it is out before I leave.

BE CONSIDERATE IN THE OUTDOORS

I will treat public and private property with respect. I will remember that use of the outdoors is a privilege I can lose by abuse.

BE CONSERVATION-MINDED

I will learn how to practice good conservation of soil, waters, forests, minerals, grasslands, and wildlife; and I will urge others to do the same. I will use sportsmanlike methods in all my outdoor activities.

Bend the wire in half. Put one end in a vise or have someone hold it with pliers while you twist the wires together. Then bend into an S. For added strength for heavy pots, twist two wires together.

The Dovetail Notch. Using this joint for making camp gadgets is a fun exercise in craftsmanship. It's easier to do than it looks.

With a saw, make a cut that slants to your right, not quite halfway through the pole. Avoid knots (a branch is a knot). Begin the notch in from the end of the pole to prevent splitting when the dovetail is driven in tight.

Now make an equal cut to the left. Notice that the cuts are almost at a right angle to each other. On thicker pieces the notch angle can be sharper.

Cut straight down to the depth of the side cuts and make another vertical cut beside the first. The side cuts outline the dovetail. The center ones break the fibers so your knife can pry the chips out.

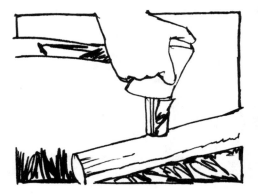

With the piece to be fitted held over the notch, shape the base and sides. Make the end a little smaller than the notch.

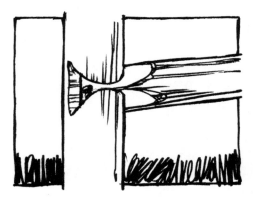

Slice out the wood in the notch, first from one side and then the other. If you haven't cut into a knot, the wood should chip out easily.

Drive the dovetail into the notch until it jams. If you want a very rigid joint—one that will support a heavy load—shape this dovetail some more so it fits through the notch.

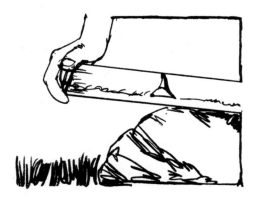

The cleaned-out notch is ready for a fitting—round stick or dovetail.

The one-legged fire crane shows the strength of a well-made dovetail joint. It can support a full kettle of water over a fire.

Kitchen Table and Rack. First lash the front crosspiece at the top of the two front legs with square lashings. Make the back section the same way, but with longer back legs to make the rack.

Then lash the front and back sections together with side rails. The whole thing can then be strengthened by lashing pieces identical to the top about a foot above the ground.

Lash a couple of crosspieces on the high back legs to make the rack. Finish the table top with pieces of wood fastened with a floor lashing.

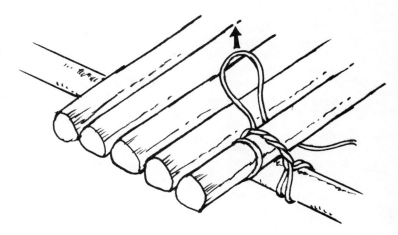

Now pull the rope under the stringer and up over the first spar—on the outside of the stringer—then repeat the second step.

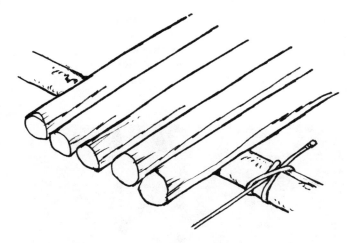

FLOOR LASHING. Start with a clove hitch around the stringer on which the floor or deck spars are to be laid.

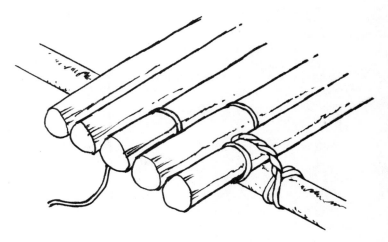

Continue this until all spars have been laid firmly in place.

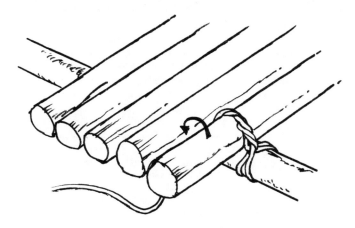

Pull a bight (loop) under the stringer and up between the first two spars and slip the bight over the end of the first spar.

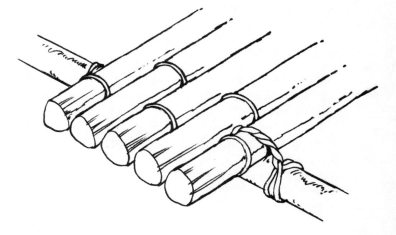

Finish with a clove hitch around the stringer.

Shower Bath. Make your own shower by lashing two spars together with a diagonal lashing. Fasten a crosspiece with square lashing so it will be about 7 feet above the ground when the spars are raised. Tie a pail to the crosspiece so when tipped with a stick lashed to it, water will spill into a #10 can with holes punched in the bottom.

Brace the shower at an angle supported by a rope to a peg in the ground.

Wash Basin Support. Lash together two spars about 5 feet long and one about 3 feet long with a tripod lashing. Put the lashing about a foot below the end of the short spars. Lash a crosspiece near the top of the two long poles with square lashings. This will make a towel rack. Put a metal basin in the space formed as shown.

Fire Buckets. Your wilderness camp won't have running water, so keep a couple of buckets of water near your tent for instant fire protection. Drive a piece of deadwood into the ground for an upright. Lash a crossbar to it with a square lashing. Hang the fire buckets from the arms formed. It will keep them from being knocked over.

Mostly For Fun Activities

The Senses

Blindfold each of your children and have them sit quietly for a period of time. Tell them to listen, smell, and feel to tell what's going on around them. At the end of the time limit, have each child list on paper the things they heard, smelled, and felt while blindfolded. Then have them describe what they noticed.

You could try this activity the first time by just blindfolding the children without telling them to listen, smell, and feel. Then do it a second time as described above. Point out the differences in the sensations recorded when they knew they were supposed to be observant. The things were all there the first time, but not observed.

Kim's Game

Rudyard Kipling's *Kim* was about a boy who developed great powers of observation through practice. Kim's Game as played today had its origins in Kipling's book.

To play the game, put 20 or 30 common objects on a table. Have your children study them for 1 minute, and then cover the objects with a cloth. Each child then lists as many items as he or she can remember. Take the lists. Remove the cloth and check the lists. Give 1 point for each item correctly listed and take 2 points off for any item listed that's not on the table.

There are variations of this game that will be fun after your children become adept at observation through practice of the first Kim's Game.

In one variation, the children study the objects for 1 minute as before, but at the end of the minute they turn their backs while you switch six to eight articles from one place to another on the table. The children have 30 seconds more to study the table, and then list which items were moved.

Another variation works the same way, but you take objects from the table. The children then look for 30 seconds, and list items that were removed.

Ranger Activities

In the National Parks and Monuments, evening programs are scheduled during the tourist season. These include campfire programs and slide-illustrated talks about the park and its flora and fauna.

During the day there are Ranger-conducted hikes to points of interest. These often include nature study to familiarize the hikers with the ecology of the park.

HINT *Weekly activity schedules of nature hikes and evening activities are posted on bulletin boards in prominent places in National Parks and Monuments. These show times and content of programs.*

Duck on the Rock

This is a good game for four to eight people, so Mom and Dad will probably want to join in.

A throwing line is marked about 30 feet from a rock called the duck rock. This rock should be about basketball size. One person, the chaser, waits near the duck rock. All others stand behind the throwing line. Each person, including the chaser, has a "duck"—a smooth round stone slightly smaller than a baseball.

To start the game, the chaser sets his duck on the duck rock. The others, in regular turns, throw or toss their rocks at the chaser's duck, trying to knock it off the duck rock. After a person throws his rock, he must try to retrieve it at the risk of being tagged by the chaser. He may try this at any time, delaying as long as he wishes, except that if he doesn't have his rock back across the line when his turn comes, he's considered as tagged, and changes places with the chaser. A person is safe and can't be tagged if he's standing with one foot on his duck, but once he picks it up he can't put it down again, and is fair game for the chaser.

Whenever a thrower knocks the chaser's duck off the duck rock, the chaser must put his duck back on the duck rock before he can tag anyone. The person who knocks the chaser's duck off can't be tagged when he retrieves his rock.

Blind trail.

Critter Crawl Race

Each person catches a bug, beetle, or other insect and puts it in a paper cup.

Mark out a 6-foot diameter circle on the ground. Put all the bugs under an inverted paper plate in the center of the circle. All contestants stand outside the circle. Lift the plate. The first bug to crawl out of the circle is the winner. No flying bugs allowed, but jumpers are great.

Hares and Hounds

This old game is lots of fun in camp. One of the grown-ups probably should be the hare. Armed with a couple of sacks of ground meal, the hare heads out on the trail. He or she pokes a small hole in the bottom corner of one of the bags so a small trickle of meal runs out on the ground. When the first sack runs out, the hare pokes a hole in the second bag and continues on.

The "hare" should have a 5-minute start before the "hounds" (the children) give chase. The object of the game is for the pack of hounds to follow the trail of the hare to its den. The den is the spot the hare reached when the ground meal ran out. The hare can hide any-

place within 100 feet of the spot where the meal runs out.

Lay the trail with ground meal, or some similar grain that won't mess up the camp. Birds and small animals will eat it within a day after the game.

This game also can be played with the hare using homemade tracking irons fastened to a pair of shoes with straps. These are made by bending ½-inch strap iron into the general shape of a deer track, and drilling holes for thongs to fit through to tie over your shoes.

Another device used in the early days of Scouting was called a whifflepoof. It was made by pounding spikes about half-way into all sides of a small log. A screw eye in one end of the log makes it possible to fasten a rope, which is used to drag the whifflepoof on the ground behind the hare. This will leave a track that can be followed.

Blind Trail

Start by tying the end of a roll of twine or string to a tree near the edge of the campground. Then walk into the woods, stringing the twine or string from tree to tree, wrapping it around a tree occasionally to keep it off the ground.

Blindfold the children and tell them to pretend they're blind. They follow the string, stopping whenever the string goes around a tree. At each stop they are to feel the tree and describe the bark. They also are to listen for any sounds and see if they can distinguish any smells.

The purpose of this activity is to give children a feeling for those who are blind, and to sharpen their powers of observation.

Water Activities

Fishing

Be sure you and your family members are in compliance with state fishing laws, including having a valid license. Most states don't require children to have licenses if they fish with a licensed adult.

Equipment for children can be as elaborate as the best to be found in a sporting goods store, or as simple as Huck Finn's cane pole, line, bobber, sinker, and hook. Let's assume the latter for a moment, and describe what's available.

A bamboo pole is probably best because it's light and strong for its weight. The line can be carpet thread, but if you're looking for big fish better use nylon. If the line is too long, it will just get tangled and frustrate a budding fisherman. A line about a length and a half of the pole is about right. Even if you don't use nylon, you'll probably want to tie a short length of nylon line at the end of the coarser line. It's easier to fool a fish with an almost transparent leader than with a chunk of cord with a hook attached.

Get a package of assorted hooks so you can use small ones when called for, and still have some larger ones if the prospects are good for sizable fish. You might consider a snelled hook or two. These are hooks that already have the nylon attached to them. The nylon has a loop at the other end to tie to your line.

Huck used a bent pin for a hook, a rusty nail for a sinker, and a cork for a bobber. Except for the pin, which doesn't have a barb, that isn't too shabby for a beginner.

Probably the best of fish baits are earthworms, which might be found by digging in your garden at home. Keep them in dirt in a small cardboard carton with a few air holes punched in the lid. Crickets, grubs, and grasshoppers make good bait, too. Strangely, lots of fish are caught with doughballs (wadded up wet bread), and also hunks of cheese.

When ready to fish, bait your hook, and swing it out into the water as gently as possible. A big splash just scares the fish. Be very still, and don't move your pole around. When your bobber dips it's your signal that a fish is nibbling at the bait. Wait a moment, then pull up quickly so you'll hook the fish, and land it on the bank.

If it's of legal size, put it in a bucket of water, or on a string tied through its mouth and gill cover. Tie the string to something solid on the shore. Put the fish in the water. If the fish isn't legal size, wet your hands before handling it, and carefully take out the hook. Let the fish slide back into the water.

When through fishing, scale your fish by holding firmly to the tail and scraping the scales off in a tail towards head motion. Slit the belly and remove the entrails. Cut the head off just back of the gills. Wash your fish thoroughly inside and out.

Cook by rolling in flour or cornmeal and frying in hot oil for just a few minutes on each side. Salt to taste.

You eat most fish by pulling the cooked flesh off the bones, leaving the skeleton behind.

Night Life—Underwater

This is a fun activity if there's a lake at your campground.

Seal a 2-cell flashlight waterproof tight in a plastic bag. Tie strong twine or rope around the center of the flashlight so it's balanced.

After dark, turn the light on through the plastic, and lower it off a dock or from a boat into 6 to 8 feet of clear water. Turn the light slowly by twisting the line.

The light will attract fish, crabs, and crayfish. Your children can see them in the light beam.

Fishscope

Make your fishscope by cutting an 8- to 10-inch viewing hole in the bottom of a 5-gallon can. Paint the inside of the can black. Cement a piece of glass on the outside of the hole, sealing watertight with windshield sealer.

To use, hold the scope with the glass a few inches underwater, and look for fish and other water creatures.

Water Games

Boat Races

Rubber Band Powered. Have each child make a simple rubber band-powered model boat using the pattern shown, but of any shape desired.

Make two holes in the propeller. Thread the rubber band through one hole and out the other. Attach it to the boat, wind it up, and let it go.

Wind the propeller this way to make your boat go forward.

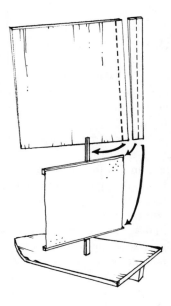

Wind Powered. Make sailboats from shingles. Cut two strips of wood off one side. One is to make a mast. The second is cut in half for top and bottom sail supports. Shape the rest of the shingle like a boat. Glue a piece of cloth or paper between the two sail supports, and glue them to the mast, making a square sail. Make a hole near the front of the shingle and glue the mast in it.

When there's no wind, have the children race their boats from one line to another by lung power—blowing. If there's a wind, have the boats race down wind. They may want to glue a strip of wood underneath as a keel to help the boats move in a straight line.

Guard the Flame

Give each child a lighted candle and a water pistol. The object of the game is to protect one's flame while trying to squirt out the flame of the others. Restrict splashing and ban physical contact. The last child with a lighted candle is the winner.

Pie Tin Race

Children are each given a pie tin, which they float in front of them at the starting line. On signal the children push the pie tins with their heads. If a pie tin sinks, its owner must retrieve, empty, and refloat it on the spot before continuing the race.

Hiking Activities

Hiking for the sake of hiking may be fun for some, but for children, a hike with a purpose is more attractive.

Photo Hike

This works best if each hiker has his or her own camera but it's not essential. The object is to hike along, constantly alert to good picture possiblities. If there's just one camera for all, then it will have to be shared. The person who first spots a potentially great picture should use the camera to record it.

If there are cameras for all, then each photographer will find the best lighting and camera angle for whatever scene is chosen. The benefit of this kind of photo hike comes when the finished pictures are compared after processing. Analysis of strengths and weaknesses of each picture of the same scene will be of value in improving photgraphic technique.

Senses Hike

This hike is so similar to the Blind Trail described earlier, except the hikers aren't blindfolded. Again, the purpose is to teach observation. This can be fun on a

---

HINT *Variety in activities is fine, but so is playing an old favorite again and again.*

---

completely informal basis with each person merely passing along to the others any impressions that come at any time. These might include sounds, sights, smells, tastes, and sensations of touch.

Mapping Hike

When your children have learned how to use a map, compass, and measuring, the mapping hike puts these skills together for fun and practice.

The first step is to pick a hike destination at least 2 miles from the starting place. Knowledge of the area can be used in picking the trail, but use of a topographic map at the time of planning will bring map reading into the picture.

This could be a separate activity for each person, but probably will be more fun and educational if the whole group works as a team.

Using a compass and measuring distance by pacing, distances and directions are recorded during the entire hike. Directions to important landmarks along the way also should be noted. Such notes might look something like this:

94 degrees – 542 feet This means the trail turned here.

55 degrees – 127 feet Another turn.

70 degrees – 32 feet Crossroad.

70 degrees – 230 feet Water tower. 121 degrees from this point — about 250 feet.

When you get to your destination, you'll have notes so you can make a rather accurate map of your route including landmarks visible from the trail.

When you get back to camp, draw a map of the hike. Record directions and distances on the map with a ruler and protractor.

A Stalking Hike

This is another activity where Dad or Mom should be the person stalked the first few times it's tried.

The rules are simple. The person being stalked pretends not to know he or she is being followed. Every so often the "quarry" stops, slowly turns around, and notes the name of any stalker seen. The quarry may turn around suddenly if he or she hears one of the followers. The stop and slow turnaround gives the followers time to hide. The rapid turnaround is justified by noise made by the stalkers.

After children become familiar with the game and how the "quarry" should act, one after another can be stalked.

Night Insect Hunt

Use a strong 2-cell flashlight. After dark, find a field, preferably grassy. Hold the flashlight in the center of your forehead so your line of sight is down the beam of the flashlight. Sweep the beam 20 to 30 feet out in front until you spot a shiny speck like a diamond. Walk toward the speck carefully, keeping it in the light. At the end of

Sightseeing by car.

the beam you'll find a moth, spider, or other insect with brilliant shining eyes.

Each family member on the hike should have a chance to use the light to spot an insect.

This might be a good time for each child to catch a bug for the Critter Crawl Race.

Bird Hike

This could be an addition to the bird identification game. The difference between this and just listing a few birds at a time is that the hike takes place at the crack of dawn. No serious bird watcher would think of missing the chance to spot early morning birds. Remember, it's the early bird that catches the worm, and since they're out early catching worms you'll see more of them.

Dress warmly—mornings often are cool. Bring field glasses, if you have them, and your bird identification book.

Hike slowly and quietly—no jerky motions or unnecessary noise. When you see a bird, freeze, and watch it carefully. If you have field glasses, bring them up to your eyes slowly and smoothly. Check the bird's markings against your bird I.D. book.

If possible, plan your hike so you are walking west. It's better to spot birds ahead of you with the sun full on them. If you hike east into the sun, they will look like dark silhouettes.

You might try to attract curious birds by holding the back of your hand against your lips and kissing it to make a squeaking sound. Who knows, it might attract a curious chipmunk, too.

Square Hike

Once your children have learned how to use a compass and figure distance by pacing, they'll enjoy a square hike as a test. They just hike a specific distance, like 1,000 feet, in each of four directions.

In turn, each hikes 1,000 feet north using compass and pacing, then the same distance east, the same south, and finally the same west. If they figure correctly, hikers should end up back where they started. The distance each is off will show the amount of error in use of either the compass or pacing.

You can use other distances as long as the legs of the hike are the same length. Different directions can be used, too. They just call for adding 90 degrees to whatever the first compass reading was, and then another 90 degrees to that for the second, and so on.

Sightseeing by Car

Many campgrounds are near areas of great scenic beauty. Part of your trip planning should include time to drive to and enjoy these sights.

In state and national forests, there are fire lookout towers. In times of minimum fire danger, these often are open to visitors. The lookout will probably welcome you because the job is a lonely one. The lookout may tell how fires are spotted, describe the use of triangulation, and share other interesting details.

If you come from a large city, your children have probably never visited a small town. Drive to a nearby town. Walk the streets and browse in the stores.

Similarly, if you live in a small town, visit a big city if one is near. Your children will enjoy seeing the hustle and bustle, and if you can stay until dark, they'll be fascinated by the colorful city lights.

Campfire Activities

Snacks

One of the delights of the small family campfire is that everyone can gather 'round, share in the warmth, and use the fire for making snacks.

Roasting Marshmallows

Roasting spits can be made from green twigs, sharpened to a point (avoid sumac or bitter tasting wood), long handled campfire forks, or coat hanger wire with one end wrapped in electricians tape to make an insulated handle. Burn off the paint on the business end of the wire before using.

The marshmallow roast is perhaps best when saved for the end of the evening. The flames will have died down, leaving hot, glowing coals, ideal for roasting. If your children are like children everywhere, they can't stand the wait necessary to produce a golden brown marshmallow so liquid in the center it barely hangs on the spit. They'll put their marshmallow so close to the coals it bursts into flame like a medieval torch. They'll blow out the fire, pop the blackened ember into their mouths and proclaim, "Just the way I like it."

Strangely, it probably is. So, don't fight it by trying to force them to roast theirs according to your taste. Ever since the marshmallow was invented, kids have been eating crispy, blackened, burned delights, and loving every bite.

Popcorn

The old open fire popcorn popper is again available in stores. This is the kind with a wire basket, a top lid that opens, and a long handle. As for the marshmallow roast, let the flames die down before starting to pop the corn. Have some melted butter or margarine and salt to add special taste.

Cereal Mixes

The basis for these mixes is dry cereal with flavoring. They can be made on your camp stove, or heated over the campfire in a foil package or in a foil-lined popcorn popper.

Puffed Stuff

3 cups puffed wheat

4 cups puffed rice

1 can salted nuts

1 cup grated Parmesan cheese

½ cup margarine

¼ teaspoon garlic powder

¼ teaspoon onion salt

½ teaspoon Worcestershire sauce

Melt margarine or butter and stir in garlic powder, onion salt, and Worcestershire sauce. Add the puffed wheat, rice, and mixed nuts. Cook over high heat for 20 minutes, stirring from time to time. Sprinkle in the Parmesan cheese, and mix well. Heat for another 10 minutes. This will make enough for 4 hungry kids or 6 normal people.

Scout Mix

6 cups of toasted square corn, wheat, and rice cereal mixed according to your own wishes

4 teaspoons Worcestershire sauce

6 tablespoons margarine or butter, melted

¼ teaspoon garlic powder

1 jar mixed nuts

Stir Worcestershire sauce and garlic powder into the melted margarine or butter. Add the cereals and nuts. Mix well in the oil. Heat over your campfire for ½ hour, stirring from time to time. Spread on paper towels to drain and cool. Makes about the same amount as the Puffed Stuff recipe.

Caramel Apples

½ pound of caramel candies

6 apples

Melt the candy in a saucepan over low heat, stirring occasionally. Spear each apple on the end of a short stick. Turn it in the melted caramel to thoroughly coat. Let cool before eating. Your campfire probably isn't the best place to melt the caramel. Better do it over a stove or small cooking fire.

Baked Apples

Package of red-hot cinnamon candy

1 apple per person

2 12 by 12-inch sheets of heavy-duty aluminum foil per person

Core the apple. Cut off about ½ inch of the bottom of the core, and put back in the apple as a stopper. Fill the cored out space with red hots. Wrap in a double thickness of foil with the Bundle wrap (see "Cooking," Chap. 4). Put each package directly on the coals and bake for 10 minutes. Cool slightly before opening the package.

Baked Banana

1 banana per person

1 12 by 12-inch piece of heavy-duty aluminum foil per person

Wrap the banana, skin and all, in foil, using the Two-Handled wrap. Bake for 10 minutes. Let cool slightly. Serve in the foil. It's less messy that way.

Hawaii Special

Leftover bread from the day's meals

Can of sweetened evaporated milk

Shredded coconut

Trim the crusts off the bread and cut trimmed bread into quarters. Spear through from side to side with a cooking spit or fork. Dip quickly into evaporated milk. Don't dip too long, or it will get soggy and fall off. Then dip into shredded coconut.

Toast over coals until brown. Repeat as long as bread and other ingredients hold out.

Try using maple syrup instead of evaporated milk if you run out of milk before you run out of bread and coconut.

Fun

Tongue Twisters

These simply are phrases that are very difficult to repeat more than two or three times without making a mistake. Try these on your children. They probably have a few others they have heard at school.

Instructions are simple. Each person in turn tries to say the words rather quickly. Keep track of how many repetitions each makes before goofing up.

In each of these, repeat the whole phrase. Some sound incredibly easy, but try them.

Toy Boat
toy boat
toy boat
toy boat...

Rubber Baby Buggy Bumpers
rubber baby buggy bumpers...

Black Bug's Blood
black bug's blood
black bug's blood
black bug's blood...

Peter Piper picked a peck of pickled peppers;

A peck of pickled peppers Peter Piper picked.

If Peter Piper picked a peck of pickled peppers,

Where's the peck of pickled peppers Peter Piper picked?

Here's another I learned as a child:

A tutor who tooted a flute
Tried to teach two young tooters to toot.
Said the two to the tooter,
"Is it harder to toot,
Or to tutor two tooters to toot?"

How much wood could a woodchuck chuck
If a woodchuck could chuck wood?

She saw sea shells by the sea shore,
By the seashore she saw sea shells.

Coordination

Instruct the family in a coordination test. Rub your stomach with your left hand, and at the same time pat the top of your head with the right. After demonstrating, and you'd better practice in private, have the family try it.

When everyone is able to do it fairly well, have them change the motion so they are now patting their stomachs and rubbing the tops of their heads. The next involves changing hands so the right hand rubs the stomach, and the left pats the top of the head. The fourth combination has the right patting the stomach while the left rubs the head.

After all have practiced the four combinations, work the group in unison following your lead as you go through the combinations in any order you want.

Crazy, Mixed-Up Kids

With everyone seated, have them slap their knees twice, clap their hands twice, and then grab their left ear with their right hand and their nose with the left hand. On signal they slap and clap again, but reverse positions—left hand to right ear, and right hand to nose. Keep repeating this routine to a definite rhythm that keeps gettng faster and faster until finally everyone is completely mixed up.

Hot or Cold

Pick one person to be "it."

"It" leaves the campfire circle and stands away

Coordination.

where he or she can't see or hear. During "its" absence, the rest of the family picks an object for "it" to touch or an action for "it" to do.

"It" is called back and, as he or she approaches the fire, family members start rhythmic clapping to indicate the closeness of "it" to the correct item or action. The louder the applause, the "hotter" "it" is. The softer the applause, the "colder" "it" is. When the object is touched or the action completed, another family member becomes "it," and the game continues with a new object or action.

Jack's Alive

Put one end of a stick or cork fastened to a stick into the campfire until it starts to burn. Put out the flame, leaving a glowing coal. Start the stick at any point in the circle. Each family member must blow once on the ember and pass the stick to the person to the left, saying "Jack's alive" as the stick is passed. The ember stick is passed rapidly around the circle until it finally dies out.

When the ember dies, the person holding the stick at the time must make a black mark on his or her face with the burned end. Be sure the end is cool!

Relight the stick and start again.

Storytelling

Help in storytelling can be found in "Getting There" (Chap. 6). It's even more appropriate as an evening campfire activity. There's something about the night and the fire that makes the storyteller more effective, and the listeners more receptive.

20 Questions

This was described as a car game in "Getting There" (Chap. 6), but makes a fine campfire game, too.

National Park Evening Programs

These already have been mentioned, but usually are so excellent they merit repeating in this campfire section.

Rainy Day Activities

Don't let rain spoil your camping trip. Be prepared for it with proper raingear, an awning or dining fly to avoid close confinement in a tent, and a few activities to fill the time.

Exploration on Wheels

Check with a camp ranger, the campground office, a travel guide, or a veteran camper for places to visit by car. It might be a local museum, a public or private cave, or a big shopping mall. In desperation, you might even check for a matinee at a theatre in a nearby town.

Games

Paper, Scissors, Rock

Your children probably already know and play this game. It's a real oldie.

The rules are simple. It's a game for two or three children. The left hand is held in front with the palm up. The right hand is clenched in a fist. On a rhythmic count of "one, two, three," each player hits his fist into his palm. On the third count, each player makes a sign with the right hand on the left palm so everyone can see. The sign must be made instantly on "three," with no hesitation to see what sign another player might be showing.

The signs are these: a clenched fist is a rock, two fingers extended are scissors, and an open palm struck with the heel of the hand on the other palm signifies paper. Easy so far. Each sign looks something like the item for which it stands.

Paper wins over a rock, a rock wins over scissors, and scissors win over paper. That's not too hard to remember. Just think of paper covering a rock, a rock dulling scissors, and scissors cutting paper. Penalty for overcoming a foe with a sign is the opportunity to slap the other player's wrist with two fingers.

Make A Square

This is a good game for two players. You just need a sheet of paper and a pencil. It takes time to make up the game, so that uses up time, too. If each player has a pencil and a piece of paper, each can prepare a sheet, and then they'll be ready to play two games.

The paper should be marked with a square of dots about ½ inch apart in each direction. If 10 dots are put down the side and 10 across the top, and dots added to fill in vertical and horizontal lines, you'll have 100 squares that can be filled in.

The object of the game is to complete as many squares as possible. The first player connects any two dots. The second player connects two more dots. They can be completely separate from the first, or join onto the line the first player made. The first player then connects another pair of dots, being careful not to form a third side of a developing square. If Player 1 does, Player 2 can complete the square when his turn comes. Players claim squares by putting an initial inside the squares they formed.

Each time a player completes a square he gets to draw another line right away. Thus, it's possible for a player to complete more than one square during a turn. The player

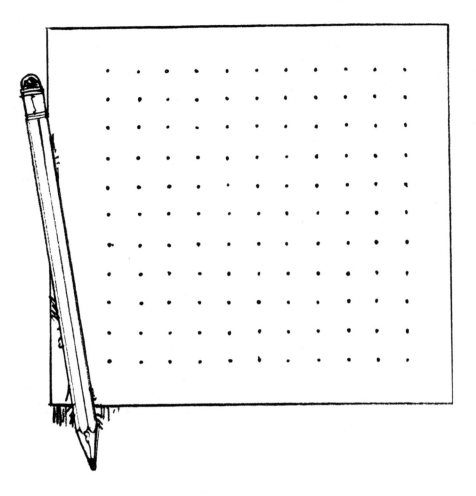

with the most inititals in squares at the end wins the game.

If you don't want the children to spend a lot of time making up the game sheets, you could make them in advance and photocopy.

Getting There Games

Don't overlook the value of almost all the ideas for car games from "Getting There" (Chap. 6). They are excellent rainy day activities.

Playing in the Rain

If it's not cold when it's raining, and you aren't too fussy, your kids can have a ball playing out in the stuff. Sure, they'll get wet, and probably muddy, too, but think of the dams and bridges to be built and the rivers and creeks to be channeled.

CHAPTER VIII

"Collect memories as a miser collects gold for that's what they'll be when your heart wants to borrow them."

Fritz Hines

The toughest part of any camping trip comes when you reach home. You're tired, glad to be home, and want to relax. But first there's that final step—the trip wrap-up. This, too, is a job for everyone.

Most of the wrap-up work should be done the day you return. In some cases you can put it off until the next day, but only when that day happens to be one when members of the family don't have to go back to jobs, or school.

better get out the home cleaner and give the inside of your RV or car a thorough vacuuming. Don't overlook the insides of drawers, cabinets, and closets. Dust and grit does tend to build up in these spots.

You'll want to scrub down the outside of your RV with a good detergent and water, followed by a rinse. Hit the underside of the vehicle, too. As mentioned earlier, dirt attracts moisture, and moisture on bare metal is the start of rust.

Check the outside of your rig for scratches. It's a good idea to carry a spray can of rustproof primer paint to cover any bare metal that might show. This will be particularly evident at the front of a trailer where small stones kicked up by the towing vehicle have marred the surface.

This is a good time for someone to inventory the things left in the RV so you'll know what's there when you plan your next trip. List things like staple foods (obviously, you'll remove all perishable foods), detergents, paper products, and other kitchen related items. Also, if you store blankets, pillows, sheets, and towels in your RV, air, sun, or fluff them in a dryer on very low heat. Inventory those items, too.

Finally, close and lock all windows and air vents. Make sure the gas is turned off. Don't leave any battery operated appliances on. Drain your fresh water tank if it will be awhile before your next trip. You'll want to fill it with fresh water at that time. Open your refrigerator door and leave it open so it will air out.

Chock your wheels, store your hitch if it's removable, and lock the doors.

The Cleanup Phase

If you put away a dull ax, it will be dull next time. You'll forget that frayed tent line unless you fix it before storing the tent.

The advice is sound. The condition of equipment won't change for the better in storage.

Tents and any other canvas or fabric need to be completely dry, brushed clean, neatly folded or rolled, and stored in their carrying bags, if they have them.

There will be times when you have to break camp in the rain. Obviously, this means arriving home with wet canvas, including the cover for your tent trailer, if you have one. You'll have to set up your tent trailer when you get home, and leave it up until it is thoroughly dry. Tents can be dried on lines in your backyard, basement, attic, or garage.

Axes, shovels, and similar metal tools should be washed clean of all dirt. Dirt on steel attracts moisture from the air—moisture that causes rust. Dry and lightly oil metal tools.

Check your pots, pans, dishes, and utensils to be sure they are clean and dry. Often, after a long trip, these items aren't in the same condition they were at the start. Open fires aren't as kind as the kitchen stove to the bottoms of pans and kettles.

Remove all clothing and other personal effects from your RV. These can be properly cleaned and stored at home. Don't leave them in the rig. They will only get in the way of a thorough cleanup.

If you carry a strong vacuum cleaner in your vehicle, and use it regularly on your trip, fine. But if you don't,

The Storage Phase

You've probably heard the expression, "A place for everything, and everything in its place." That's the best approach for camping gear, too. That way you won't have to frantically hunt for items before leaving on your next trip.

If you camp in an RV, it provides a good place to store your gear after it's all cleaned, packaged, and inventoried. Tent campers will need to make shelf space at home, probably in a basement, attic, or garage. You can store your staples, cooking gear, and eating utensils in a chuck box as suggested in "Camping Gear" (Chap. 2).

Try to store your camping gear in a clean, dry area.

The Memories Phase

Unlike cleanup and storage, this activity can and should wait until your family camping trip pictures are back. In the meantime, you can start arranging your collection of souvenirs, probably in chronological order by days. You'll have the daily logbook pages to remind you where to put the trip mementos, which will become a big part of your total camping log.

You'll recall it was suggested that a record of daily expenses be kept. This serves two purposes. The record will become part of the logbook, and it also will be useful in analyzing how well you kept to the budget established before you left. This budget comparison will prove valuable as you look forward to future trips.

Collect memories as a miser collects gold for that's what they'll be when your heart wants to borrow them. Memories are like TV images on video cassettes, filed away in your mind, ready for instant replay whenever they're needed.

The mind has a method of recall that is strengthened by repetition, by photos, by keepsakes, and by "Remember whens" at family reunions over the years.

The memories of shared activities, hardships overcome, and joyous times forge lasting bonds that hold family members one to another. The family camp is a great place to build these memories.

Happy Camping!

APPENDIX

State Governments

Each of the 50 states will send you free camping information about itself. The amount and kind of information will vary. Some states send a complete listing of state camping facilities, while others reply with promotional brochures describing the wonders of their states.

ALABAMA

Bureau of Publicity and Information
532 S. Perry St.
Montgomery, AL 36130

ALASKA

Div. of Tourism
Dept. of Commerce and Economic
    Devel.
Pouch E
Juneau, AK 99881

ARIZONA

Office of Tourism
112 N. Central Ave.
Phoenix, AZ 85004

ARKANSAS

Dept. of Parks and Tourism
One Capitol Mall
Little Rock, AR 72201

CALIFORNIA

Distribution Center
Dept. of Parks and Recreation
Box 2390
Sacramento, CA 95811

COLORADO

Div. of Parks and Outdoor
    Recreation
1313 Sherman St.
Denver, CO 80203

CONNECTICUT

Office of Parks and Recreation
Dept. of Environment Protection
165 Capitol Ave., Room 265
Hartford, CT 06106

DELAWARE

State Travel Service
Box 1401
Dover, DE 19901

FLORIDA

Dept. of Natural Resources
Bureau of Education and
    Information
3900 Commonwealth Blvd.
Tallahassee, FL 32303

GEORGIA

Dept. of Natural Resources
Parks and Historical Sites Division
270 Washington St., S.W.
Atlanta, GA 30334

HAWAII

Visitors Bureau, Suite 801
Waikiki Business Plaza
2270 Kalakaua Ave.
Honolulu, Oahu, HI 96815

IDAHO

Parks and Recreation Dept.
2177 Warm Springs Ave.
Boise, ID 83720

ILLINOIS

Dept. of Conservation,
    Land, and Historic
    Sites
405½ E. Washington St.
Springfield, IL 62706

INDIANA

Div. of State Parks
616 State Office Bldg.
Indianapolis, IN 46204

IOWA

State Conservation Commission
Wallace State Office Bldg.
Des Moines, IA 50319

KANSAS

State Park and Recreation
    Authority
Box 977
Topeka, KS 66601

KENTUCKY

Dept. of Parks
Capital Plaza, 10th Floor
Frankfort, KY 40601

LOUISIANA

Office of Tourism
Dept. of Culture, Recreation, and
    Tourism
Box 44291
Baton Rouge, LA 70804

MAINE

Publicity Bureau
97 Winthrop St.
Hallowell, ME 04347

MARYLAND

Dept. of Natural Resources
Forest and Park Service
Tawes Office Bldg.—B-2
Annapolis, MD 21401

MASSACHUSETTS

Dept. of Commerce and Devel.
Saltonstall Office Bldg.
100 Cambridge St.
Boston, MA 02202

MICHIGAN

Travel Bureau
Box 30226
Lansing, MI 48909

MINNESOTA

Dept. of Natural Resources,
    Parks, and Recreation
Box 39
Centennial Bldg.
St. Paul, MN 55155

MISSISSIPPI

Dept. of Economic Devel.
1200 Walter Sillers Bldg.
Box 849
Jackson, MS 39205

MISSOURI

Div. of Parks and Historic
    Preservation
Box 176
Jefferson City, MO 65102

MONTANA

Dept. of Commerce
Travel Promotion
1424 N. Ave.
Helena, MT 59620

NEBRASKA

Div. of Travel and Tourism
Dept. of Economic Devel.
Box 94666
Lincoln, NE 68509

NEVADA

Dept. of Economic Devel.
Div. of Tourism
Capitol Complex
Carson City, NV 89701

NEW HAMPSHIRE

Office of Vacation Travel
Box 856
State House Annex
Concord, NH 03301

NEW JERSEY

Div. of Travel and Tourism
Box CN384
Trenton, NJ 08625

NEW MEXICO

State Park and Recreation Div.
Box 1147
Santa Fe, NM 87501

NEW YORK

Office of Parks, Recreation, and
 Historic Preservation
Empire State Plaza
Albany, NY 12238

NORTH CAROLINA

Div. of Travel and Tourism
Dept. of Commerce
430 N. Salisbury St.
Raleigh, NC 27611

NORTH DAKOTA

Tourism Promotion Div.
1050 E. Interstate Ave.
Bismarck, ND 58505

OHIO

Div. of Parks and Recreation
Bldg. C-3
Fountain Square
Columbus, OH 43224

OKLAHOMA

Tourism and Recreation Dept.
500 Will Rogers Memorial Bldg.
Oklahoma City, OK 73105

OREGON

Travel Information Section
Dept. of Transportation
101 Transportation Bldg.
Salem, OR 97310

PENNSYLVANIA

Press Office
Dept. of Environmental Resources
Box 2063
Harrisburg, PA 17120

RHODE ISLAND

Tourism Promotion Div.
Dept. of Economic Dev.
7 Jackson Walkway
Providence, RI 02903

SOUTH CAROLINA

Div. of Tourism
Box 71
Columbia, SC 29202

SOUTH DAKOTA

Dept. of Economic and
 Tourism Devel.
221 S. Central
Pierre, SD 57501

TENNESSEE

Div. of State Parks
Dept. of Conservation
701 Broadway
Nashville, TN 37203

TEXAS

Parks and Wildlife Dept.
4200 Smith School Rd.
Austin, TX 78744

UTAH

Div. of Parks and Recreation
1636 W. North Temple St.
Salt Lake City, UT 84116

VERMONT

Dept. of Forests, Parks, and
 Recreation
Agency of Environmental
 Conservation
Montpelier, VT 05602

VIRGINIA

State Travel Service
202 N. 9th St.
Suite 500
Richmond, VA 23219

WASHINGTON

State Parks and Recreation
 Commission
7150 Cleanwater Lane
Olympia, WA 98504

WEST VIRGINIA

Office of Economic and
 Community Devel.
Communications Div.
1900 Washington St. E.
Bldg. 6, Room B-564
Charleston, WV 25305

WISCONSIN

Dept. of Natural Resources
Box 7921
Madison, WI 53707

WYOMING

Travel Commission
I-25 at College Dr.
Cheyenne, WY 82002

Canadian Provincial Government

ALBERTA

Travel Alberta
Capitol Square
10065 Jasper Ave. 14th Floor
Edmonton, Alta. T5J OH4

BRITISH COLUMBIA

Tourism British Columbia
1117 Wharf St.
Victoria, B.C. V8W 2Z2

MANITOBA

Travel Manitoba
Dept. 2045, Legislative Bldg.
Winnipeg, Man. R3C 0V8

NEW BRUNSWICK

Tourism, New Brunswick
Box 12345
Fredericton, N.B. E3B 5C3

NEWFOUNDLAND

Newfoundland and Labrador Dept.
 of Devel.
Tourism Branch
Box 2016
St. John's, NFLD. A1C 5R8

NORTHWEST TERRITORIES

Travel Arctic
Govt. Of the N.W.T.
Yellowknife, N.W.T. X1A 2L9

NOVA SCOTIA

Dept. of Tourism
Box 130
Halifax, N.S. B3J 2M7

ONTARIO

Ontario Travel
Queens Park
Toronto, Ont. M7A 2E5

PRINCE EDWARD ISLAND

Dept. of Tourism
Box 940
Charlottetown, P.E.I. C1A 7M5

QUEBEC

Tourism Quebec
CP20,000
Quebec, Que, G1K 7X2

SASKATCHEWAN

Saskatchewan Travel Service
3211 Albert St.
Regina, Sask. S4S 5W6

YUKON TERRITORY

Tourism Yukon
Box 2703
Whitehorse, Y.T. Y1A 2C6

United States Government

National Park Service Regional Offices

Address requests to the National Park Service and the Regional Office desired as listed below.

ALASKA REGIONAL OFFICE

540 W. 5th Ave.
Room 202
Anchorage, AK 99501

MID-ATLANTIC REGIONAL OFFICE

(For PA, MD, WV, DE, VA)
143 S. Third St.
Philadelphia, PA 19106

MIDWEST REGIONAL OFFICE

(For OH, IN, MI, IL, MN, IA, NE, KS)

1709 Jackson St.
Omaha, NE 68102

NATIONAL CAPITAL REGIONAL OFFICE

(For Metro D.C., Western MD, and Harpers Ferry, WV

1100 Ohio Dr., S.W.
Washington, D.C. 20242

NORTH ATLANTIC REGIONAL OFFICE

(For ME, NH, VT, MA, RI, CT, NY, NJ)

15 State St.
Boston, MA 02109

PACIFIC NORTHWEST REGIONAL OFFICE

(For ID, OR, WA)
2001 6th Ave.
Seattle, WA 98121

ROCKY MOUNTAIN REGIONAL OFFICE

(For MT, ND, SD, WY, UT, CO)

Box 25287
Denver, CO 80225

SOUTHEAST REGIONAL OFFICE

(For KY, TN, NC, SC, MS, AL, GA, FL, and Puerto Rico)

75 Spring St., S.W.
Atlanta, GA 30303

SOUTHWEST REGIONAL OFFICE

(For AR, LA, TX, OK, NM)

Box 728
Santa Fe, NM 87501

WESTERN REGIONAL OFFICE

(For CA, NV, AZ, HI)

Box 36063
San Francisco, CA 94102

United States Forest Service

Address requests to the United States Forest Service at the Regional Offices listed below.

ALASKA REGIONAL OFFICE

Federal Office Bldg.
Box 1628
Juneau, AK 99802

EASTERN REGIONAL OFFICE

(For CT, DE, IL, IN, IA, ME, MD, MA, MI, MN, MO, NH, NJ, NY, OH, PA, RI, VT, WV, WI)
633 W. Wisconsin Ave.
Milwaukee, Wi 53203

INTERMOUNTAIN REGIONAL OFFICE

(For Southern ID, NV, UT and Western WY)
324 25th St.
Ogden, UT 84401

PACIFIC NORTHWEST REGIONAL OFFICE

(For OR, WA)
Box 3623
Portland, OR 97208

PACIFIC SOUTHWEST REGIONAL OFFICE

(For CA, HI)
630 Sansome St.
San Francisco, CA 94111

ROCKY MOUNTAIN REGIONAL OFFICE

(For CO, KS, NE, SD, Eastern WY)
11177 W. 8th Ave.
Lakewood, CO 80225

United States Army Corps of Engineers

There are more than 1,000 campgrounds on Corps lakes and reservoirs. For information write to:

Office of the Chief of Engineers
Department of the Army
Washington, D.C. 20314

SOUTHERN REGIONAL OFFICE
(For AL, AR, FL, GA, KY, MS, NC, OK, SC, TN, TX, VA, and Puerto Rico)
1720 Peachtree Rd., N.W.
Atlanta, GA 30367

SOUTHWESTERN REGIONAL OFFICE
(For AZ, NM)
517 Gold Ave., S.W.
Albuquerque, NM 87102

United States Bureau of Land Management

Nearly 300 developed campgrounds are open to the public on lands managed by the Bureau. For information write to:

Bureau of Land Management
    U.S. Department of Interior
    at the following state offices.

ALASKA

Box 13
Anchorage, AK 99513

ARIZONA

2400 Valley Bank Center
Phoenix, AZ 85073

CALIFORNIA

Federal Bldg.
Room E-2841
2800 Cottage Way
Sacramento, CA 95825

COLORADO

1037 20th St.
Denver, CO 80205

IDAHO

Box 042
Boise, ID 83724

MONTANA

Granite Tower Bldg.
Box 30157
Billings, MT 59107

NEVADA

Federal Bldg.
Box 12000
Reno, NV 89520

NEW MEXICO

U.S. Post Office and Federal Bldg.
Box 1449
Santa Fe, NM 87501

OREGON

Box 2965
Portland, OR 97208

UTAH

University Club Bldg.
136 E. South Temple
Salt Lake City, UT 84111

VIRGINIA

350 S. Picket St.
Alexandria, VA 22304

WYOMING

U.S. Post Office and Court House Bldg.
Box 1828
Cheyenne, WY 82001

United States Fish and Wildlife Service

Selected refuges in the National Wildlife Refuge System have primitive campgrounds. Arrangements for use must be made with the refuge manager in advance. For information about these facilities write to:

Director, U.S. Fish and Wildlife Service
Department of the Interior
Washington, D.C. 20240

Tennessee Valley Authority

TVA runs about 50 developed campgrounds in its area. For information write to:

TVA Information Services
Division of Land and Forest Resource
Norris, TN 37828

Franchise Campgrounds

BEST HOLIDAY TRAV-L PARKS

7400 Cypress Gardens Blvd.
Winter Haven, FL 33880
Call toll-free 813-324-7400 for free
  delivery

JELLYSTONE PARK CAMP-RESORTS/ SAFARI CAMPGROUNDS

Leisure Systems, Inc.
30 N. 18th Ave., Unit 9
Sturgeon Bay, WI 54235
Call toll-free 800-558-2954 for
  reservations or directory

KAMPGROUNDS OF AMERICA (KOA)

Pick up free campground directory
at any local KOA

OUTDOOR RESORTS OF AMERICA

2400 Crestmoor Road
Nashville, TN 37215
Request free brochure of condo
  resort parks with rental sites

WALT DISNEY WORLD

Central Reservations
Box 40
Lake Buena Vista, FL 32830

BOY SCOUTS OF AMERICA

Open for use by persons registered
with the BSA.

Write for BSA Campground
Directory:

  Boy Scouts of America
  1325 Walnut Hill Lane
  Irving, TX 75062-1296
Or check with your council
service center.

Campground Information for Sale

Check your local bookstore for these:

National Park Guide

National Forest Guide

Mobil Travel Guides (Sectional)

Rand McNally Campground & Trailer
  Park Guide for the United States,
  Canada, and Mexico

Rand McNally Campground and
  Trailer Park Guide, Eastern
  Edition

Rand McNally Campground and
  Trailer Park Guide, Western
  Edition

Trailer Life Campground and Service Directory

Woodall's Campground Directory,
  covering United States, Canada,
  and Mexico

Woodall's Campground Directory,
  Eastern Edition

Woodall's Campground Directories,
  State and Regional

Woodall's Campground Directory,
  Western Edition

Bibliography

Camping How-To Books

All About Camping, Merrill

Boy Scout Handbook, The Official, BSA

Campers Bible, Riviere

Camping and Woodcraft, Kephart

Camping merit badge pamphlet, BSA

Complete Book of Camping, Miracle/Decker

Golden Book of Camping and Camp Crafts, Lynn

Eddie Bauer Guide to Family Camping, Bauer

Family Camping, Meredith Press

Family Camping Guide, Newman

Fieldbook, BSA

Handbook of Auto Camping & Motorists Guide to
  Public Campgrounds, Wells

L.L. Bean, Guide to the Outdoors, Riviere

Roughing It Easy #1 and #2, Thomas

Sunset Ideas for Family Camping, Lane Publishing Co.

Your Family Goes Camping, Patterson

Camping Activities How-To Books

Be Expert With Map and Compass, Kjellstrom

Boy Scout Songbook, BSA

Complete Book of Campfire Programs, Thurston

Enjoying the Outdoors with Children, Hein

Games on the Go, Beram

Golden Nature Guides (over 20 titles), Zim

Fieldbook of Natural History, Palmer

Field Guide to Nature Tracks, Murie

Field Guide to Butterflies, Klots

Field Guide to Mammals, Burt & Grossenheider

Field Guide to Nature Study, Mohr

Field Guide to Reptiles and Amphibians, Conant

Field Guide to Rocky Mountain Wildflowers, Craigheads & Davis

Field Guide to Rocks and Minerals, Pough

Field Guide to Shells of the Pacific Coast & Hawaii, Morris

Field Guide to the Birds, Peterson

Field Guide to the Ferns, Cobb

Field Guide to the Shells of Our Atlantic and Gulf Coasts, Morris

Field Guide to the Stars and Planets, Menzel

Field Guide to Trees and Shrubs, Petrides

Field Guide to Western Birds, Peterson

Field Guide to Wildflowers of the Northeastern and Central States, McKenney & Peterson

Guide to Fresh and Salt Water Fishing; Zim, Fichter, & Francis

Historic Trails Guide, BSA Publication

Insect Guide, Swain

Things To Do While Traveling, Grossett & Dunlap

Wildwood Wisdom, Jaege

Cooking How-To Books

All Outdoors Cookbook, McMorris

Betty Crocker's New Outdoor Cookbook, Golden Press

Camp Cookery, Kephart

Camping & Outdoor Cooking, Oetting & Robison

Campsite Cookbook, Woodall

Cookbook for Family Camping, Williams

Cooking merit badge pamphlet, BSA

Jack-Knife Cookery, Wilder

Outdoorsman's Cookbook, Carhart

Sportman's Cookbook, Karry

Wilderness Cookery, Angier

INDEX